ENGINEERING GRAPHICS ESSENTIALS

FIFTH EDITION

Kirstie Plantenberg
University of Detroit Mercy

SDC
Publications

SDC Publications
P.O. Box 1334
Mission, KS 66222
913-262-2664
www.SDCpublications.com
Publisher: Stephen Schroff

ISBN-13: 978-1-63057-052-1
ISBN-10: 1-63057-052-4

Printed and bound in the United States of America.

Second Printing

PREFACE

Engineering Graphics Essentials is specifically designed to be used in a 1 or 2 credit introduction to engineering graphics course. It covers the main topics of engineering graphics, including tolerancing and fasteners, and gives engineering students a basic understanding of how to create and read engineering drawings.

This text is designed to encourage students to interact with the instructor during lecture. It has many exercises that require student participation.

Instructor Resources

Power Point Lecture Material

Power Point lecture materials accompany the *Engineering Graphics Essentials* text. The presentations cover the entire book.

Solution Manual

A PDF solution manual file accompanies the *Engineering Graphics Essentials* text. There are solutions to the questions and the end of the chapter problem sets.

Student Supplements

Engineering Graphics Essentials comes with additional independent learning material. It allows the learner to go through the topics of the book independently. The main media content of the material is html (web pages). It contains html pages that summarize the topics covered in the book. Each page has voice-over content that simulates a lecture environment. There are also interactive examples that allow the learner to go through the *Exercise* found in the book on their own. Video examples are included to supplement the learning process.

Independent Learning Material Download

The independent learning material can be downloaded from the publisher's website by following the instructions on the inside of the front cover. After you download the files, move it to the location of your choice, then upzip the download. Next, open the new folder, navigate to index.htm and double click. This will open the content in your web browser, then you can start browsing the material. The independent learning material contains the following:

- Web-based summary pages with voice-over lecture content
- Interactive exercises
- Video examples
- Supplemental problem solutions

Have questions? Please e-mail: ege5@engineeringessentials.com

Found a mistake? Please e-mail a detailed description of the errata to:
ege5@engineeringessentials.com

This book is dedicated to my family for their support and help.

Nassif, Summer and Lias Rayess
and
Phyllis Plantenberg

CONTENTS AT A GLANCE

TABLE OF CONTENTS

Chapter 4: Dimensioning

Chapter 5: Sectioning

Chapter 6: Advanced Drawing Techniques

Chapter 7: Tolerancing

Chapter 8: Threads and Fasteners

Chapter 9: Assembly Drawings

Appendix A: Limits and Fits

Appendix B: Threads and Fastener Tables

Appendix C: References

CHAPTER 1

INTRODUCTION TO ENGINEERING DRAWINGS

CHAPTER OUTLINE

CHAPTER SUMMARY

In this chapter you will learn the importance of engineering drawings, how they relate to design and manufacturing, and the general arrangement and placement of the components on a print. In addition, the information that is contained within the various blocks (e.g. title block) will be described.

1.1) DESIGN

Design is a strategic approach to problem solving. The design process may involve considerable research, thought, modeling, adjustments, and redesign. In the field of Engineering, the design process leads to the creation of a plan for the construction of an object or system. These plans define things such as the specifications, parameters, costs, processes, and constraints of the system. Designing often necessitates considering the aesthetics, functionality, economics, and sociopolitical aspects of the system. In mechanical engineering, the designed object is most likely a manufactured part or machine that performs a required function. In the field of electrical engineering, the design could be a computer algorithm or a circuit. In civil engineering, the design could be subdivision or bridge plans. No matter what kind of design is required, you will be required to communicate this design to someone. Your audience may vary from your classmates, instructor, boss, or potential investors.

1.2) COMMUNICATING A DESIGN

Why would you want to communicate your design? Most likely, you want to attract, inspire, and motivate people to respond to your design. Methods of design communications can be written or oral. Written communication could be in the form of reports, memos, or drawings. Design communication through drawings may be as simple as a sketch or as complex as a computer generated technical drawing.

1.2.1) Sketching

A sketch is a quickly executed freehand drawing that is not intended to be a drawing used to manufacture a finished part. It is only used to express an idea. Sketching is a useful skill that may be used to quickly convey an idea in a design meeting or to have as a record of an idea for later use.

1.2.2) Technical Drawing

Technical drawing may be used as both a noun and a verb. **Technical drawing** is the process of creating an engineering drawing. Technical drawing is governed by a set of rules or standards that allow you to create an engineering drawing that is understandable and unambiguous.

A **technical drawing** is a drawing or a set of drawings that communicate an idea, design, schematic, or model. They are often used to show the look and function of an object or system. Each engineering field has its own type of technical drawings. For example, electrical engineers draw circuit schematics and circuit board layouts, civil engineers draw plans for bridges and road layouts, and mechanical engineers draw parts and assemblies that need to be manufactured. This book focuses on the technical drawings of parts and systems for manufacture. This is not to say that only students in a mechanical engineering curriculum will benefit from learning the skills necessary to read and create part drawings. It benefits everyone from the weekend carpenter who wants to draw plans for his/her new bookshelf to the electrical engineer who wants to analyze electrical component cooling using a CAE (i.e. computer aided engineering) program. Technical drawing teaches you how to visualize and see all sides of an object in your mind. Being able to visualize in your mind will help you in several aspects of critical thinking.

Engineering drawings, a type of technical drawing, are used to fully and clearly define requirements for an engineered part or system. It communicates all the needed information from the engineer who designed the part to the machinist who will make it. The process of producing an engineering drawing is often referred to as technical drawing or drafting. The person that generates the drawing may be called the designer or drafter. Before the advent of computers, copies of the engineering drawing were duplicated through the process of blueprinting. Therefore, engineering drawings are often referred to as prints. Figure 1.2-1 shows one example of an engineering drawing.

Figure 1.2-1: Engineering drawing example

1.2.3) Computer-Aided Drawing

Today, the mechanics of drafting have been automated through the use of **computer-aided drawing or design** (i.e. CAD) systems. Computer-aided drawing or design refers to computer software that allows an engineer to create drawings of their design ideas. There are two types of CAD systems used to create technical drawings. The first type allows you to draw two-dimensional drawings from scratch. The other types, and more prevalent today, are programs that start from a three-dimensional model and automatically create the two-dimensional drawing from the model. Communicating ideas is critical for developing the best possible solution, and solid models allow you to show a three dimensional version of your system instead of the traditional two-dimensional drawing. Many people are able to more quickly understand the idea if they are shown a three-dimensional representation of the design.

Figure 1.2-2: Three-dimensional CAD model

1.3) STANDARDS

An **engineering drawing** is a legal document because it communicates all the needed information about what is wanted to the people who will expend resources turning the idea into reality. Therefore, if the resulting product is wrong, the manufacturer is protected from liability as long as they have faithfully executed the instructions conveyed by the drawing. Mistakes made by the designer during the drawing phase and manufacturers misreading prints are costly. This is the biggest reason why the conventions and standards of engineering drawings have evolved over decades toward a very precise and unambiguous state.

In the pursuit of unambiguous communication, engineering drawings often follow certain national and international standards, such as ASME Y14.5M or a group of ISO standards. Standardization also aids with globalization. Standards allow people from different countries who speak different languages to share a common language of engineering drawing.

Standards define how to create an orthographic projection, apply dimensions, symbols use, perspectives, and layout conventions among many other things. This enables the drafter to communicate more concisely by using a commonly understood convention.

1.4) HISTORY OF TECHNICAL DRAWING

For centuries, all engineering drawings were done manually by using pencil and paper. This process took time, precision, and a certain degree of artistic ability. Since the advent of computers, an increasing number of engineering drawings are drawn within the virtual world of a computer-aided design or drawing (i.e. CAD) program. Currently, it is very hard to find any company that still practices manual drafting.

Some of the tools used in manual drafting include pencils, erasers, straightedges, T-square, French curves, triangles, rulers, protractor, compass, and drawing board. The English saying "Go back to the drawing board" means to rethink something altogether. It was inspired by the literal act of discovering design errors and returning to a drawing board to revise the design.

An engineering drawing is usually reproduced multiple times. These copies are distributed to the shop floor, vendors, supervisors, and to the company archives. Historically, a process called **blueprinting** was used which produced a copy that was blue in appearance. This is why engineering drawings are still referred to as blueprints or simply prints. Drawings today are simply reproduced using a plotter or printer.

Figure 1.4-1: Drafting implements

1.5) MANUFACTURING

Engineering drawings provide an understanding of how a product will function and be manufactured. Historically, two-dimensional engineering drawings have served as the sole method of transferring information from design into a manufactured part. However, there are always challenges involved in trying to describe a 3D world in a 2D drawing. Many companies are realizing that two-dimensional drawings alone are not sufficient and often lead to design errors and higher manufacturing costs.[1] Recently, 3D solid modeling software has been developed that take the computer drawing or model information and produce a G-code, which is executed by a CNC (i.e. computer numerical control) machine. However, two-dimensional drawings still play an important role in the design process by providing tolerancing, annotations, parts lists and other information that is critical to manufacturing and quality control.[1]

Engineering drawings transform ideas into products and communicate information between engineering and manufacturing. Drawings originate in the engineering department and give the manufacturing department all the information that is needed to manufacture the part. These prints also give the inspection department all the information that is needed to inspect the part.

1.6) ENGINEERING DRAWING FORMAT AND CONTENTS

The drawing format, arrangement, and organization of information within a drawing is controlled by ASME Y14.1 and Y14.1M. A drawing sheet's main elements are the drawing, various blocks, notes and zones as shown in Figure 1.6-1. However, there are other components that are optional and may be included on the drawing sheet. First and foremost, engineering drawings contain all the information needed to make the product. A drawing could be anything from a simple part print to a complex assembly drawing. Note that the drawing format may vary slightly depending on the drawing size and orientation.

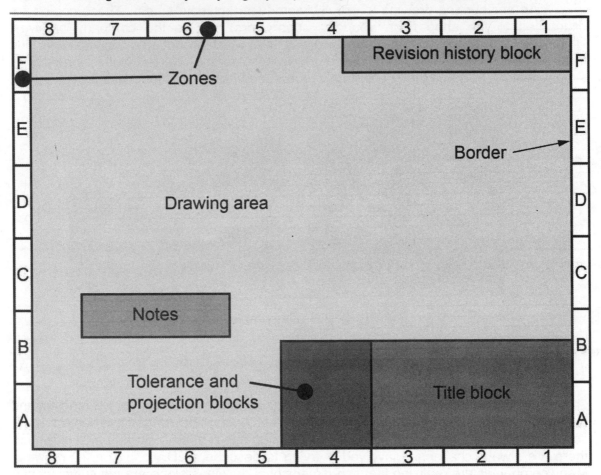

Figure 1.6-1: Engineering drawing format

1.6.1) Sheet Sizes

The physical size of the printed drawing is controlled by ASME Y14.1 and ASME Y14.1M. Each drawing size is identified by a letter or a letter number combination. For example, drawing size A is an 8.5 x 11 inch sheet. A complete list of drawing sizes are given in Tables 1.6-1 through 1.6-4. Note that a flat sheet is a sheet that is usually stored flat, and a roll or elongated sheet is rolled due to its elongated length.

Format size designation	Vertical (in)	Horizontal (in)	Recommended number of zones
A (Horizontal)	8.50	11.00	2 x 2
A (Vertical)	11.00	8.50	2 x 2
B	11.00	17.00	2 x 4
C	17.00	22.00	4 x 4
D	22.00	34.00	4 x 8
E	34.00	44.00	8 x 8
F	28.00	40.00	6 x 8

Table 1.6-1: Drawing sheet flat sizes [2]

Format size designation	Vertical (in)	Horizontal (in)	Recommended number of zones
G	11.00	22.50 - 90.00	4 x (6 - 24)
H	28.00	44.00 - 143.00	8 x (8 - 26)
J	34.00	55.00 - 176.00	8 x (10.32)
K	40.00	55.00 - 176.00	8 x (10.32)

Table 1.6-2: Drawing sheet roll sizes [2]

Designation	Vertical (mm)	Horizontal (mm)	Recommended number of zones
A0	841	1189	16 x 24
A1	594	841	12 x 16
A2	420	594	8 x 12
A3	297	420	6 x 8
A4	297	210	6 x 4

Table 1.6-3: Basic sheet sizes (metric) [3]

Designation	Vertical (mm)	Horizontal (mm)	Recommended number of zones
A1.0	594	1189	12 x 24
A2.1	420	841	8 x 16
A2.0	420	1189	8 x 24
A3.2	297	594	6 x 12
A3.1	297	841	6 x 16
A3.0	297	1189	6 x 24

Table 1.6-4: Elongated sheet sizes (metric) [3]

1.6.2) Drawing

The most important part of a print is the drawing and the most important part of reading the print is the ability to visualize the part. The drawing area (see Figure 1.6-1) may contain an orthographic projection and a pictorial of the object as shown in Figure 1.6-2. The orthographic projection is a two-dimensional representation of a three-dimensional object. It usually contains three views (e.g. front view, top view, right side view) but it may contain more or less than three. The number of views needed is determined by the complexity of the part. A pictorial is a pseudo 3D drawing. Pictorials are very useful in helping the reader visualize the object.

Dimensions are an important part of the drawing that give the size, shape and finish of the part. Without the dimensions, the part would not be able to be manufactured. Dimensions communicate more than just the size of the part, they also give the manufacturing department an idea of the object's function and important surfaces.

Figure 1.6-2: The drawing component of an engineering drawing

1.6.3) Zoning

The zone letters and numbers are located in the drawing margins outside the border. The letter-number combinations allow you to indicate a specific location on an engineering drawing. Zones are similar to how cells are identified in a spread sheet application. For example, zone B6 is located where row B and column 6 intersect (see Figure 1.6-1). On inch drawings, zone sizes are equal, not less than 1 inch, and not more than 5.50 inches. On metric drawings, the zone size selected is equal on the horizontal and the vertical, except that the upper and far left zones may be an odd size to accommodate the size of the sheet.

1.6.4) Scale

The drawing scale expresses the ratio of the object's size as printed to its actual physical size. If a drawing is printed full-scale, it implies that a feature dimensioned as 1 inch measures 1 inch with a ruler on the printed drawing. This is referred to as a 1 to 1 scale. Printing full scale, in most cases, is difficult to achieve unless you have access to a large plotter. In a classroom setting, most engineering drawings are printed on a standard 8.5" x 11" sheet of paper regardless of the object's size. The scale at which the part is printed should allow all details of the part to be seen clearly and accurately. **Even though a drawing may not be able to be printed full scale, they should always be drawn full scale in the CAD environment.**

Since it is impractical to print all drawings full scale, we employ printing to half scale, quarter-scale and so on. For example, if a drawing is printed half-scale, a feature that is dimensioned 1 inch will measure 0.5 inch on the printed drawing. The scale at which the drawing is printed should be indicated in the drawing's title block next to the text "SCALE." On a drawing, half-scale may be denoted in the following ways.

1/2   or   1:2   or   0.5

Although it is nice to print to scale, the ASME standard states that no dimension should be measured directly from the printed drawing. For drawings that are not prepared to any scale, the word "NONE" should be entered after "SCALE" in the title block.

1.6.5) Notes

Drawing notes provide information that clarify a particular requirement or specifies new information necessary to manufacture the object correctly. This concept will be discussed in the chapter on dimensioning.

1.6.6) Title Block

Every engineering drawing should have both a border and a title block. The border defines the drawing area and the **title block** gives pertinent information about the part or assembly being drawn. There are several different types of title blocks, but they all contain similar information. The information that is included depends on the drawing type, field of engineering, and viewing audience.

The title block is located in the lower right corner of the sheet as shown in Figure 1.6-1. The information common to all drawings is shown in Figure 1.6-3 where the identification letters refer to the following information. For a more complete explanation, see ASME Y14.100.

A. Company name and address.
B. Drawing title.
C. Drawing number.
D. Sheet revision. This block may be omitted when a revision history block is included.
E. This block may contain sub-blocks such as DRAFTER, CHECKER, and ENGINEER.
F. This block is used for approval by the design activity when different from the source preparing the drawing. This block may be necessary when a contractor-subcontractor condition exists.
G. Approval by an activity other than those described for blocks E and F.
H. Scale of the drawing sheet.
I. DAI (Design activity identification).
J. Drawing size.
K. Actual or estimated weight of the item.
L. Sheet number.

Figure 1.6-3: Title block contents

1.6.7) Revision History Block

The revision history block is used to record changes to the drawing and is located in the upper right corner of the drawing sheet as shown in Figure 1.6-1. The block is extended downward as required. Revisions are necessary when the part is redesigned. The information contained in the revision history block is shown in Figure 1.6-4 where the identification letters refer to the following information. For a more complete explanation, see ASME Y14.100.

A. Specifies the zone location of the revision.
B. The revision letter or number is found in this location.
C. Gives a short description of the change.
D. The revision date is given numerically in order of *year-month-day*. For example, the date, May 31, 2016, would be indicated as 2016-05-31 or 2016/05/31.
E. The initials of the person approving the change.

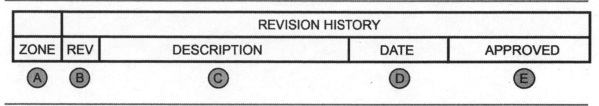

Figure 1.6-4: Revision history block

1.6.8) Tolerance and Projection Blocks

The *tolerance* and *projection blocks* are located to the left of the title block as shown in Figure 1.6-1. The *angle of projection block* shown in Figure 1.6-5 indicates the projection method that was used to create the drawing. The two methods of projection are third angle projection and first angle projection. What projection is and how to interpret it will be discussed in the chapter on orthographic projection.

The *dimension and tolerancing block* shown in Figure 1.6-5 gives information relating to dimensioning and tolerancing that apply to the drawing as a whole. Dimensioning and tolerancing will be discussed in later chapters.

Figure 1.6-5: Tolerance and projection blocks

NOTES:

INTRODUCTION TO ENGINEERING DRAWINGS QUESTIONS

Name: _____   Date: _____

Q1-1) Design is _____. (fill in the blank)

Q1-2) A technical drawing is one way of communicating... (circle all that apply)

    a) an idea.
    b) a design.
    c) information used to manufacture a part.
    d) inspection specifications.

Q1-3) The two organizations that control the content of **engineering drawings**.

    a) ASME
    b) AMCE
    c) ISO
    d) EAU

Q1-4) Historically, engineering drawings are also called...

    a) copies.
    b) drafting.
    c) prints.
    d) details.

Q1-5) CAD stands for... (circle all that apply)

    a) computer achieved drafting.
    b) computer aided drawing.
    c) computer aided design.
    d) computer aided development.

Q1-6) What are the four basic components of an engineering drawing?

Q1-7) What is the most important part of a print?

    a) Title block
    b) Zones
    c) Drawing
    d) Notes

Q1-8) How many views are generally used to describe the shape of a part?

    a) 1
    b) 2
    c) 3
    d) 4

Q1-9) What is the function of dimensions?

Q1-10) The letters and numbers along the margins that allow you to specify a location on the drawing is called...

    a) referencing.
    b) zoning.
    c) mapping.
    d) celling.

Q1-11) The area inside the border lines and outside the various blocks is called the...

    a) drawing area.
    b) zone
    c) revision area.
    d) plot.

Q1-12) The scale of a drawing is the ratio of the...

    a) printed size of the part to its actual size.
    b) actual size of the part to its printed size.
    c) the part's size to the sheet size.
    d) sheet size to the part's size.

Q1-13) What scale should a part be drawn in the CAD environment?

Q1-14) This block gives information about the drawing such as title, sheet size and scale.

    a) Revision history block
    b) Dimension and tolerance block
    c) Angle of projection block
    d) Title block
    e) Note

Q1-15) This block gives information about the drawing's projection method.

    a) Revision history block
    b) Dimension and tolerance block
    c) Angle of projection block
    d) Title block
    e) Note

Q1-16) This block gives information about the drawing's modifications.

    a) Revision history block
    b) Dimension and tolerance block
    c) Angle of projection block
    d) Title block
    e) Note

Q1-17) This block gives information about general dimensions and tolerancing specifications.

    a) Revision history block
    b) Dimension and tolerance block
    c) Angle of projection block
    d) Title block
    e) Note

<u>NOTES:</u>

INTRODUCTION TO ENGINEERING DRAWINGS PROBLEMS

Name: _____ Date: _____

P1-1) Given the following title block, name and briefly describe each space.

A	
B	
C	
D	
E	
F	
I	
J	
K	
L	
M	
N	
O	

NOTES:

Name: _____ Date: _____

P1-2) Given the following revision history block, name and briefly describe each space.

		REVISION HISTORY		
ZONE	REV	DESCRIPTION	DATE	APPROVED
Ⓐ	Ⓑ	Ⓒ	Ⓓ	Ⓔ

A	
B	
C	
D	
E	

<u>NOTES:</u>

Name: _____ Date: _____

P1-3) Given the print shown on the next page, fill in the following information.

Company name	
Print title	
Print number	
Print scale	
Sheet size	
Number of revisions	
Revision A zone location	
Number of sheets	
Material	
Projection method	
Finish requirements	
Approving drafter	
Approving checker	
Approving engineer	
Tolerance for a .XXX dimension	
Number of notes	

Name: _____ Date: _____

P1-4) Given the print shown below, fill in the following information.

Company name	
Print title	
Print number	
Print scale	
Sheet size	
Number of revisions	
Revision A zone location	
Sheet number	
Number of sheets	
Material	
Projection method	
Finish requirements	
Approving drafter	
Approving checker	
Approving engineer	
Tolerance for a .XX dimension	

Name: _____ Date: _____

P1-5) Using the ruler provided, determine the scale that should be indicated in the drawing title block for the following objects.

Scale = _____

Scale = _____

Scale = _____

NOTES:

CHAPTER 2

ORTHOGRAPHIC PROJECTIONS

CHAPTER OUTLINE

CHAPTER SUMMARY

In this chapter you will learn how to create orthographic projections. An orthographic projection describes the shape of an object. It is a two-dimensional representation of a three-dimensional object. Different line types are used to indicate visible features, hidden features and symmetry. By the end of this chapter, you will be able to create a technically correct orthographic projection and visualize its three-dimensional form.

2.1) ORTHOGRAPHIC PROJECTION INTRODUCTION

An *orthographic projection* enables us to represent a three-dimensional object in two dimensions (see Figure 2.1-1). An orthographic projection is a drawing that shows different sides of an object on a sheet of paper (i.e. in two dimensions). The drawing is formed by projecting the edges of the object onto a projection plane from different viewing perspectives. Orthographic projections allow us to represent the shape of an object usually using three views; however, a part may be represented completely with only one or two views. These views together with dimensions and notes are sufficient to manufacture the part.

3D Representation   2D Orthographic Projection

Figure 2.1-1: Orthographic projection.

2.1.1) The Six Principal Views

The six principal viewing directions of an orthographic projection and their associated view names are shown in Figure 2.1-2. These viewing directions are used to create the six principal views. Each principal view is created by looking at the object in the directions indicated in Figure 2.1-2 and drawing what is seen, as well as, what is hidden from view.

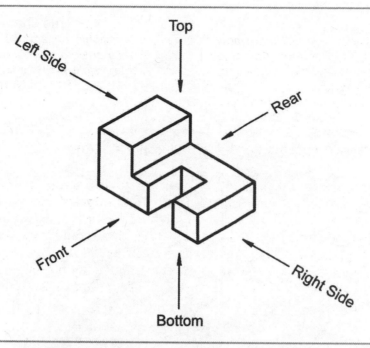

Figure 2.1-2: The six principal viewing directions

2.2) THE GLASS BOX METHOD

The glass box method is a very convenient way of visualizing how an orthographic projection is created. To obtain an orthographic projection, an object is placed in an imaginary glass box as shown in Figure 2.2-1. The sides of the glass box represent the six principal planes. Images of the object are projected onto the sides of the box to create the six principal views. The box is then unfolded to lie flat, showing all views in a two-dimensional plane. Figure 2.2-2 shows the glass box being unfolded to create the orthographic projection of the object.

True shape of surface A.

Foreshortened shape of surface B.

Projection Planes (Sides of the Box)

Top View

Projectors

A

B

Front View

Right Side View

Figure 2.2-1: Object in a glass box

Figure 2.2-2: Glass box being unfolded

Exercise 2.2-1: Principal views

Label the five remaining principal views with the appropriate view name. Figure 2.1-1 indicates the six principal viewing directions as well as their associated view names.

Front View

What are the differences between the *Right Side* and *Left Side* views?

What are the differences between the *Top* and *Bottom*, and *Front* and *Rear* views?

Which view(s) have the least number of hidden or dashed lines?

2.3) THE STANDARD VIEWS

When constructing an orthographic projection, we need to include enough views to completely describe the true shape of the part. The more complex a part, the more views are needed to completely describe its shape. Most objects require three views to be completely described. **The standard views used in an orthographic projection are the *front, top,* and *right side* views.** The other views (bottom, rear, left side) are omitted since they usually do not add any new information. The top, front, and bottom views are all aligned vertically and share the same width dimension. The left side, front, right side, and rear views are all aligned horizontally and share the same height dimension.

It is not always necessary to use the three standard views. Some objects can be completely described in one or two views. For example, a sphere only requires one view, and a block only requires two views. No matter how many views are used, the viewing directions should be chosen to minimize the use of hidden lines and convey maximum clarity.

2.3.1) The Front View

The *front view* shows the most features or characteristics of the object. It usually contains the least number of hidden lines. The exception to this rule is when the object has a predefined or generally accepted front view. All other views are based on the orientation chosen for the front view.

2.4) LINE TYPES USED IN AN ORTHOGRAPHIC PROJECTION

Line type and ***line weight*** **provide valuable information to the print reader.** For example, the type and weight of a line can answer the following questions: Is the feature visible or hidden from view? Is the line part of the object or part of a dimension? Is the line indicating symmetry? There are four commonly used line types: continuous, hidden, center and phantom. Important lines are thicker than less important thin lines. The following is a list of common line types and widths used in a basic orthographic projection that has no section views or dimensions.

1. Visible lines: Visible lines represent visible edges and boundaries. The line type is **continuous** and the line weight is **thick**.
2. Hidden lines: Hidden lines represent edges and boundaries that cannot be seen. The line type is **dashed** and the line weight is **medium thick**.
3. Center lines: Center lines represent axes, center points, planes of symmetry, circle of centers, and paths of motion. A *circle of centers* is usually a hole pattern that exists on the circumference of a circle. A *path of motion* indicates the path a feature takes when moving from one position to the next. The line type is **long dash – short dash** and the line weight is **thin**.
4. Phantom lines: Phantom lines are used to indicate imaginary features. For example, they are used to indicate the alternate positions of moving parts, adjacent positions of related parts, repeated detail, reference planes between adjacent views, and filleted and rounded corners. The line type is **long dash – short dash – short dash** and the line weight is usually **thin**.
5. Break lines: Break lines are used to show imaginary breaks in objects. A break line is usually made up of a series of connecting arcs. The line type is **continuous** and the line weight is usually **thick**.

Exercise 2.4-1: Line types

Using the line type definitions, match each line type name with the appropriate line type.

- Visible Line

- Hidden Line

- Center Line

- Phantom Line

- Dimension and Extension Lines

- Cutting Plane Line

- Section Lines

- Break Line

Exercise 2.4-2: Line identification

In the following orthographic projection, identify the line type of each line that is pointed to. Then, identify the associated feature (using a letter) of the selected lines.

Line width and type are controlled by the ASME Y14.2 standard. The standard recommends using, no less than, two line widths. Important lines should be twice as thick as the less important thin lines. Thick lines should be at least 0.6 mm in width and thin lines should be at least 0.3 mm in width. However, to further distinguish line importance, it is recommended to use four different thicknesses or weights: thin, medium, thick, and very thick. The actual line thickness should be chosen such that there is a visible difference between the line weights; however, they should not be too thick or thin making it difficult to read the print. The thickness of the lines should be adjusted according to the size and complexity of the part. Table 2.4-1 contains a list of common line types and widths used in an orthographic projection.

Line type name	Line type	Use	Thickness
Visible	————————	visible edges	0.5 - 0.6 mm
Hidden	– – – – – – – –	hidden edges	0.35 - 0.45 mm
Center	——— — — ———	symmetry, circle of centers, paths of motion	0.3 mm
Phantom	——— — — ———	imaginary features	0.3 mm
Break	∿	imaginary brakes in the part	0.5 – 0.6 mm

Table 2.4-1: Common line types and their thicknesses

2.5) RULES FOR LINE CREATION AND USE

The rules and guide lines for line creation should be followed in order to create lines that are effective in communicating the drawing information. However, due to computer automation, some of the rules may be hard to follow. The rules of line creation and use are in accordance with the ASME Y14.2 and ASME Y14.3 standards.

2.5.1) Hidden Lines

Hidden lines represent edges and boundaries that cannot be seen.

Rule 1.   The length of the hidden line dashes may vary slightly as the size of the drawing changes. For example, a very small part may require smaller dashes in order for the hidden line to be recognized.

Rule 2.   Hidden lines should always begin and end with a dash, except when the hidden line begins or ends at a parallel visible line (see Figure 2.5-1).

Rule 3.   Hidden line dashes should join at corners (see Figure 2.5-2).

Figure 2.5-1: Drawing hidden lines

Figure 2.5-2: Hidden lines at corner

2.5.2) Center Lines

Center lines are used to identify planes and axes of symmetry and are important for interpreting cylindrical shapes as shown in Figure 2.5-3. If a center line is used to indicate part symmetry, two short thick parallel lines are placed on the center line, outside the part, and perpendicular to the center line (see Figure 2.5-4). Center lines are also used to indicate circle of centers and paths of motion as shown in Figure 2.5-5. Short center lines may be left unbroken if it is certain that they won't be confused with another line type. However, every measure should be taken to produce a break.

Rule 1.   Center lines should start and end with long dashes (see Figure 2.5-3).

Rule 2.   Center lines should intersect by crossing either the long dashes or the short dashes (see Figure 2.5-6).

Rule 3.   Center lines should extend a short distance beyond the object or feature. They should not terminate at other lines of the drawing (see Figure 2.5-7).

Rule 4.   Center lines may be connected within a single view to show that two or more features lie in the same plane as shown in Figure 2.5-8. However, they should not extend through the space between views.

Figure 2.5-3: Axes of symmetry

Figure 2.5-4: Part symmetry

Figure 2.5-5: Center line uses

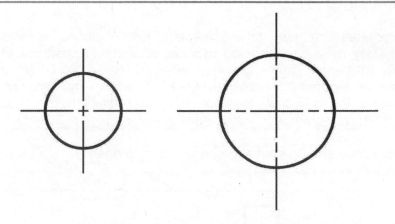

Figure 2.5-6: Crossing center lines.

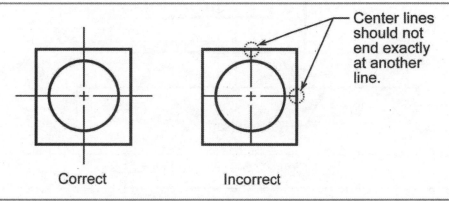

Correct   Incorrect

Figure 2.5-7: Terminating center lines.

Figure 2.5-8: Connecting center lines.

2.5.3) Phantom Lines

Phantom lines are used to indicate alternate positions of moving parts (see Figure 2.5-5). They may also be used to indicate adjacent positions of related parts, repeated detail, reference planes between adjacent views, and filleted and rounded corners as shown in Figures 2.5-9 through 2.5-11. Phantom lines are only used to show fillets and rounds in the view that does not show the radius. In this case, the phantom lines are used to show a change in surface direction (see Figure 2.5-11).

Rule 1. Phantom lines should start and end with a long dash.

Figure 2.5-9: Related part.

Figure 2.5-10: Repeated detail.

Figure 2.5-11: Phantom lines used to indicate a change in surface direction

2.5.4) Break Lines

Break lines are used to shorten the length of a detail and indicate where the part contains an imaginary break. For example, when drawing a long rod, it may be broken and drawn at a shorter length as shown in Figure 2.5-12. When a break is used, the drawing should indicate the characteristic shape of the cross section.

Figure 2.5-12: Using break lines.

There are two types of break lines. A break line may be a series of connecting arcs, as shown in Figure 2.5-12, or a straight line with a jog in the middle as shown in Figure 2.5-13. If the distance to traverse is short, the series of connecting arcs is used. This series of arcs is the same width as the visible lines on the drawing. If the distance is long, the thin straight line with a jog is used.

Short distances
(thick)

Long distances
(thin)

Figure 2.5-13: Types of break lines.

2.5.5) Line Type Precedence

Some lines are considered more important than other lines. **Two lines may occur in the same place, however, only the line that is considered to be the most important is shown.** Lines in order of precedence/importance are as follows:

1. Cutting plane line
2. Visible line
3. Hidden line
4. Center line

Try Exercise 2.5-1

Exercise 2.5-1: Line use in an orthographic projection

Fill the following dotted orthographic projection with the appropriate line types.

2.6) CREATING AN ORTHOGRAPHIC PROJECTION

The steps presented in this section are meant to help you create a technically correct orthographic projection using the third-angle projection standard. Once you become experienced and proficient at creating orthographic projections, you will develop short cuts and may not need to follow the steps exactly as written. These steps are visually illustrated in Figure 2.6-1.

1. **Choose a front view**. This is the view that shows the most about the object.
2. **Decide how many views are needed** to completely describe the object. If you are unable to determine which views will be needed, draw the standard views (front, top and right side).
3. **Draw the visible features of the front view**.
4. **Draw projectors off of the front view** horizontally and vertically in order to create the boundaries for the top and right side views.
5. **Draw the top view**. Use the vertical projectors to fill in the visible and hidden features.
6. **Project from the top view back to the front view.** Use the vertical projectors to fill in any missing visible or hidden features in the front view.
7. **Draw a 45° projector** off of the upper right corner of the box that encloses the front view.
8. **From the top view, draw projectors over to the 45° line and down** in order to create the boundaries of the right side view.
9. **Draw the right side view.**
10. **Project back to the top and front view** from the right side view as needed.
11. **Draw center lines where necessary.**

Following the aforementioned steps will ensure that the orthographic projection is technically correct. That is, it will ensure that:

√ The front and top views are vertically aligned.
√ The front and right side views are horizontally aligned.
√ Every point or feature in one view is aligned on a projector in any adjacent view (front and top, or front and right side).
√ The distance between any two points of the same feature in the related views (top and right side) are equal.

Figure 2.6-1 identifies the *adjacent* and *related* views. Adjacent views are two adjoining views aligned by projectors. Related views are views that are adjacent to the same view.

Figure 2.6-1: Features of a technically correct orthographic projection

2.6.1) Projection Symbol

Two internationally recognized systems of projection used to create orthographic projections are third-angle projection and first-angle projection. In the United States, we use third-angle projection to create an orthographic projection. This is the method of creating orthographic projections that is described in this chapter. In some parts of Europe, and elsewhere, first-angle projection is used. To inform the print reader what projection method was used to create the drawing, the projection symbol is placed in the projection block. If the drawing uses metric units, the text "SI" is placed in front of the projection symbol. The projection symbols are shown in Figure 2.6-2 and 2.6-3.

It is extremely important to let the print reader know which projection method was used to create the orthographic projection. Without knowledge of the projection method, reading a drawing may be confusing and lead to interpretation mistakes. The glass box method described in a previous section will produce a drawing in third-angle projection. Figures 2.6-4a and b show an object represented in both third-angle and first-angle projection.

To understand and visually see how views are created using the third-angle projection standard, put your right hand on a table palm up. You are looking at the front view of your hand. Now rotate your hand so that your thumb points up and your little finger is touching the table. This is the top view of your hand. Put your hand back in the front view position. Now rotate your hand so that your finger tips are pointing down and your wrist is off the table. This is the right side view of your hand. Now let's see how that changes when we are creating a first-angle projection drawing. Put your right hand on the table with your palm down. The back of your hand is the front view. Now, rotate your hand so that your thumb is pointing up and your little finger is on the table. This is the top view of your hand. Put your hand back in the front view position. Rotate your hand so that your fingers are pointing up. This is the right side view of your hand. To be more technical, **third-angle projection** forms the orthographic projection by placing the projection plane between the object and the observer, and **first-angle projection** places the object between the observer and the projection plane. Note that the geometry of the views for both first-angle and third-angle projections are the same, it is just the placement of the views that are different.

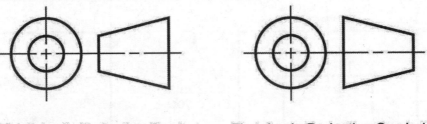

Third-Angle Projection Symbol
(Our national standard)

First-Angle Projection Symbol

Figure 2.6-2: First and third-angle projection symbols

H = Text height

Figure 2.6-3: Projection symbol proportions.

Figure 2.6-4a: Third-angle projection methods

Figure 2.6-4b: First-angle projection methods

Exercise 2.6-1: Projection methods

Identify which drawing was created using third-angle projection and which was created using first-angle projection.

Video Exercise 2.6-2: Beginning Orthographic Projection

This video exercise will take you through creating an orthographic projection for the object shown.

Video Exercise 2.6-3: Intermediate Orthographic Projection

This video exercise will take you through creating an orthographic projection for the object shown.

Video Exercise 2.6-4: Advanced Orthographic Projection

This video exercise will take you through creating an orthographic projection for the object shown. Note: The object is not completely dimensioned; however, the missing dimensions will be made apparent in the video.

NOTES:

2.7) APPLYING WHAT WE HAVE LEARNED

Exercise 2.7-1: Missing lines 1

Name: _____   Date: _____

Fill in the missing lines in the front, right side, and top views. **Hint:** The front view has one missing visible line. The right side view has one missing visible line and two missing hidden lines. The top view has five missing visible lines and two missing hidden lines.

TOP

FRONT   RIGHT SIDE

Exercise 2.7-2: Missing lines 2

Name: _____   Date: _____

Fill in the missing lines in the top, front, and right side views. **Hint:** The top view has one missing visible line. The front view has four missing visible lines and four missing center lines. The right side view has two missing hidden lines and one missing center line.

TOP

FRONT   RIGHT SIDE

Exercise 2.7-3: Drawing an orthographic projection 1

Name: _____   Date: _____

Shade in the surfaces that will appear in the front, top, and right side views. Estimating the distances, draw the front, top, and right side views. Identify the surfaces with the appropriate letter in the orthographic projection.

TOP ↓

FRONT   RIGHT SIDE

Exercise 2.7-4: Drawing an orthographic projection 2

Name: _____ Date: _____

Identify the best choice for the front view. Estimating the distances, draw the front, top, and right side views.

ORTHOGRAPHIC PROJECTIONS QUESTIONS

Name: _____   Date: _____

Orthographic projection

Q2-1) An orthographic projection is a _____ representation of a three-dimensional object? (fill in the blank)

Q2-2) In the United States, is first or third-angle projection used as the standard?

Q2-3) Are the front and right side views aligned vertically or horizontally?

Q2-4) Are the front and top views aligned vertically or horizontally?

Q2-5) The projection symbol, indicating the projection method used to create the drawing, is placed in the _____ block. (fill in the blank)

Q2-6) The standard views used in an orthographic projection are… (circle all that apply)

    a) front
    b) top
    c) back
    d) right side
    e) left side
    f) bottom

Q2-7) The view that generally shows the most characteristics of the part and contains the least number of hidden lines.

    a) front
    b) top
    c) right side

Line types and their uses

Q2-8) Hidden lines are used to indicate...

    a) edges and boundaries that you can see.
    b) edges and boundaries that you cannot see.
    c) imaginary features.
    d) symmetric features.

Q2-9) Phantom lines are used to indicate... (circle all that apply)

    a) alternate positions.
    b) repeated detail.
    c) related parts.
    d) change in surface direction.

Q2-10) Center lines are used to indicate... (circle all that apply)

    a) axes of symmetry.
    b) paths of motion.
    c) circles of center.
    d) change in surface direction.

Q2-11) To indicate line importance we draw lines using different line...

    a) texture
    b) thicknesses
    c) colors
    d) symbols

Q2-12) The thickest line type on a non-sectioned orthographic projection.

    a) visible
    b) hidden
    c) center line
    d) dimension

Q2-13) If a hidden line and center line appear in exactly the same location on a drawing, which one do you delete?

Q2-14) Projection or construction lines are not shown on the final drawing. (true, false)

Q2-15) Should a center line end at the boundary of an object? (yes, no)

ORTHOGRAPHIC PROJECTIONS PROBLEMS

Name: _____ Date: _____

P2-1) Match the solid part with its correct orthographic projection.

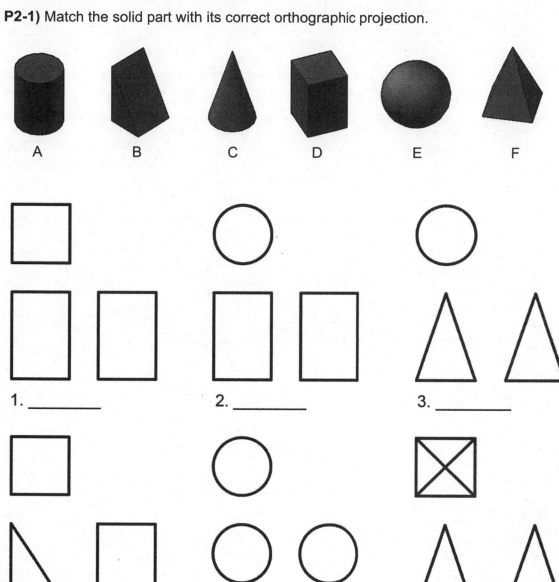

NOTES:

Name: _____   Date: _____

P2-2) Match the solid part with its correct orthographic projection.

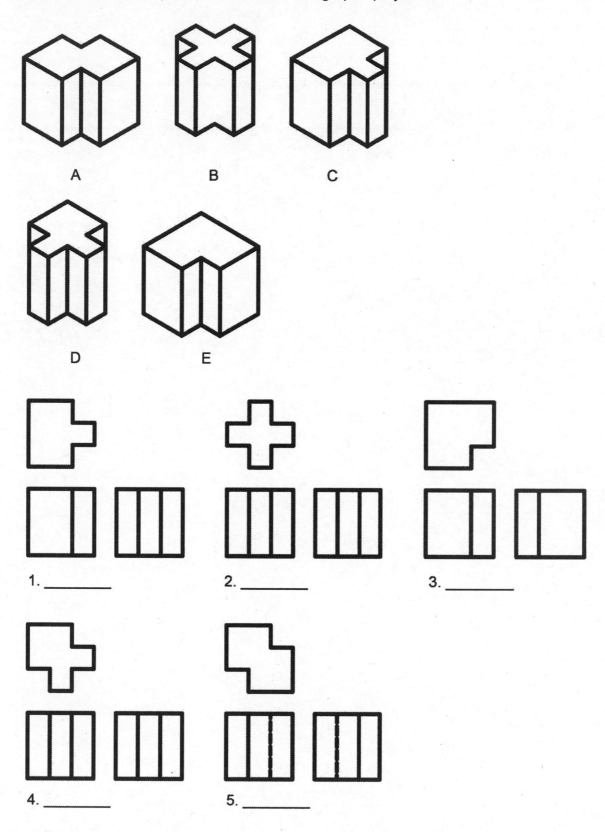

A   B   C

D   E

1. _____   2. _____   3. _____

4. _____   5. _____

NOTES:

Name: _____ Date: _____

P2-3) Match the solid part with its correct orthographic projection.

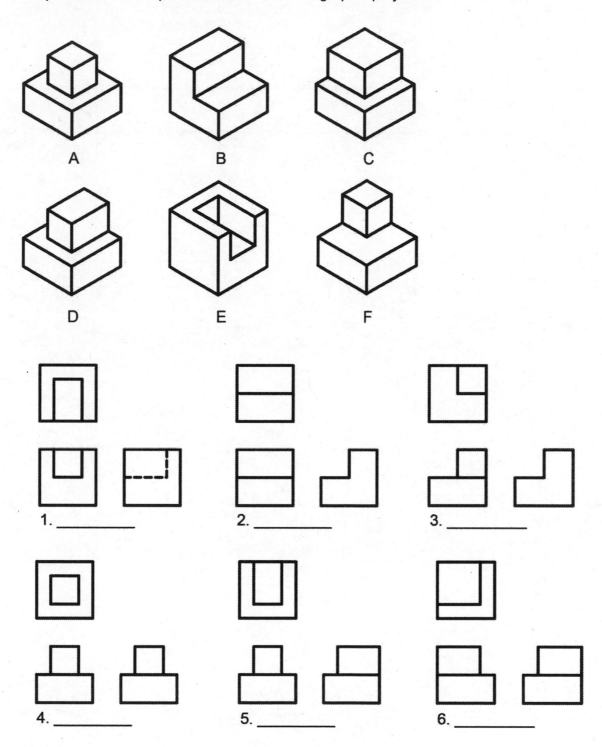

1. _____

2. _____

3. _____

4. _____

5. _____

6. _____

NOTES:

Name: _____ Date: _____

P2-4) Answer the following questions related to the orthographic projection shown.

1. View name	
2. View name	
3. View name	
4. View name	
5. View name	
6. View name	
7. Line type	
8. Line type	
9. Line type	
10. Line type	
11. Line type	
12. Line type	
Are all the views needed to fully describe the part?	
Which views should be used to fully describe the part?	

Name: _____ Date: _____

P2-5) Answer the following questions related to the orthographic projection shown.

1. View name	
2. View name	
3. View name	
4. View name	
5. View name	
6. View name	
7. Line type	
8. Line type	
9. Line type	
10. Line type	
11. Line type	
12. Line type	
Are all the views needed to fully describe the part?	
Which views should be used to fully describe the part?	

Name: _____ Date: _____

P2-6) Answer the following questions related to the orthographic projection shown.

1. View name	
2. View name	
3. View name	
4. View name	
5. View name	
6. View name	
7. Line type	
8. Line type	
9. Line type	
10. Line type	
11. Line type	
12. Line type	
Are all the views needed to fully describe the part?	
Which views should be used to fully describe the part?	

Name: _____ Date: _____

P2-7) Match the numbers in the orthographic projection with the letters in the pictorial.

	A	B	C	D	E
FRONT			7		
TOP			5		
RIGHT SIDE			12		

NOTES:

Name: _____ Date: _____

P2-8) Match the numbers in the orthographic projection with the letters in the pictorial.

	A	B	C	D	E	F	G
FRONT							
TOP							
RIGHT SIDE							

NOTES:

Name: _____ Date: _____

P2-9) Match the numbers in the orthographic projection with the letters in the pictorial.

	FRONT	TOP	RIGHT SIDE
A			
B			
C			
D			
E			
F			
G			
H			
I			
J			
K			
L			
M			

NOTES:

Name: _____ Date: _____

P2-10) Match the object with its correct views. Note that views should not be aligned on an orthographic projection as shown in this problem.

NOTES:

Name: _____ Date: _____

P2-11) Match the object with its correct views. Note that views should not be aligned on an orthographic projection as shown in this problem.

FRONT VIEW

FRONT VIEW

TOP VIEW

RIGHT SIDE VIEW

NOTES:

Name: _____ Date: _____

P2-12) Circle the correct front, top and right side views. Note that this problem does not show correct view alignment.

FRONT VIEW

FRONT VIEW

TOP VIEW

RIGHT SIDE VIEW

NOTES:

Name: _____ Date: _____

P2-13) Sketch the front, top and right side views of the following object. Use the grid provided.

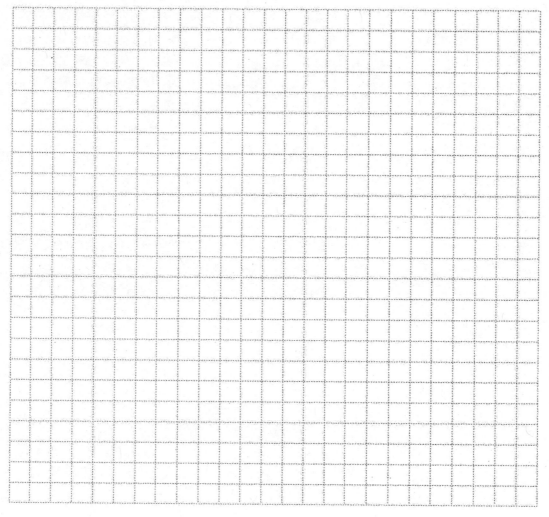

NOTES:

Name: _____ Date: _____

P2-14) Sketch the front, top and right side views of the following object. Use the grid provided.

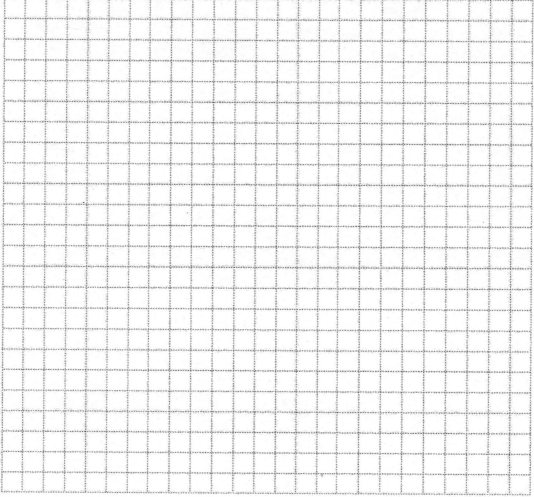

NOTES:

Name: _____ Date: _____

P2-15) Sketch the front, top and right side views of the following object. Use the grid provided.

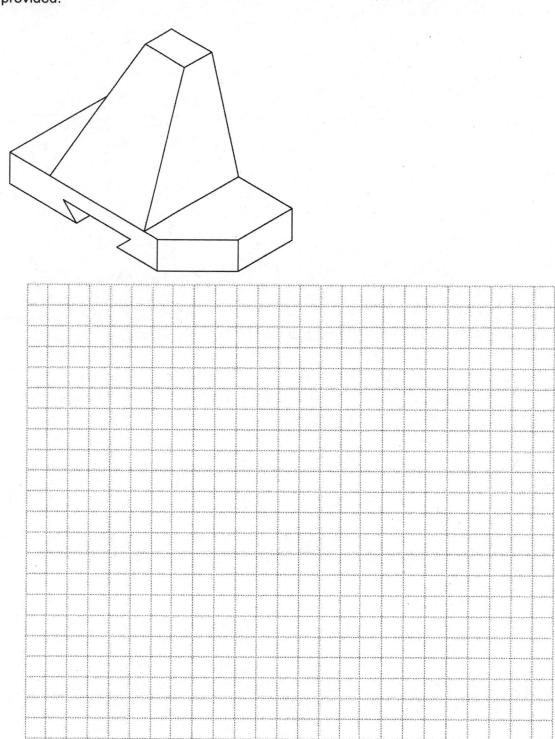

NOTES:

Name: _____ Date: _____

P2-16) Sketch the front, top and right side views of the following object. Use the 5x5 mm grid provided.

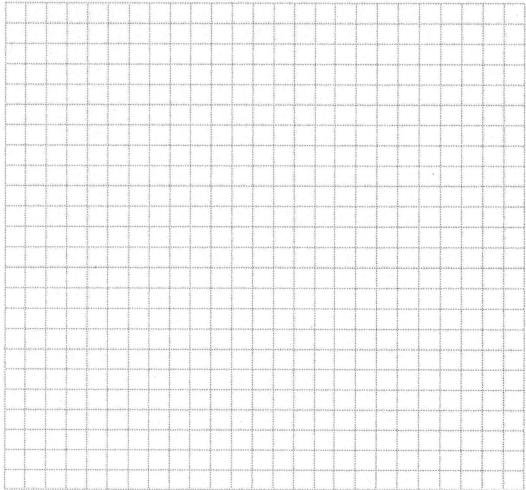

NOTES:

Name: _____ Date: _____

P2-17) Sketch the front, top and right side views of the following object. Use the grid provided.

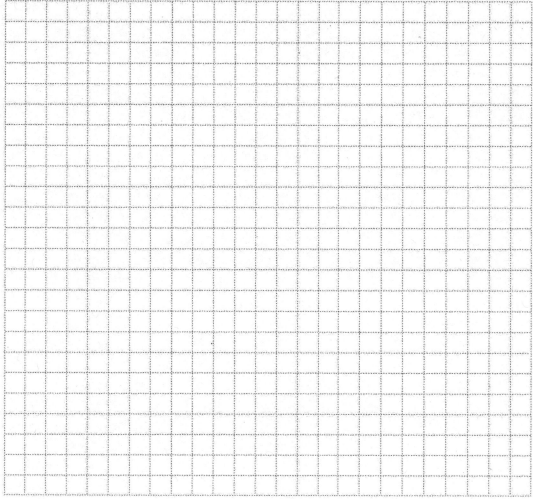

NOTES:

Name: _____   Date: _____

P2-18) Sketch the front, top and right side views of the following object. Use the grid provided.

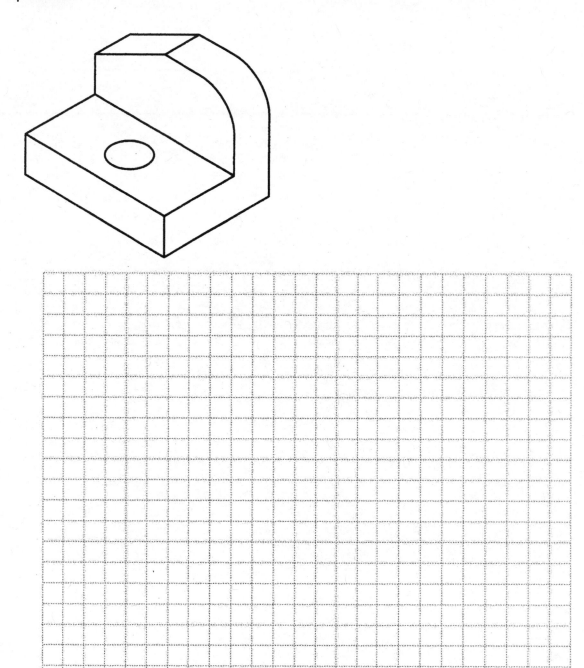

NOTES:

Name: _____   Date: _____

P2-19) Sketch the front, top and right side views of the following object. Use the grid provided.

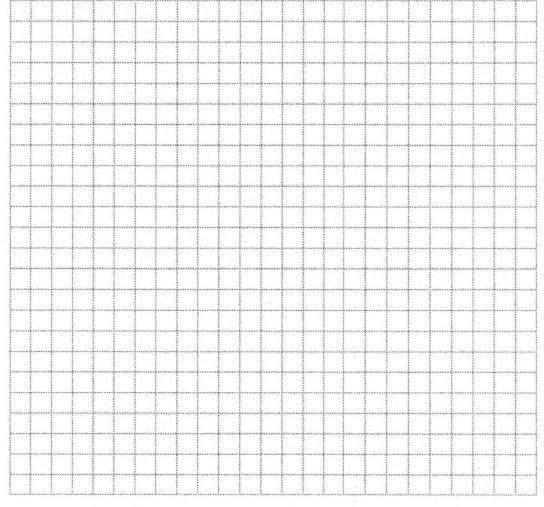

NOTES:

Name: _____ Date: _____

P2-20) Sketch the front, top and right side views of the following object. Use the grid provided.

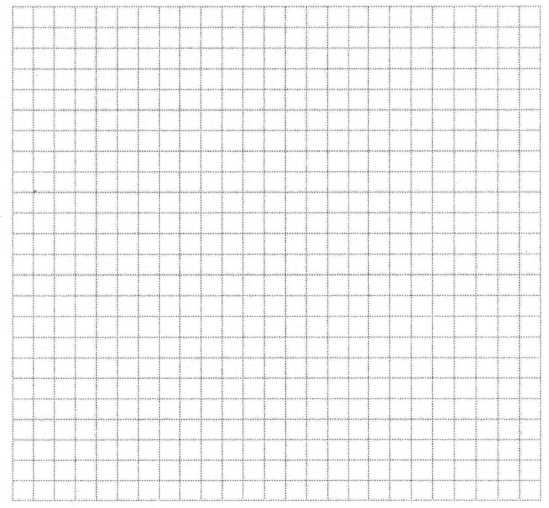

NOTES:

NOTES:

Name: _____ Date: _____

P2-21) Sketch the front, top and right side views of the following object. Use the grid provided.

NOTES:

Name: _____ Date: _____

P2-22) Sketch the front, top and right side views of the following object. Use the grid provided.

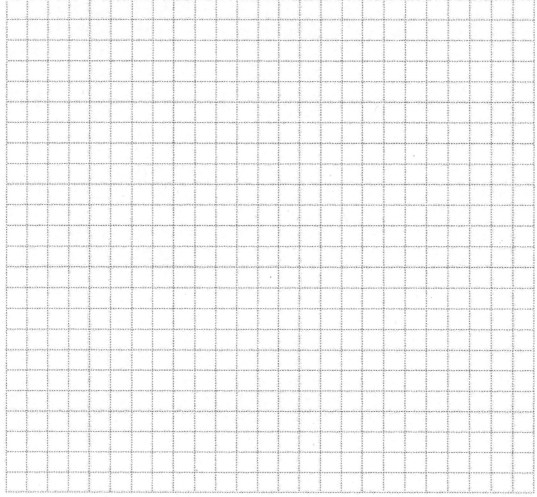

NOTES:

Name: _____ Date: _____

P2-23) Sketch the front, top and right side views of the following object. Use the grid provided.

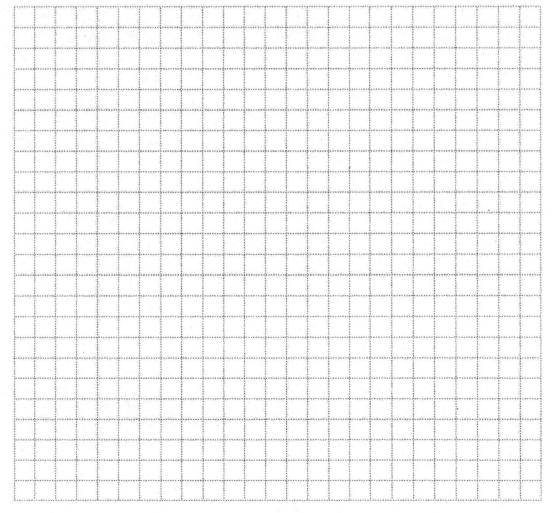

NOTES:

Name: _____ Date: _____

P2-24) Sketch the front, top and right side views of the following object. Use the grid provided.

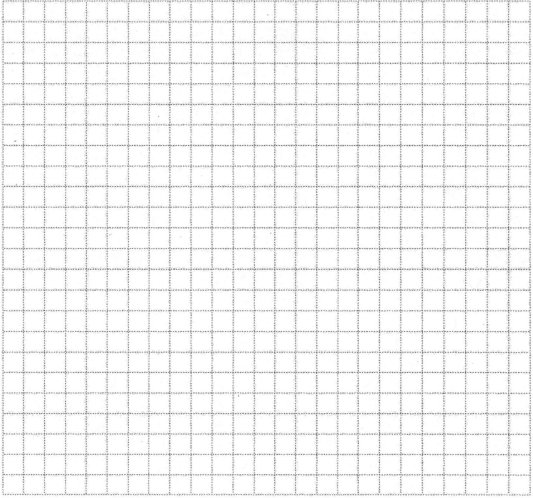

NOTES:

Name: _____ Date: _____

P2-25) Sketch the front, top and right side views of the following object. Use the grid provided.

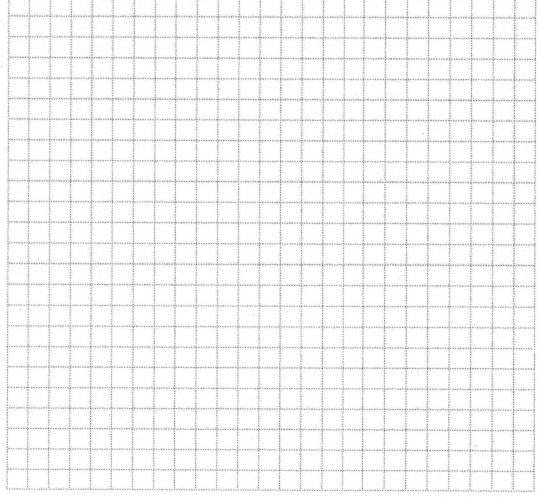

NOTES:

Name: _____ Date: _____

P2-26) Sketch the front, top and right side views of the following object. Use the grid provided.

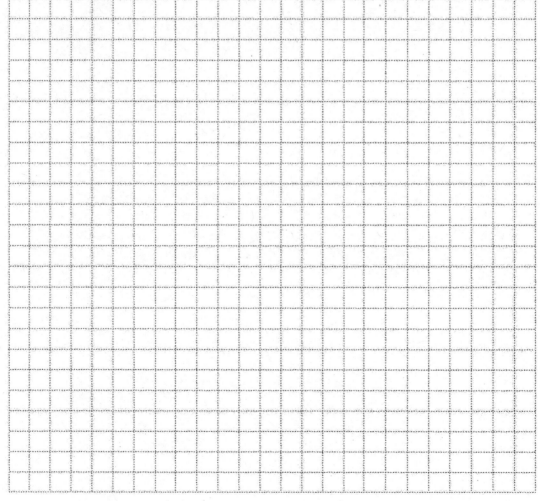

NOTES:

Name: _____ Date: _____

P2-27) Sketch the front, top and right side views of the following object. Use the grid provided.

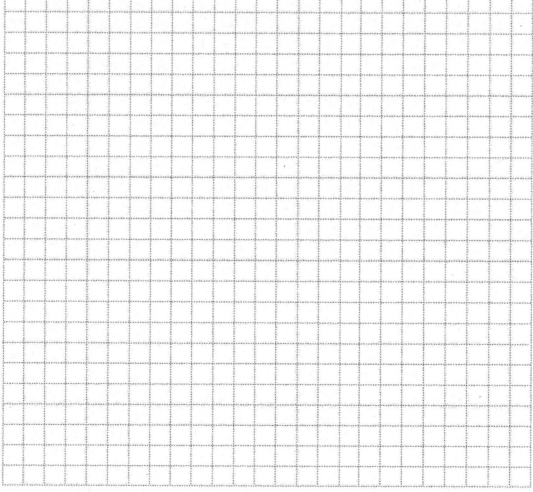

NOTES:

Name: _____ Date: _____

P2-28) Sketch the front, top and right side views of the following object. Use the grid provided.

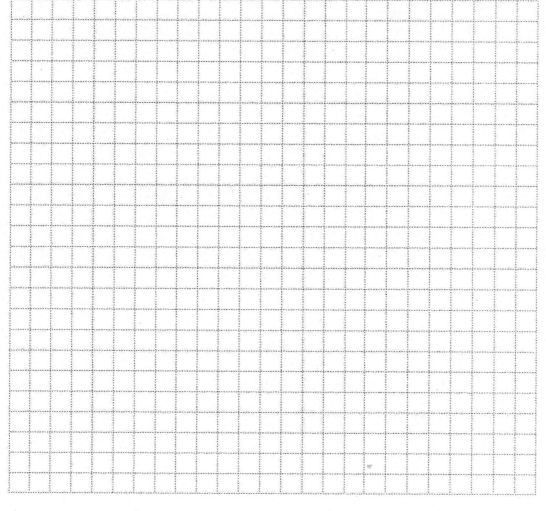

NOTES:

NOTES:

Name: _____ Date: _____

P2-29) Sketch the front, top and right side views of the following object. Use the grid provided.

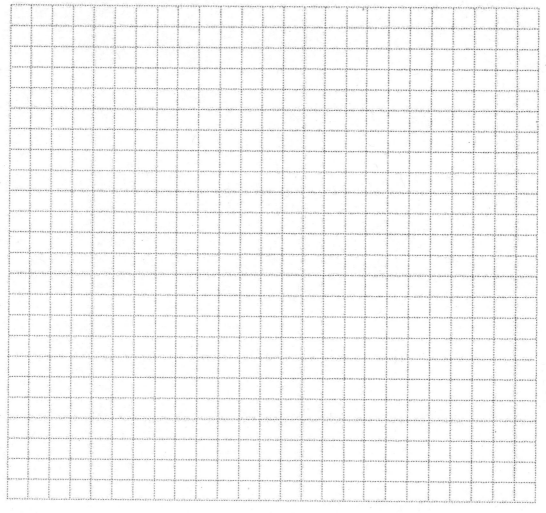

NOTES:

Name: _____ Date: _____

P2-30) Sketch the front, top and right side views of the following object. Use the grid provided.

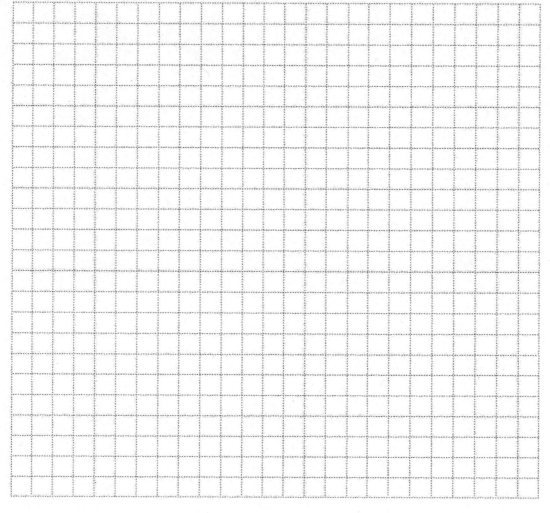

NOTES:

Name: _____ Date: _____

P2-31) Given two complete views, sketch in the missing view.

NOTES:

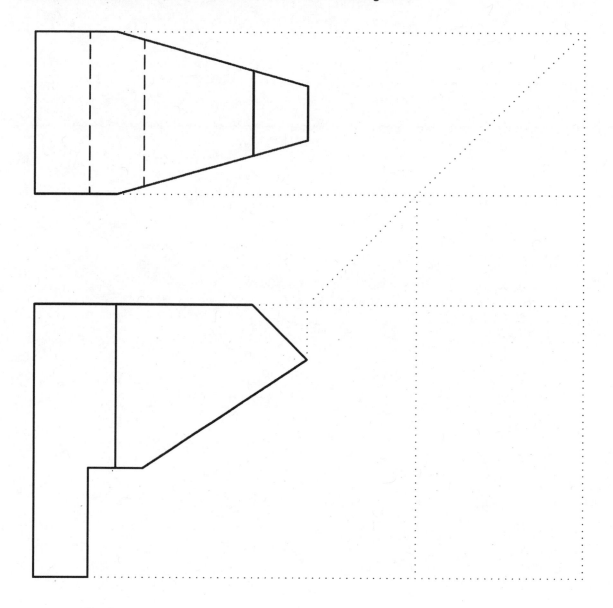

Name: _____ Date: _____

P2-32) Given two complete views, sketch in the missing view.

NOTES:

Name: _____ Date: _____

P2-33) Given two complete views, sketch in the missing view.

NOTES:

Name: _____ Date: _____

P2-34) Given two complete views, sketch in the missing view.

NOTES:

Name: _____ Date: _____

P2-35) Given two complete views, sketch in the missing view.

NOTES:

Name: _____ Date: _____

P2-36) Given two complete views, sketch in the missing view.

<u>NOTES:</u>

Name: _____ Date: _____

P2-37) Given two complete views, sketch in the missing view.

NOTES:

Name: _____ Date: _____

P2-38) Given two complete views, sketch in the missing view.

NOTES:

P2-39) Create an orthographic projection of the following object. Draw the three standard views.

P2-40) Create an orthographic projection of the following object. Draw the three standard views.

P2-41) Create an orthographic projection of the following object. Draw the three standard views.

P2-42) Create an orthographic projection of the following object. Draw the three standard views.

P2-43) Create an orthographic projection of the following object. Draw the three standard views.

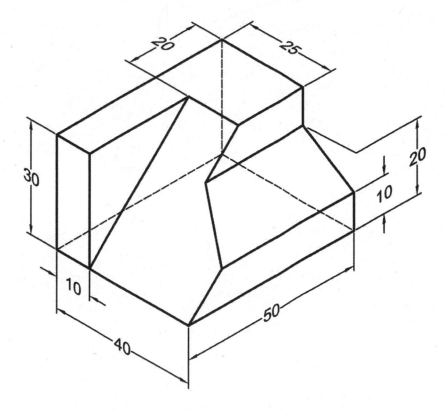

P2-44) Create an orthographic projection of the following object. Draw the three standard views.

P2-45) Create an orthographic projection of the following object. Draw the three standard views.

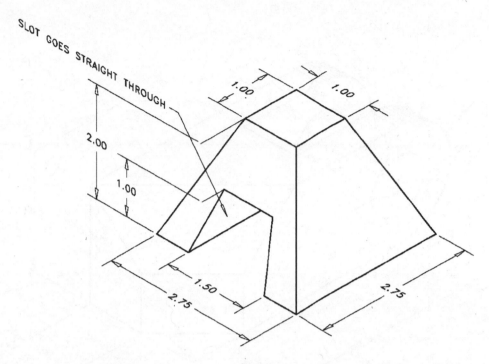

P2-46) Create an orthographic projection of the following object. Draw the three standard views.

P2-47) Create an orthographic projection of the following object. Draw the three standard views.

P2-48) Create an orthographic projection of the following object. Draw the three standard views.

P2-49) Create an orthographic projection of the following object. Draw the three standard views.

P2-50) Create an orthographic projection of the following object. Draw the three standard views.

P2-51) Create an orthographic projection of the following object. Draw the three standard views.

P2-52) Create an orthographic projection of the following object. Draw the three standard views.

P2-53) Create an orthographic projection of the following object. Draw the three standard views.

P2-54) Create an orthographic projection of the following object. Draw the three standard views.

P2-55) Create an orthographic projection of the following object. Draw the three standard views.

P2-56) Create an orthographic projection of the following object. Draw the three standard views.

SP2-1) Sketch the front, top and right side views of the following object. Use the grid provided. The answer to this problem is given in the *Independent Learning Content*.

SP2-2) Sketch the front, top and right side views of the following object. Use the grid provided. The answer to this problem is given in the *Independent Learning Content*.

SP2-3) Sketch the front, top and right side views of the following object. Use the grid provided. The answer to this problem is given in the *Independent Learning Content*.

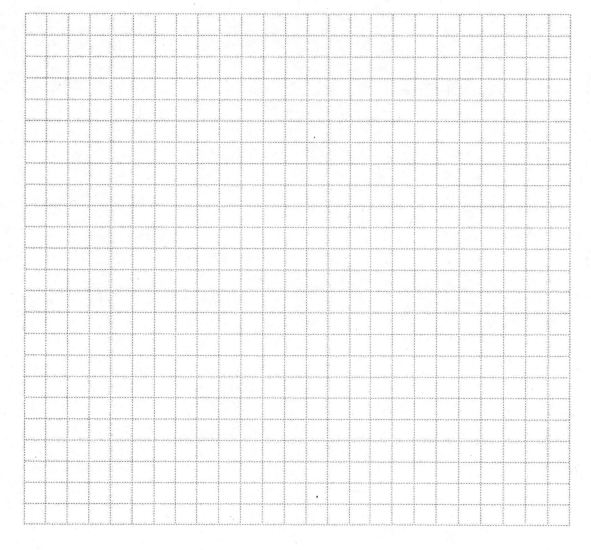

NOTES:

CHAPTER 3

PICTORIAL DRAWINGS

CHAPTER OUTLINE

CHAPTER SUMMARY

In this chapter you will learn about pictorial drawings and how to draw them. A pictorial drawing is a representation of an object created in two dimensions, which appears three dimensional. Pictorials are very helpful when trying to interpret a complex part print or when you are trying to communicate design ideas to an audience that is unfamiliar with orthographic projections. By the end of this chapter you will be able to recognize the different types of pictorials and be able to sketch isometric and oblique pictorials based on an orthographic projection of the part.

3.1) PICTORIALS INTRODUCTION

Pictorials are pseudo three-dimensional drawings. That is, they are drawings of an object created in two dimensions that look three dimensional. Pictorials are very useful when trying to communicate design ideas to an audience that may be unfamiliar with orthographic projections. Being able to efficiently and effectively create a pictorial sketch will enable you to get your idea across to your design team quickly and with less possibility of misinterpretation (see Figure 3.1-1). A pictorial of a part is often included on a detailed drawing to help with the visualization of the part (see Figure 3.1-2). Pictorials are also used to illustrate how parts fit together in an exploded assembly drawing (see Figure 3.1-3).

Figure 3.1-1: Pictorial sketches of design ideas

Figure 3.1-2: Pictorial representation added to a detailed drawing

Figure 3.1-3: Exploded assembly drawing

3.2) PICTORIAL TYPES

There are three basic types of pictorial drawings: **axonometric**, **oblique**, and **perspective**. These three pictorial types differ in their relationship between the object and the point of sight. Before computer assisted drawing, the two most commonly used pictorials were *isometric* and *oblique* (see Figure 3.2-1). Notice that they both look three dimensional, but their orientations are different. They are both useful techniques. You will find yourself choosing one or the other method depending on your part geometry. The procedure for creating isometric and cabinet oblique pictorials will be discussed in detail. Most computer drawing and modeling packages are set up to create pictorial drawings. Some programs let you choose the type of pictorial, however, many others create the pictorial based on your current model view which rarely coincides with one of the three types of pictorials mentioned.

The pictorial types discussed in this book and how they are constructed are in accordance with the ASME – Y14.3 standard.

Isometric Pictorial   Oblique Pictorial

Figure 3.2-1: Common pictorial types

3.3) AXONOMETRIC PROJECTIONS

An axonometric projection is one in which the projectors are perpendicular to the plane of projection and parallel to each other as shown in Figure 3.3-1. All the principal edges are drawn on or parallel to the axonometric axes. On the real object, the principal edges are 90° apart and lie on or parallel to the x-y-z coordinate system. In order to produce the illusion of a three-dimensional object, the axonometric axes are not 90° apart. To the eye, circular features represented in an axonometric pictorial look perfectly circular. However, if you look closely, circular features such as holes, cylinders, and radii are drawn as ellipses as shown in Figure 3.3-1 and 3.3-2.

There are three types of axonometric projections: **isometric**, **dimetric**, and **trimetric**. Each type has a different axonometric axes configuration as shown in Figure 3.3-2. The type of axonometric projection used should be chosen based on which type will give the most accurate description of the object.

3.3.1) Types of axonometric pictorials

Isometric pictorials are drawn in a coordinate system where one axis is vertical and the other two are 30 degrees above the horizontal as shown in Figure 3.3-2. The height of the object is drawn along the vertical axis and the width and depth are drawn along the axes that are at a 30 degree angle from the horizontal. Isometric pictorials are drawn at a uniform scale. The most realistic looking scale is 80%. Linear dimensions along or parallel to the isometric axes are to scale. Features at an angle to the axes are not to scale.

Dimetric pictorials are drawn in a coordinate system where one axis is vertical and the other are equal and may vary between 0 and 45 degrees above the horizontal as shown in Figure 3.3-2. If the angle becomes 30 degrees, it is identified as an isometric pictorial. The height of the object is drawn along the vertical axis and the width and depth are drawn along angled axes. The scaling of a dimetric pictorial is equal along the angled axes and may be different on the vertical axis. Features at an angle to the dimetric axes are not to scale.

Trimetric pictorials are drawn in a coordinate system where one axis is vertical and the other axes may vary in angle above the horizontal as shown in Figure 3.3-2. The varying axis angles are not equal to each other and may not be zero degrees. If the angle becomes equal, it is identified as a dimetric pictorial. The sum of the two angles of the non-vertical axes may not exceed 90 degrees. The height of the object is drawn along the vertical axis and the width and depth are drawn along angled axes. Each axis may use a different scale. Features at an angle to the trimetric axes are not to scale.

Figure 3.3-1: Axonometric projection

Isometric

30°   30°

Drawn to scale

Trimetric

θ

φ

Different scale on each axis

θ = variable (not 0°)
φ = variable (not 0°)
θ + φ ≤ 90°

Dimetric

Same scale

θ   θ

θ = varies between 0° - 45°, (not 30°)

Figure 3.3-2: Axonometric projection types

Exercise 3.3-1: Axonometric pictorial identification

Identify what type of axonometric pictorial is used to represent the following object.

3.4) OBLIQUE PROJECTIONS

An oblique projection is one in which the projectors are not perpendicular to the plane of projection but are parallel to each other as shown in Figure 3.4-1. All the principal edges are drawn on or parallel to the oblique axes. On the real object, the principal edges are 90° apart and lie on or parallel to the x-y-z coordinate system. Oblique pictorials are drawn in a coordinate system where two of the axes make a 90 degree angle with each other. Only one of the axes is at an angle from the horizontal. The angle of this axis may range between 0 and 90 degrees; however, the most commonly used angle is 45 degrees.

There are three types of oblique pictorials: **cavalier**, **cabinet**, and **general**. Each type is created by drawing the height in a vertical axis, the width along the horizontal axis and the depth along the axes that is at an angle from the horizontal. The features drawn on the axes that are parallel to the projection plane (i.e. vertical and horizontal axes) are drawn at full scale and true shape. The linear features drawn on the angled axis may be full scale (cavalier projection) or may be drawn foreshortened. The most common, is a half scale cabinet projection. The cabinet projection approach looks more realistic (see Figure 3.4-2).

3.4.1) Types of oblique pictorials

A **cavalier projection** is an oblique projection where all features drawn parallel to the oblique pictorial axes are drawn full scale. A **cabinet projection** is an oblique projection where all features drawn on the angled axis are drawn at half scale. A **general oblique projection** is where all features drawn on the angled axis are drawn at scale but not at full or half scale. Figure 3.4-3 shows an example of each type of oblique pictorial.

Projectors <u>not</u> perpendicular to the projection plane but are parallel to each other.

Projection plane

Oblique Projection

Figure 3.4-1: Oblique projection

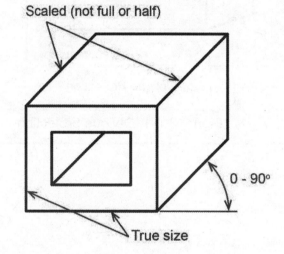

Figure 3.4-2: Oblique pictorial types

3.5) PERSPECTIVE PROJECTIONS

A perspective projection is one in which the projectors are not parallel, instead they converge to a point of sight as shown in Figure 3.5-1. That means that edges that are parallel on the real object will not necessarily be parallel in a perspective projection. There are three types of perspective projections: **one-point**, **two-point**, and **three-point**.

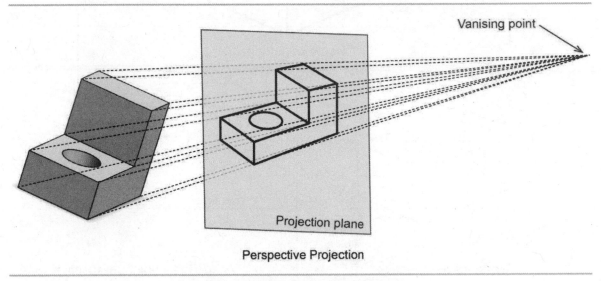

Perspective Projection

Figure 3.5-1: Perspective projection

3.5.1) Types of perspective projections

A **one-point perspective projection** is created by placing two of the principal axes of the object parallel to the projection plane. The remaining axis is perpendicular to the projection plane. In a one-point perspective, the height and width of the object are shown vertically and horizontally, and the depth axis will converge to a single vanishing point (see Figure 3.5-2).

A **two-point perspective projection** is created by placing one of the principal axes of the object parallel to the projection plane. This is usually the vertical axis. The other two axes are inclined to the projection plane. The height is shown vertically and the width and depth axes each converge to their own vanishing point.

A **three-point perspective projection** is created by placing all three principal axes neither parallel nor perpendicular to the projection plane. The height, width, and depth axes will each converge to their own vanishing point. Figure 3.5-2 shows examples of each type of perspective projection.

One-point perspective

Two-point perspective

Three-point perspective

Figure 3.5-2: Perspective projection types

3.6) VISUALIZATION

With solid modeling becoming the main method of constructing part prints, teaching visualization skills has been deemphasized. Visualization is the ability to picture in your mind how a 3D part would look as a 2D orthographic projection and visa-versa. Being able to visualize a part is important for two reasons. First, if you create a part print from a solid model, it is important that you can inspect the computer generated drawing and be able to determine whether or not the CAD program created a technically correct orthographic projection. Second, if you are given a part print you should have the skills to turn that drawing into a solid model.

Exercise 3.6-1: Pictorial matching

Based on the orthographic projection shown, circle the pictorial that represents the true shape of the object?

3.7) DRAWING ISOMETRIC PICTORIALS

Isometric pictorials are drawn in a coordinate system where the axes are 60° apart as shown in Figure 3.7-1. The height of the object is drawn along the vertical axis and the width and depth are drawn along the axes that are at a 30 degree angle from the horizontal. The linear features on or parallel to these three axes are drawn at 80% of full scale to represent true size. However, isometric pictorials may be drawn at any scale as long as the scale is uniform on all axes. Note that even though round features such as holes appear to the eye as being perfectly circular, they are really ellipses (see Figure 3.7-2).

Figure 3.7-1: Isometric pictorial axes

Figure 3.7-2: Isometric pictorial

3.7.1) Drawing linear features in an isometric pictorial

The steps used to draw an isometric pictorial depend on the method of its creation. For example, you may use pencil and paper to sketch an isometric pictorial, or a computer drawing and/or solid modeling package such as AutoCAD® or SOLIDWORKS®. If you are sketching an isometric pictorial, it is best to start with a box that contains or frames in your part. When using a 2-D drawing package, it is best to start with an isometric grid that will guide you along the appropriate axes. If you are using a 3-D modeling package, you don't have to draw an isometric pictorial at all because it will automatically generate one for you. The following steps describe a method that may be used to draw an isometric drawing by hand or with a 2-D drawing package. The object shown in Figure 3.7-3 will be used to illustrate the steps. Note that, for ease of illustration, the following steps produce a full scale isometric. A more realistic isometric is one that is drawn at 80% of full scale.

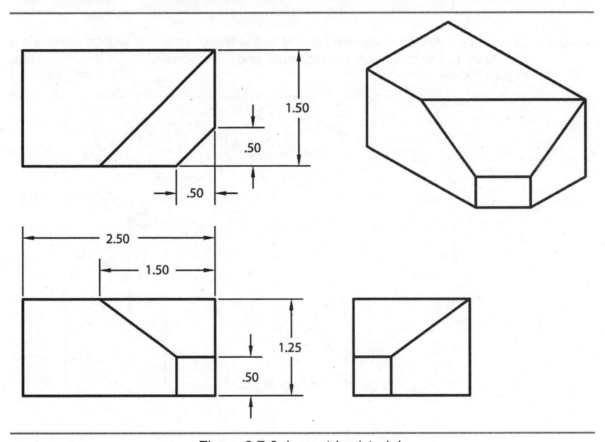

Figure 3.7-3: Isometric pictorial

Step 1) Draw three construction lines that represent the isometric axes (see Figure 3.7-4).

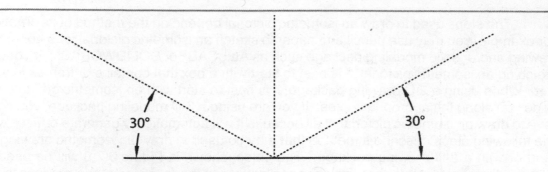

30°   30°

Figure 3.7-4: Creating an isometric pictorial step 1

Step 2) Draw a box whose sides are parallel to the three axes and whose dimensions are equal to the maximum height, width and depth dimension of the object (see Figure 3.7-5).

2.50

1.25

1.50

Figure 3.7-5: Creating an isometric pictorial step 2

Step 3) Draw the lines of the object that are parallel to the axes. These lines will be drawn to scale (see Figure 3.7-6).

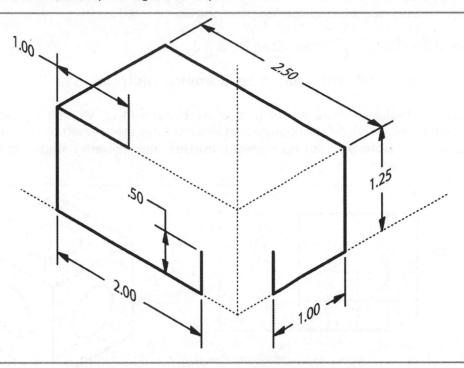

Figure 3.7-6: Creating an isometric pictorial step 3

Step 4) The lines of the object that are not parallel to one of the axes are added by connecting the ends of existing lines (see Figure 3.7-7). Note that these lines are not to scale.

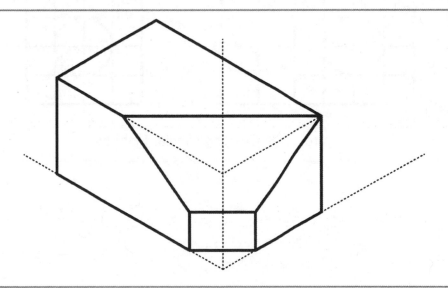

Figure 3.7-7: Creating an isometric pictorial step 4

Step 5) Erase or remove the construction lines.

If you plan to sketch an isometric pictorial by hand, a 30/60 triangle, an isometric (80%) ruler and an isometric ellipse template should be used.

Try Exercise 3.7-1 and view Video Exercise 3.7-2

3.7.2) Drawing circles and radii in an isometric pictorial

Circular features of an object appear as ellipses in an isometric pictorial. The object shown in Figure 3.7-8 will be used to illustrate the steps used to create isometric circular features. Note that, for illustrative purposes, the following steps produce a full scale isometric.

Figure 3.7-8: Creating circular features

Exercise 3.7-1: Isometric pictorial linear features

Create an isometric pictorial of the following object. The grid spacing is 10 mm.

<u>Video Exercise 3.7-2: Beginning Isometric Pictorial</u>

This video exercise will take you through creating an isometric pictorial based on the orthographic projection shown.

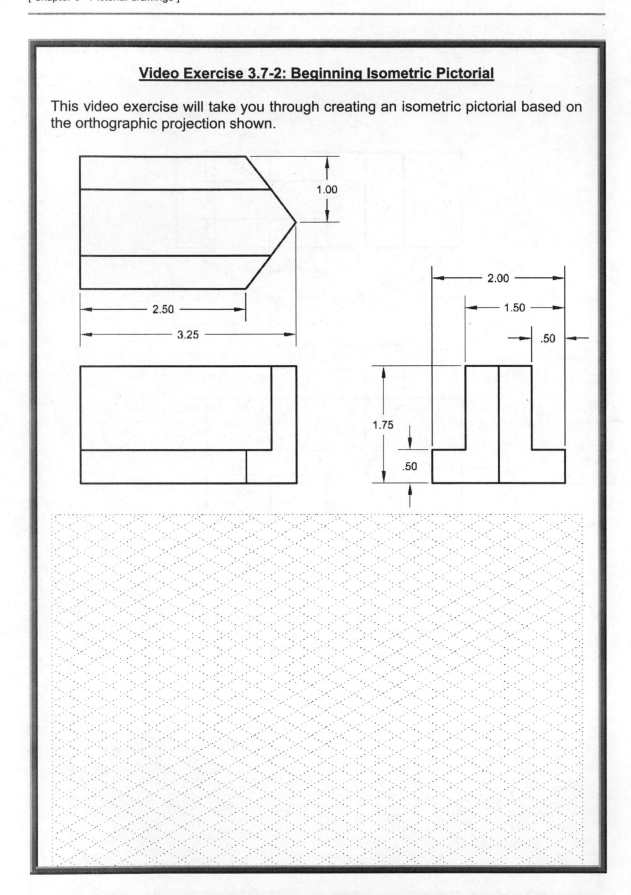

Step 1) Draw the linear features of the object using the procedure previously described (see Figure 3.7-9).

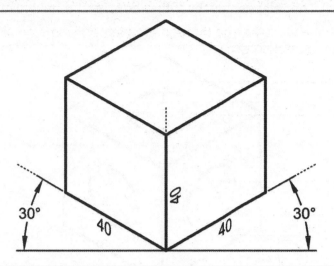

Figure 3.7-9: Creating circular features step 1

Step 2) For each circular feature, draw a box whose diagonals meet at the center of the circle and side dimensions are equal to the circle's diameter (see Figure 3.7-10).

Figure 3.7-10: Creating circular features step 2

Step 3) Draw an ellipse in the box whose major axis is aligned with the long diagonal of the box. The ellipse touches the box at the midpoint of its sides (see Figure 3.7-11).

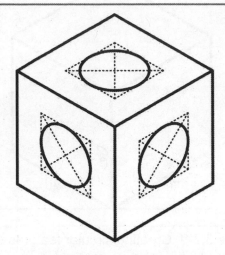

Figure 3.7-11: Creating circular features step 3

Step 4) Erase or remove the construction lines.
Step 5) If the drawing is produced in a 2-D drawing package, it should be scaled by 80%.

The same procedure is used to create radii except that the unwanted part of the ellipse is erased or trimmed. To sketch a more accurate isometric pictorial, an isometric ellipse template should be used.

3.7.3) Drawing cylinders in an isometric pictorial

Drawing cylinders in an isometric pictorial is just a matter of drawing two isometric circles and adding some connecting lines (see Figure 3.7-12).

Step 1) Draw a defining box whose height is equal to the height of the cylinder and whose width and depth dimensions are equal to the diameter of the cylinder.
Step 2) Draw the diagonals and ellipses in the boxes that define the beginning and end of the cylinder.
Step 3) Draw two lines that connect the two ellipses. The lines will start and end at the intersection between the ellipse and the major axis diagonal.
Step 4) Erase all construction lines and any lines that fall behind the cylinder.
Step 5) If the drawing is produced in a computer drawing package, it should be scaled by 80%.

Figure 3.7-12: Drawing cylinders

Try Exercise 3.7-3 and view Video Exercises 3.7-4 and 3.7-5.

Exercise 3.7-3: Isometric pictorial circular features

Create an isometric pictorial of the following object. The grid spacing is 10 mm.

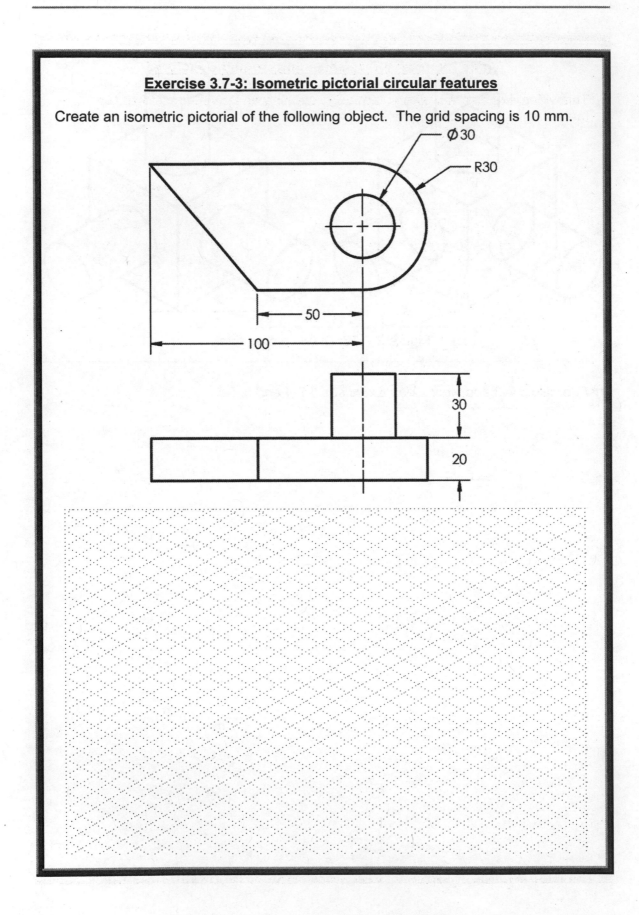

Video Exercise 3.7-4: Beginning Isometric Pictorial

This video exercise will take you through creating an isometric pictorial based on the orthographic projection shown.

Video Exercise 3.7-5: Intermediate Isometric Pictorial

This video exercise will take you through creating an isometric pictorial based on the orthographic projection shown.

3.8) DRAWING CABINET OBLIQUE PICTORIALS

Oblique pictorials are drawn in a coordinate system where only one axis is at an angle from the horizontal. The angle of this axis may range between 0 and 90 degrees; however, the most commonly used angle is 45 degrees as shown in Figure 3.8-1. Oblique pictorials are created by drawing the height in a vertical axis, the width along the horizontal axis and the depth along the axis that is at an angle from the horizontal. The features drawn on the plane defined by the vertical and horizontal axes are drawn at full scale and true shape. The linear features drawn on the angled axis may be full scale (cavalier projection) or may be drawn foreshortened. The most common, is a half scale cabinet projection (see Figure 3.8-1). The cabinet projection approach looks more realistic.

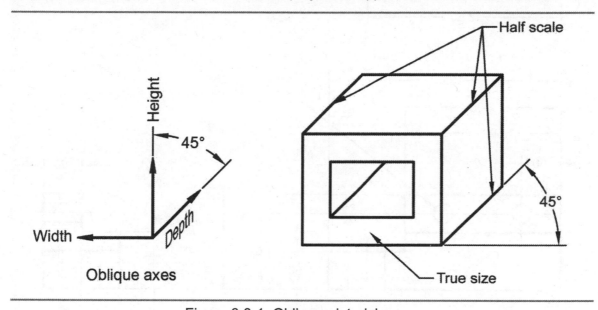

Figure 3.8-1: Oblique pictorial axes

3.8.1) Drawing features of a cabinet oblique pictorial

Just as with an isometric pictorial, the steps used to draw an oblique pictorial depend on the method of its creation. The following steps describe a method that may be used to draw a cabinet oblique pictorial by hand. Most CAD packages are not set up to draw oblique pictorials. The object shown in Figure 3.8-2 will be used to illustrate the steps.

Figure 3.8-2: Cabinet oblique pictorial

Step 1) Draw three construction lines that represent the oblique axes (see Figure 3.8-3). We will use an angle of 45° for the third axis.

Figure 3.8-3: Creating a cabinet oblique pictorial step 1

Step 2)   Draw a box whose sides are parallel to the three axes and whose dimensions are equal to the maximum height, width and half of the maximum depth dimension of the object (see Figure 3.8-4).

Figure 3.8-4: Creating an isometric pictorial step 2

Step 3)   Draw the lines of the object that are parallel to the sides of the box (see Figure 3.8-5).

Features on or parallel to the shaded plane are drawn **full** scale.

Features on or parallel to the shaded plane are drawn **half** scale.

Figure 3.8-5: Creating an isometric pictorial step 3

Step 4)   Add any lines of the object that are not parallel to one of the axes by connecting the ends of existing lines. Note that these lines are not to scale.

Step 5)   Add any circular features. Note that the circular features that are drawn on a plane that is parallel to the plane created by the height and width axes are true size and shape. Any circular features that are not parallel to these axes are not true shape (see Figure 3.8-6). The procedure for drawing these circular features is similar to that of an isometric circular feature except for the scaling of the depth dimension.

Figure 3.8-6: Creating an isometric pictorial step 5

Step 6)   Erase or remove the construction lines.

Figure 3.8-7: Creating an isometric pictorial step 6

If you plan to sketch a cabinet oblique pictorial by hand, a 45° triangle, a half scale ruler and a 45° ellipse template should be used.

Try Exercise 3.8-1 and 3.8-2, and watch Video Exercise 3.8-3 and 3.8-4.

Exercise 3.8-1: Cabinet oblique pictorial linear features

Create a cabinet oblique pictorial of the following object. The grid spacing is 10 mm.

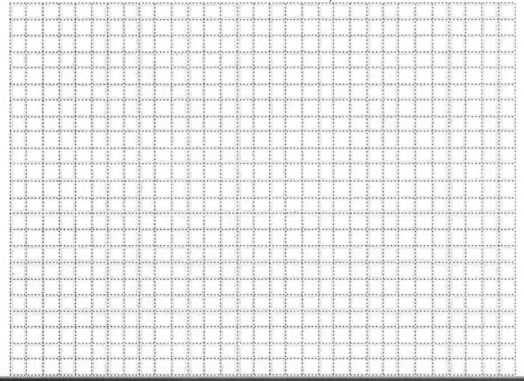

Exercise 3.8-2: Cabinet oblique pictorial circular features

Create a cabinet oblique pictorial of the following object. The grid spacing is 10 mm.

Video Exercise 3.8-3: Beginning Oblique Pictorial

This video exercise will take you through creating cabinet oblique pictorial based on the orthographic projection shown.

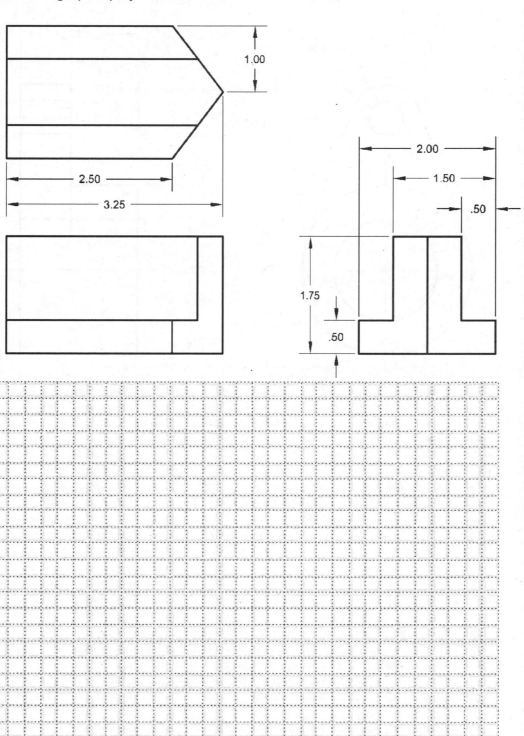

<u>Video Exercise 3.8-4: Creating a cabinet oblique pictorial</u>

This video exercise will take you through creating cabinet oblique pictorial based on the orthographic projection shown.

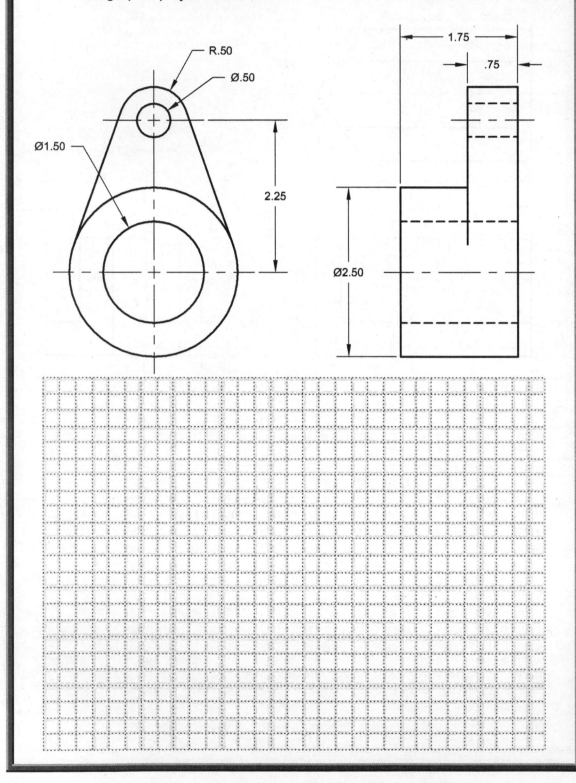

3.9) APPLYING WHAT WE HAVE LEARNED

Exercise 3.9-1: Creating pictorials 1

Name: _____ Date: _____

Create an isometric pictorial and then a cabinet oblique pictorial of the following object. The grid spacing is 0.25 inches.

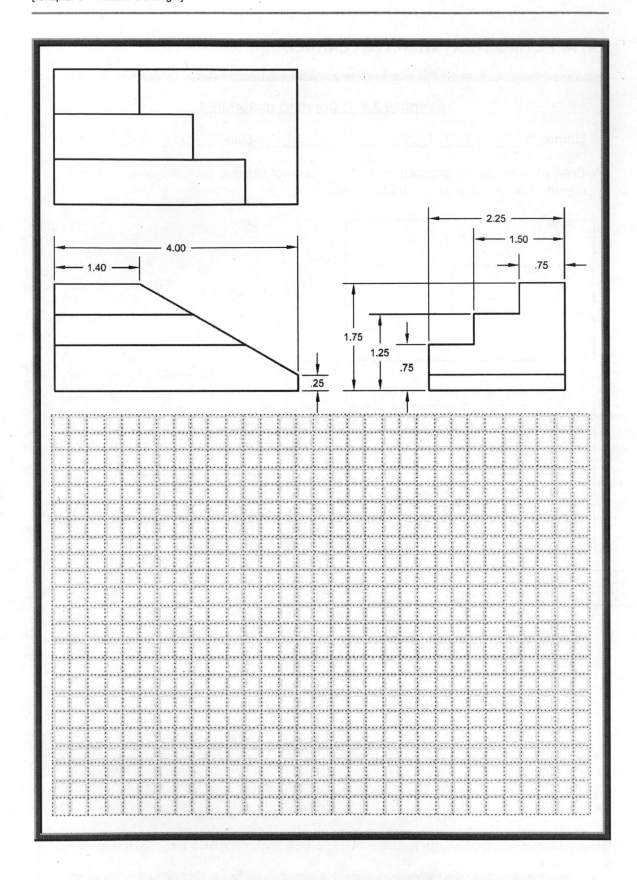

Exercise 3.9-2: Creating pictorials 2

Name: _____ Date: _____

Create an isometric pictorial and then a cabinet oblique pictorial of the following object. The grid spacing is 10 mm.

R35

35

55

Ø30

Ø20

60

30

15

(35)

Ø10
Ø20
▽10

Ø20

(15)

(35)

PICTORIAL DRAWINGS QUESTIONS

Name: _____ Date: _____

Q3-1) A pictorial drawing is a two-dimensional rendering of a part, but the drawing still looks _____. (Fill in the blank)

Q3-2) Pictorials help us... (Circle all that apply.)

a) be expressive.
b) visualize a part or assembly.
c) communicate ideas.

Q3-3) A pictorial may be included on a detailed drawing. (true, false)

Q3-4) List the three different types of axonometric projections?

Q3-5) List the three different types of oblique projections?

Q3-6) List the three different types of perspective projections?

Q3-7) Why is developing the ability to sketch pictorials by hand important?

Q3-8) Two of the isometric axes are drawn .... degrees above the horizontal.

    a) 10
    b) 15
    c) 30
    d) 45

Q3-9) Two of the oblique pictorial axes are drawn horizontally and vertically. The other axis is most commonly drawn .... degrees above the horizontal.

    a) 10
    b) 15
    c) 30
    d) 45

Q3-10) An isometric pictorial looks more realistic if it is drawn at a/an .... percent scale.

    a) 30
    b) 50
    c) 80
    d) 90

Q3-11) Circular features in a pictorial are drawn as _____. Fill in the blank.

PICTORIAL DRAWINGS PROBLEMS

Name: _____ Date: _____

P3-1) Match the correct pictorial to the orthographic projection.

NOTES:

Name: _____ Date: _____

P3-2) Match the correct pictorial to the orthographic projection.

NOTES:

Name: _____ Date: _____

P3-3) Match the correct pictorial to the orthographic projection.

NOTES:

Name: _____ Date: _____

P3-4) Draw a full scale isometric pictorial and a cabinet oblique pictorial by hand or in a drawing package per instructions. The grid spacing is 0.25 inch.

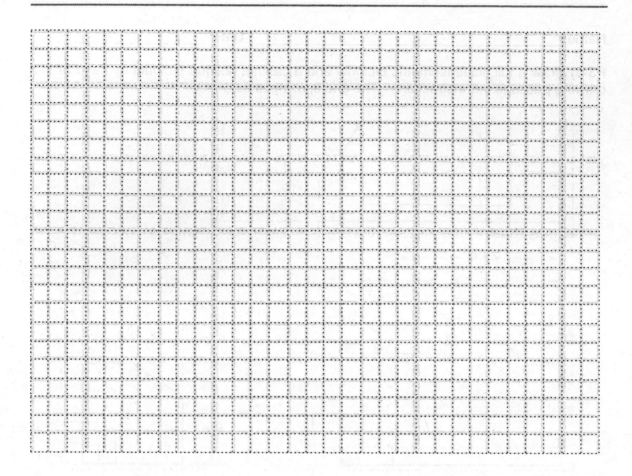

Name: _____ Date: _____

P3-5) Draw a full scale isometric pictorial and a cabinet oblique pictorial by hand or in a drawing package per instructions. The grid spacing is 10 mm.

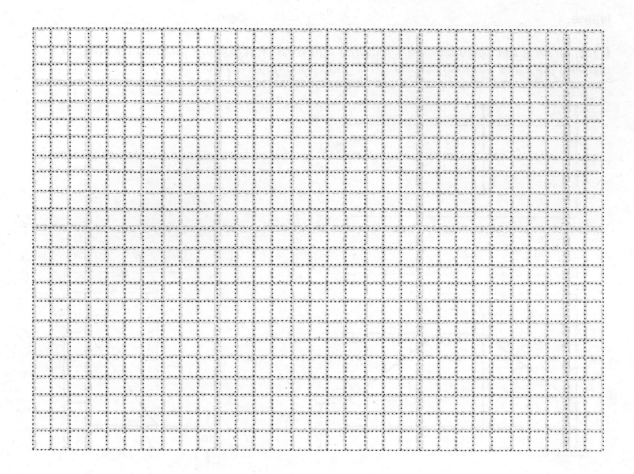

Name: _____ Date: _____

P3-6) Draw a full scale isometric pictorial and a cabinet oblique pictorial by hand or in a drawing package per instructions. The grid spacing is 0.25 inch.

Name: _____ Date: _____

P3-7) Draw a full scale isometric pictorial and a cabinet oblique pictorial by hand or in a drawing package per instructions. The grid spacing is 10 mm.

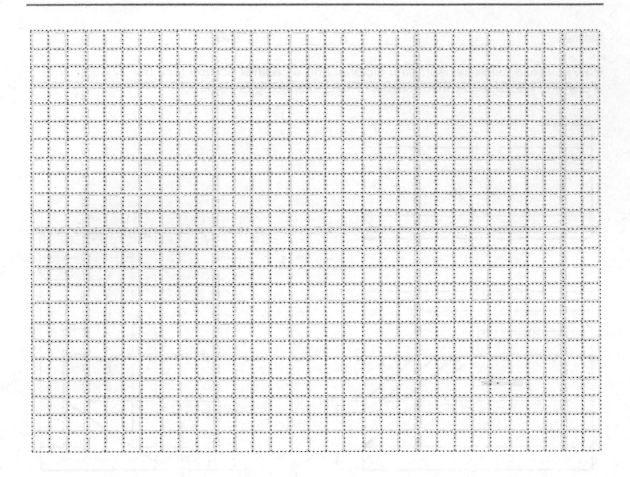

Name: _____ Date: _____

P3-8) Draw a full scale isometric pictorial and a cabinet oblique pictorial by hand or in a drawing package per instructions. The grid spacing is 0.25 inch.

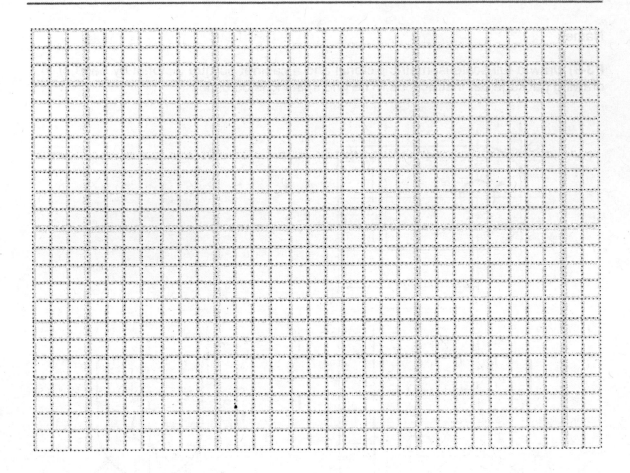

Name: _____ Date: _____

P3-9) Draw a full scale isometric pictorial and a cabinet oblique pictorial by hand or in a drawing package per instructions. The grid spacing is 10 mm.

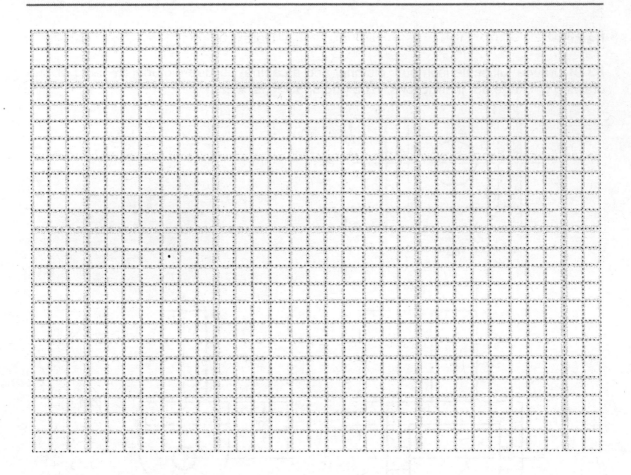

P3-10) Draw an isometric and cabinet oblique pictorial drawing of the following object.

P3-11) Draw an isometric and cabinet oblique pictorial drawing of the following object.

P3-12) Draw an isometric and cabinet oblique pictorial drawing of the following object.

P3-13) Draw an isometric and cabinet oblique pictorial drawing of the following object.

P3-14) Draw an isometric and cabinet oblique pictorial drawing of the following object.

P3-15) Draw an isometric and cabinet oblique pictorial drawing of the following object. Include all hidden lines.

SP3-1) Draw a full scale isometric pictorial and a cabinet oblique pictorial by hand or in a drawing package. The answer to this problem is in the *Independent Learning content*.

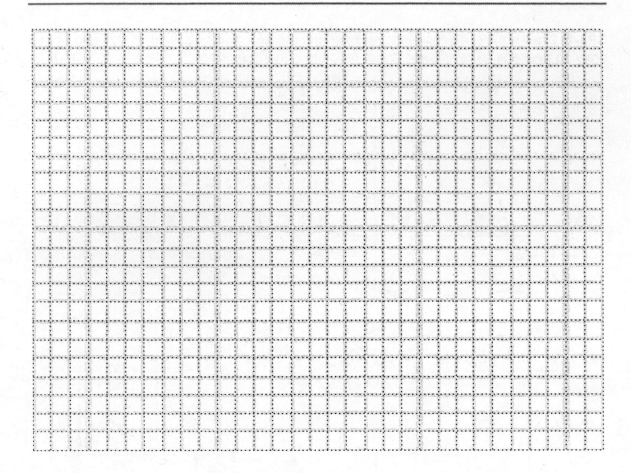

SP3-2) Draw a full scale isometric pictorial and a cabinet oblique pictorial by hand or in a drawing package. The answer to this problem is in the *Independent Learning content*.

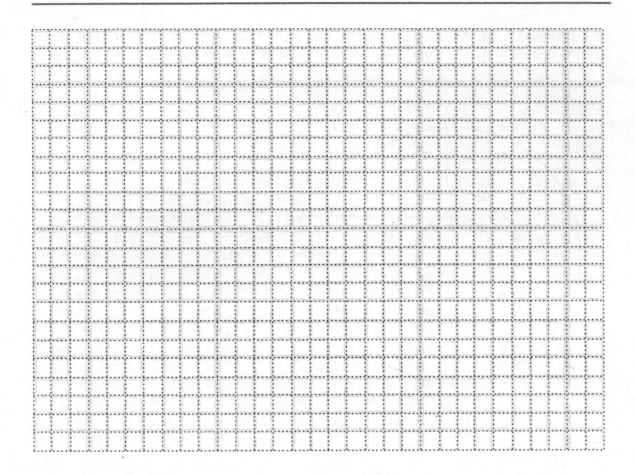

CHAPTER 4

DIMENSIONING

CHAPTER OUTLINE

CHAPTER SUMMARY

In this chapter you will learn how to dimension an orthographic projection using proper dimensioning techniques. This may seem like a simple task; however, dimensioning a part is not as easy as inserting the sizes used to draw the part. Dimensions affect how a part is manufactured. A small change in how an object is dimensioned may produce a part that will not pass inspection. The type and placement of the dimensions and the dimension text is highly controlled by ASME standards (American Society of Mechanical Engineers). By the end of this chapter, you will be able to dimension a moderately complex part using proper dimensioning techniques. Dimensioning complex/production parts requires the knowledge of x-y coordinate tolerancing and GD&T (Geometric Dimensioning & Tolerancing). Tolerancing is covered in another chapter.

4.1) DETAILED DRAWINGS

In addition to the shape description of an object given by an orthographic projection, engineering drawings must also give a complete size description using dimensions. This enables the object to be manufactured. **An orthographic projection, complete with all the dimensions and specifications needed to manufacture the object is called a *detailed drawing*.** Figure 4.1-1 shows a simple example of a detailed drawing.

Figure 4.1-1: Detailed drawing

4.2) LEARNING TO DIMENSION

Dimensioning a part correctly entails conformance to many rules. It is very tempting to dimension an object using the measurements needed to draw the part. But, these are not necessarily the dimensions required to manufacture it. Generally accepted dimensioning standards should be used when dimensioning any object. In basic terms, dimensions should be given in a clear and concise manner and should include all the information needed to produce and inspect the part exactly as intended by the designer. There should be no need to measure the size of a feature directly from the drawing.

The dimensioning standards presented in this chapter are in accordance with the ASME Y14.5-2009 standard. This standard was created to establish a uniform way of dimensioning an engineering drawing. This also minimizes errors that could occur while reading or interpreting an engineering drawing. When a drawing conforms to the standard, it is noted in the tolerance block as shown in Figure 4.2-1. Other common sense practices will also be presented.

UNLESS OTHERWISE SPECIFIED
DIM ARE IN INCHES
TOL ON ANGLE ±.XX°
2 PL ±.XX   3 PL ±.XXX
INTERPRET DIM AND TOL PER
ASME Y14.5 - 2009

THIRD ANGLE PROJECTION

Figure 4.2-1: ASME Y14.5 – 2009 designation

4.3) DIMENSION APPEARANCE

4.3.1) Lines Used in Dimensioning

Dimensions require the use of *dimension*, *extension* and *leader lines*. **All lines used in dimensioning are drawn thin so that the print reader does not confuse them with visible lines.** Thin lines should be drawn at approximately 0.016 inch (0.3 mm). Figure 4.3-1 illustrates the different features of a dimension and Figure 4.3-2 illustrates different leader line configurations.

- Dimension line: A dimension line is a thin solid line terminated by arrowheads, which indicates the direction and extent of a dimension. A number is placed near the midpoint to specify the feature's size.
- Extension line: An extension line is a thin solid line that extends from a point on the drawing to which the dimension refers. There should be a visible gap between the extension line and the object, and long extension lines should be avoided.
- Leader line: A leader line is a straight inclined thin solid line that is usually terminated by an arrowhead. It is used to direct a dimension, note, symbol, item number, or part number to the intended feature on a drawing. Leader lines should not be drawn vertical or horizontal, except for a short horizontal portion extending to the first or last letter of the note. The horizontal part should not underline the note and may be omitted entirely. Leader lines may be terminated by an arrow if it ends on the outline of an object or without an arrow head or with a dot (∅1.5 mm, minimum) if it ends within the outline of an object (see Figure 4.3-2). You should avoid creating long leaders, crossing leaders, or leaders that are parallel to features on the drawing.

Figure 4.3-1: Features of a dimension

Figure 4.3-2: Leader line configurations

4.3.2) Types of Dimensions

Dimensions are given in the form of *linear distances*, *angles*, and *notes*.

- Linear distances: A linear dimension is used to give the distance between two points. They are usually arranged horizontally or vertically, but may also be aligned with a particular feature of the part.
- Angles: An angular dimension is used to give the angle between two surfaces or features of a part.
- Notes: Notes are used to dimension diameters, radii, chamfers, threads, and other features that cannot be dimensioned by the other two methods. Notes can be local (i.e. applies to one feature), or general (i.e. applies to the whole drawing).

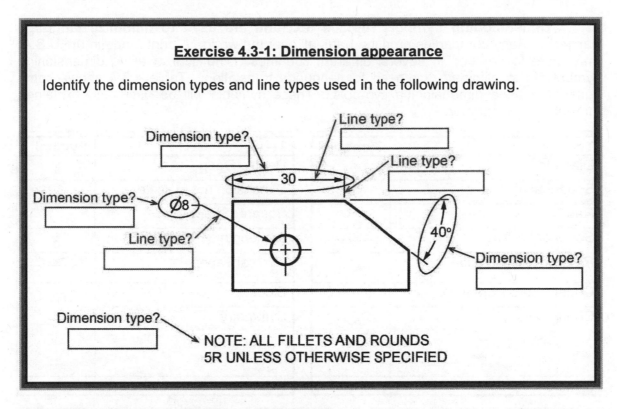

Exercise 4.3-1: Dimension appearance

Identify the dimension types and line types used in the following drawing.

4.3.3) Arrowheads, lettering, and symbols

The length and width ratio of an **arrowhead** should be 3 to 1 and the width should be proportional to the line thickness. A single style of arrowhead should be used throughout the drawing. Arrowheads are drawn between the extension lines if possible. If space is limited, they may be drawn on the outside. Figure 4.3-3 shows the most common arrowhead configurations.

Lettering should be legible, easy to read, and uniform throughout the drawing. **Upper case letters** should be used for all lettering unless a lower case is required. The minimum lettering height is **0.12 inch (3 mm)**.

Figure 4.3-3: Arrowhead and feature size placement.

Dimensioning symbols replace text and are used to minimize language barriers. Many companies produce parts all over the world. A print made in the U.S.A. may have to be read in several different countries. The goal of using dimensioning symbols is to eliminate the need for language translation. Table 4.3-4 shows some commonly used dimensioning symbols. These symbols will be used and explained throughout the chapter.

Term	Symbol	Term	Symbol
Diameter	⌀	Depth / Deep	⤓
Spherical diameter	S⌀	Dimension not to scale	<u>10</u>
Radius	R	Square (Shape)	□
Spherical radius	SR	Arc length	$\hat{5}$
Reference dimension	(8)	Conical Taper	▷
Counterbore / Spotface	⊔	Slope	◺
Countersink	⋁	Symmetry	÷ or =
Number of places	4X		

Table 4.3-4: Dimensioning symbols

4.4) FEATURE DIMENSIONS

The following section illustrates the standard ways common features are dimensioned.

a) A circle is dimensioned by its diameter and an arc by its radius using a leader line and a note or linear dimension. Diameter dimensions of solid parts, such as a cylinder, is given as a linear dimension. A diameter dimension is preceded by the symbol "⌀", and a radial dimension is preceded by the symbol "R". On older drawings you may see the abbreviation "DIA" placed after a diameter dimension and the abbreviation "R" following a radial dimension. Figure 4.4-1 illustrates the diameter and radius dimensions.

| Diameter of hole | Radius | Diameter of solid part |

Figure 4.4-1: Diameter and radius dimensions

b) The depth ($\overline{V}$) of a blind hole is specified under the hole's diameter dimension and is the depth of the full diameter from the surface of the object. Figure 4.4-2 illustrates how a dimension for a blind hole (i.e. a hole that does not pass completely through the object) is given.

Figure 4.4-2: Dimensioning a blind hole.

c) If a hole goes completely through the feature and it is not clearly shown on the drawing, the abbreviation "THRU" follows the dimension.

d) If a dimension is given to the center of a radius, a small cross is drawn at the center. Where the center location of the radius is unimportant, the drawing must clearly show that the arc location is controlled by other dimensioned features such as tangent surfaces. Figure 4.4-3 shows several different radius configurations.

Figure 4.4-3: Dimensioning radial features.

e) A complete sphere is dimensioned by its diameter and an incomplete sphere by its radius. A spherical diameter is indicated by using the symbol "S⌀" and a spherical radius by the symbol "SR". Figure 4.4-4 illustrates the spherical diameter and spherical radius dimensions.

Spherical Diameter   Spherical Radius

Figure 4.4-4: Dimensioning spherical features.

<u>Exercise 4.4-1: Feature dimensions 1</u>

Indicate the size of the following features using appropriate feature dimensions and symbols.

Dimension the
diameter of the hole.

Dimension the radius.

Dimension the blind hole.

Draw the hole's side view.

Ø10 - THRU

Dimension the sphere and the rod with a spherical end.

f) Holes are dimensioned by giving their diameter and location in the circular view. Cylinders are dimensioned by giving their diameter and length in the rectangular view, and are located in the circular view. By giving the diameter of a cylinder in the rectangular view, it is less likely to be confused with a hole.

Try Exercise 4.4-2

g) Repetitive features or dimensions are specified by using the symbol "X" along with the number of times the feature is repeated. There is no space between the number of times the feature is repeated and the "X" symbol, however, there is a space between the symbol "X" and the dimension (i.e. 8X $\varnothing$10).

h) Equally spaced features are specified by giving the number of spaces followed by the repeated feature symbol "X", a space, and then the dimension value of the space as shown in Figure 4.4-5. The total distance may be given in parentheses after the dimension and one spacing may be dimensioned and given as a reference value.

Figure 4.4-5: Equally spaced features

Try Exercise 4.4-3

Exercise 4.4-2: Circular and rectangular views

Below is shown the front and top view of a part. Consider the hole and cylinder features of the part when answering the following questions.

- Which view is considered the circular view and which is considered the rectangular view?
- Looking at just the top view, can you tell the difference between the hole and the cylinder?
- Why do we dimension the diameter of the cylinder in the rectangular view?

Exercise 4.4-3: Feature dimensions 2

Fill in the repeated pattern dimension if there are a total of 11 holes all equally spaced.

i) If the center of a radius is outside the drawing or interferes with another view, the dimension lines are foreshortened. In this case, a false center and jogged dimensions are used to give the size and location from the false center as shown in Figure 4.4-6. The false center is indicated by a small cross.

Figure 4.4-6: Jogged radius

j) Solid parts that have rounded ends are dimensioned by giving their overall dimensions (see Figure 4.4-7). If the ends are partially rounded, the radii are also given. For fully rounded ends, the radii are indicated but the value is not given. This is because the width of the part is two times the radius.

Fully rounded ends   Partially rounded ends

Figure 4.4-7: Rounded ends

k) Slots are dimensioned by giving their overall dimensions or by giving the overall width and the distance between centers as shown in Figure 4.4-8. The radii are indicated but the value is not given. This is because the width of the slot is two times the radius.

Figure 4.4-8: Slots

Exercise 4.4-4: Feature dimensions 3

Indicate the size of the following features using appropriate feature dimensions and symbols.

Dimension these solid parts.	Dimension this slot.

l) The length of an arc is dimensioned using the arc length symbol as shown in Figure 4.4-9.

Figure 4.4-9: Arc length

m) If a part is symmetric, dimensions on one side of the center line of symmetry may only be given. The center line of symmetry is indicated by using the symbol "⹀" or "=". On older drawings you might see the symbol "₵" used instead. Figure 4.4-10 illustrates the use of the symmetry symbol.

Figure 4.4-10: Center line of symmetry.

n) Counterbored holes are specified by giving the diameter ($\emptyset$) of the drill (and depth if appropriate), the diameter ($\emptyset$) of the counterbore ($\sqcup$), and the depth ($\overline{\mathbb{V}}$) of the counterbore in a note as shown in Figure 4.4-11. If the thickness of the material below the counterbore is significant, this thickness rather than the counterbore depth is given.

Figure 4.4-11: Counterbored holes.

Application Question 4.4-1

What is the purpose of a counterbored hole? (See Figure 4.4-11)

o) Spotfaced holes are similar to counterbored holes. The difference is that the machining operation occurs on a curved surface. Therefore, the depth of the counterbore drill is not given in the note. It must be specified in the rectangular view as shown in Figure 4.4-12.

Figure 4.4-12: Spotfaced holes.

p) Countersunk holes are specified by giving the diameter ($\emptyset$) of the drill (and depth if appropriate), the diameter ($\emptyset$) of the countersink ($\vee$), and the angle of the countersink in a note as shown in Figure 4.4-13.

Figure 4.4-13: Countersunk holes.

q) Chamfers are dimensioned by a linear dimension and an angle, or by two linear dimensions. A note may be used to specify 45 degree chamfers because the linear value applies in either direction (see Figure 4.4-14). Notice that there is a space between the 'X' symbol and the linear dimension. The space is inserted so that it is not confused with a repeated feature.

Figure 4.4-14: Chamfers.

Exercise 4.4-5: Feature dimensions 4

Fill in the feature size if
- drill = 10 mm
- counterbore drill and max. countersink dia. = 20 mm
- countersink angle = 90°
- counterbore depth = 12 mm
- blind hole depth = 25 mm
- chamfer size is 2 mm and angle is 45°

4.4.1) Drawing Notes

Drawing notes give additional information that is used to complement conventional dimensions. Drawing notes provide information that clarify the manufacturing requirements for the part. They cover information such as treatments and finishes among other manufacturing processes. A note may also be used to give blanket dimensions, such as the size of all rounds and fillets on a casting or a blanket tolerance. Notes may apply to the entire drawing or to a specific area. A general note applies to the entire drawing. A local note is positioned near and points to the specified area to which it applies. A general note area is identified with the heading "NOTE:". Listed below are a few examples of general drawing notes.

NOTE: ALL FILLETS AND ROUNDS 3 MM UNLESS
OTHERWISE SPECIFIED.

NOTE: REMOVE BURRS AND BREAK SHARP EDGES.

NOTE: APPLICABLE STANDARDS: ASME Y14.5-2009,
ASME Y14.41-2003.

4.5) DIMENSIONING RULES

The ASME Y14.5M – 2009 standard specifies 16 fundamental rules. The rules that are relevant to interpreting basic to intermediate engineering drawing dimensions are explained below. Note that these rules are not necessarily given in the same order as listed in the standard.

4.5.1) Dimension placement, spacing and readability

Rule 1) Dimensions should be arranged for maximum readability.

Dimensions should be easy to read and minimize the possibility for conflicting interpretations and should be placed in such a way as to enhance the communication of your design. Dimensions should be given clearly and in an organized fashion. They should not be crowded or hard to read.

The following are guidelines that govern the logical and practical arrangement of dimensions to insure maximum legibility:

a) The **spacing** between dimension lines should be uniform throughout the drawing. The space between the first dimension line and the part should be at least **10 mm**; the space between subsequent dimensions should be at least **6 mm**. However, the above spacing is only intended as a guide.

b) **Do not dimension inside an object** or have the dimension line touch the object unless clearness is gained.

c) **Dimension text should be horizontal** which means that it is read from the bottom of the drawing.

d) Dimension text should not cross dimension, extension or visible lines.

e) Dimension lines should not cross extension lines or other dimension lines. To avoid this, shorter dimensions should be placed before longer ones. Extension lines can cross other extension lines or visible lines. However, this should be minimized. Where extension lines cross other lines, the extension lines are not broken. If an extension line crosses an arrowhead or is near an arrowhead, a break in the extension line is permitted.

Try Exercise 4.5-1.

f) Extension lines and centerlines should not connect between views.

g) Leader lines should be straight, not curved, and point to the center of the arc or circle at an angle between 30°-60°. The leaders should *float up* or, in other words, lead from the arrow up to the text.

Try Exercise 4.5-2.

h) Dimensions should be grouped whenever possible.

i) Dimensions should be placed between views, unless clearness is promoted by placing some outside.

j) Dimensions should be attached to the view where the shape is shown best.

k) Do not dimension hidden lines.

Try Exercises 4.5-3

Exercise 4.5-1: Spacing and readability 1

Consider the incorrectly dimensioned object shown. There are 5 types of dimensioning mistakes. List them and then dimension the object correctly.

1)   4)
2)   5)
3)

Exercise 4.5-2: Spacing and readability 2

Consider the incorrectly dimensioned object shown. There are 4 types of dimensioning mistakes. List them and then dimension the object correctly.

1)   3)

2)   4)

Exercise 4.5-3: Dimension placement

Consider the incorrectly dimensioned object shown. There are 6 types of dimensioning mistakes. List them and then dimension the object correctly.

1)   4)

2)   5)

3)   6)

4.5.2) Over/Under dimensioned parts

Rule 2) Your part should be completely dimensioned, but not over defined. Dimensions should not be duplicated or the same information given in two different ways. It is not allowable for the print reader to measure directly from the drawing. The standard does list a few exceptions, but none are relevant here.

Exercise 4.5-4: Missing dimensions

Find and draw the missing dimensions. There are three.

Exercise 4.5-5: Duplicate dimensions

Find the duplicate dimensions and cross out the ones that you feel should be omitted.

Rule 3) The use of reference (duplicated) dimension should be minimized. If a reference dimension is used, the size value is placed within parentheses (e.g. (10)). Duplicate dimensions may cause needless trouble. If a change is made to one dimension, the reference dimension may be overlooked causing confusion. If the reference dimension and the dimension it references do not match, the reference dimension should be ignored.

Exercise 4.5-6: Reference dimensions

Match the reference dimension with the dimension it references. Are there any inconsistencies?

Rule 4) Features drawn at 90° to each other (e.g. two center lines, a corner) **are assumed to be 90° if no angle dimension is given.** The angle tolerances in this case are controlled by the drawing's block tolerance.

Exercise 4.5-7: Dimensioning

Dimension the following object.

4.5.3) Manufacturing

Rule 5) Don't specify manufacturing processes with your dimension. For example, words such as "DRILL", "REAM", and "PUNCH" should not be placed with the feature size. On old prints, you may see a hole dimension specified as ".12 DRILL". This dimension specifies a manufacturing process. The dimension should read "$\varnothing$.12". The exception is when the process is essential to the definition of the engineering requirements.

Rule 6) Parts identified by gage or code numbers are dimensioned using their actual decimal size. The gage or code number may be shown in parenthesis next to the dimension. Sometimes you may encounter a drawing that specifies standard drills, broaches, and the like by a number or letter.

Rule 7) All dimensions are applicable at 20°C unless otherwise specified. If the material has a high thermal expansion coefficient, compensations may be made.

Rule 8) Part sizes prior to processing may be specified on a drawing. In general, final part dimensions are specified on a drawing, however, non-mandatory processing dimensions may also be present. These dimensions are identified using the note "NONMANDATORY (MFG DATA)". Non-mandatory processing dimensions specify part sizes prior to processing such as finishing the part or part shrinkage.

Your choice of dimensions will directly influence the method used to manufacture a part. However, your **choice of dimensions should depend on the function and the mating relationship of the part**, and then on manufacturing. Learning the topics in this section and the upcoming sections will guide you when choosing your dimension units, decimal places and the dimension's starting point. Even though dimensions influence how the part is made, the manufacturing process is not specifically stated on the drawing. Listed are a few examples of how dimension placement and dimension text influence how the part gets manufactured.

- ✓ Increasing the number of decimal places (e.g. 1.00 goes to 1.000) will increase the cost of manufacturing. Some manufacturing processes are not as accurate as other processes (e.g. *casting* is not very accurate, *grinding* is more accurate). More accurate processes are generally more expensive.
- ✓ Identifying a datum feature (i.e. a surface from which most dimensions originate) will influence the surfaces used in the manufacturing process. This topic is covered in section 4.5.4.
- ✓ Dimension placement also influences error build up. This is how much error is allowed during the manufacturing process. This topic is covered in section 4.5.5.

a) On drawings where all the dimensions are given either in millimeters or inches, individual identification of the units is not necessary. However, the drawing should contain a note stating UNLESS OTHERWISE SPECIFIED, ALL DIMENSIONS ARE IN MILLIMETERS (or INCHES). If some inch dimensions are used on a millimeter drawing or visa versa, the abbreviations **IN** or **mm** shall follow the dimension value.

b) Metric dimensions are given in 'mm' and typically given to 0 or 1 decimal place (e.g. 10, 10.2). When the dimension is less than a millimeter, a zero should precede the decimal point (e.g. 0.5).

c) English dimensions are given in 'inches' and typically given to 2 decimal places (e.g. 1.25). A zero is not shown before the decimal point for values less than one inch (e.g. .75).

There is no such thing as an "exact" measurement. **The more accurate a dimension is, the more expensive it is to manufacture.** To cut costs it is necessary to round off fractional dimensions. If, for example, we are rounding off to the second decimal place and the third decimal place number is less than 5, we truncate after the second decimal place. If the number in the third decimal place is greater than 5, we round up and increase the second decimal place number by 1. If the number is exactly 5, whether or not we round up depends on if the second decimal place number is odd or even. If it is odd, we round up and if it is even, it is kept the same.

Exercise 4.5-8: Dimension accuracy

Consider the figure shown below.

- Does the arrow indicate an increasing or decreasing accuracy?

- Write down the range in which the dimension values are allowed to vary.

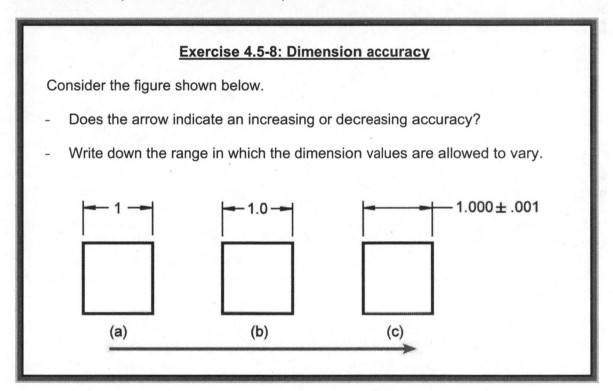

Exercise 4.5-9: Rounding off

Round off the following fractions to two decimal places according to the rules stated above.

(5/16) .3125 →   (1/8) .125 →

(5/32) .1562 →   (3/8) .375 →

Exercise 4.5-10: Advanced dimensioning

Consider the incorrectly dimensioned object shown. There are 7 types of dimensioning mistakes. List them and then dimension the object correctly.

1)   5)

2)   6)

3)   7)

4)

4.5.4) Functional dimensioning

Rule 9) Dimensions imply function. When reading a print, the dimensions give you clues to the part's function and mating relationships. Figure 4.5-1 shows examples of this.

Figure 4.5-1: Dimensions imply function

Choose your dimensions based on the function of your part. In general, dimensions should originate from a datum feature. However, if the distance between two features is critical, it will not originate from the datum feature. Datum features will be covered in more detail in the next paragraph. Figure 4.5-2 shows an assembly where two parts are aligned using pins. Notice that the surface of the HUB that touches the BASE is designated as datum feature A. In general, all the dimensions originate from datum features. Without seeing the assembly, we can determine the importance of surfaces based on which surfaces are chosen to be the datum features. If a dimension does not originate from a datum feature it means that the distance between the two features is important. For example, the HUB center extrusion and the pin holes must match the distances between the BASE center hole and the pin holes. Therefore, this distance is given as opposed to the distance from the datum feature. Note that the HUB is not completely dimensioned in this figure. This figure is used for illustrative purposes only.

Figure 4.5-2: Dimensions indicate function

Consider three mutually perpendicular datum planes as shown in Figure 4.5-3. These planes are imaginary and theoretically exact. Now, consider a part that touches all three datum planes. The surfaces of the part that touch the datum planes are called datum features. Most of the time, features on a part are located with respect to these features. **A datum feature is a functionally important surface.** Datum features on a drawing are identified by a datum feature symbol as shown in Figure 4.5-4. A letter is used to identify and differentiate between the datum features. If no datum feature symbols are given, datums may be identified by the use of dimensions. Usually, datum features are the origin of all the dimensions.

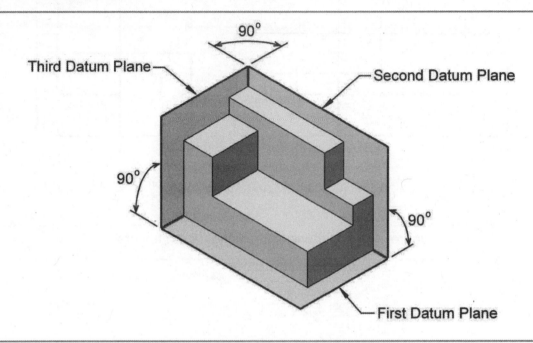

Figure 4.5-3: Datums and datum features.

Datum feature selection is based on the function of the part. When selecting datum features, think of the part as a component of an assembly. Functionally important surfaces and features should be selected as datum features. For example, to ensure proper assembly, mating surfaces should be used as datum features. A datum feature should be big enough to permit its use in manufacturing the part. If the function of the part is not known, take all possible measures to determine its function before dimensioning the part. In the process of learning proper dimensioning techniques, it may be necessary to make an educated guess as to the function of the part.

Figure 4.5-4: Dimensioning using datum features.

Exercise 4.5-11: Dimension choice

Consider the incorrectly dimensioned object shown. There are 6 types of dimensioning mistakes. List them and then dimension the object correctly.

1)   4)

2)   5)

3)   6)

Video Exercise 4.5-12: Beginning Dimensioning

This video exercise will take you through dimensioning the following objects using proper dimensioning techniques.

<u>Video Exercise 4.5-13: Intermediate Dimensioning</u>

This video exercise will take you through dimensioning the following objects using proper dimensioning techniques.

<u>Video Exercise 4.5-14: Advanced Dimensioning 1</u>

This video exercise will take you through dimensioning the following objects using proper dimensioning techniques.

Video Exercise 4.5-15: Advanced Dimensioning 2

This video exercise will take you through dimensioning the following objects using proper dimensioning techniques.

4.5.5) Tolerancing

Rule 10) Every dimension is toleranced. A toleranced dimension is not a single value, but states the maximum and minimum size that a feature may be and still function correctly. Dimensions that are not toleranced are called **basic dimensions**. These dimensions are used to locate and dimension features to their theoretically exact location. Basic dimensions are identified by placing them in a box.

Rule 11) All dimensions and tolerances apply to the non-deformed part (i.e. the free state condition).

Tolerances may be explicitly stated or covered by the block tolerance. If a dimension is not explicitly stated and there is no block tolerance, the tolerance is implied and depends on the number of decimal places in the dimension value. The exceptions are basic dimensions, reference dimensions, maximum/minimum dimensions, and stock sizes. A basic dimension provides a nominal location or size from which permissible variations are established by geometric tolerances (GD&T) which is not covered in this chapter. Figure 4.5-5 illustrates a few different examples of explicit and implied tolerances, and basic dimensions.

Try Exercise 4.5-11

Figure 4.5-5: Tolerances

Exercise 4.5-16: Tolerances

Identify which dimensions have explicitly stated tolerances, which are covered by the block tolerance, which dimensions are implied, and which are basic dimensions.

UNLESS OTHERWISE SPECIFIED
DIM ARE IN MM
TOL ON ANGLE ± .2°
1 PL ± 0.1
INTERPRET DIM AND TOL PER
ASME Y14.5 - 2009

Figure 4.5-6 shows two different styles of dimensioning. One is called *Continuous Dimensioning*, the other *Datum Dimensioning*. Continuous dimensioning has the disadvantage of accumulating error. **It is preferable to use datum dimensioning to reduce error buildup.**

Consider the part shown in Figure 4.5-6. It is dimensioned using both continuous and datum dimensioning. The implied tolerance of all the dimensions is on the first decimal place. If we look at the continuous dimensioning case, the actual dimensions are x.*e*, where 0.*e* is the error associated with each dimension. Adding up the individual dimensions, we get an overall dimension of 3x + 3*(0.*e*). The overall dimension for the datum dimensioning case is 3x + 0.*e*. As this example shows, continuous dimensioning accumulates error.

Another advantage for the use of datum dimensioning is the fact that many manufacturing machines are programmed using a datum or origin. Therefore, it makes it easier for the machinist to program the machine if datum dimensioning is used.

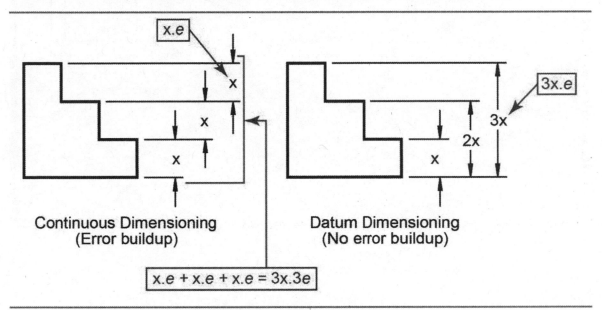

Figure 4.5-6: Error buildup.

NOTES:

4.6) APPLYING WHAT WE HAVE LEARNED

Exercise 4.6-1: Dimensioning 1

Name: _____ Date: _____

Dimension the following object using proper dimensioning techniques. Did we need to draw the right side view?

This way is up

Exercise 4.6-2: Dimensioning 2

Name: _____ Date: _____

Dimension the following object using proper dimensioning techniques.

This way is up

Exercise 4.6-3: Dimensioning 3

Name: _____ Date: _____

Dimension the following object using proper dimensioning techniques.

This way is up

Exercise 4.6-4: Dimensioning 4

Name: _____ Date: _____

Dimension the following object using proper dimensioning techniques.

DIMENSIONING QUESTIONS

Name: _____   Date: _____

Dimension appearance

Q4-1) A detailed drawing is an orthographic projection with ... (Circle all that apply.)

   a) dimensions.
   b) notes.
   c) manufacturing specifications.
   d) everything necessary to manufacture and inspect the part as intended by the designer.

Q4-2) Dimensions generally take the form of ... (Circle all that apply.)

   a) linear dimensions.
   b) extension lines.
   c) angular dimensions.
   d) notes.

Q4-3) Dimension and extension lines are thin so that they will not be mistaken for ... lines.

   a) visible
   b) hidden
   c) center
   d) cutting plane

Q4-4) Which line type does not ever have arrowheads? (dimension, extension, leader)

Q4-5) Leader lines should not be ... (Circle all that apply.)

   a) horizontal.
   b) straight.
   c) curved.
   d) vertical.

Q4-6) Lettering should measure ... on the printed drawing.

   a) 2 mm
   b) 3 mm
   c) 4 mm
   d) 5 mm

Q4-7) All dimension text should be ...

   a) vertical
   b) horizontal
   c) lower case
   d) bold

Dimensioning and locating features

Q4-8) What is this symbol? ▽

    a) repeated feature
    b) depth
    c) counterbore
    d) countersink
    e) symmetry

Q4-9) What is this symbol? ∨

    a) repeated feature
    b) depth
    c) counterbore
    d) countersink
    e) symmetry

Q4-10) What is this symbol? ⊵ or =

    a) repeated feature
    b) depth
    c) counterbore
    d) countersink
    e) symmetry

Q4-11) X is the symbol used for repeated features. What else is this symbol used for?

    a) chamfer
    b) concentricity
    c) counterbore
    d) symmetry

Q4-12) A reference dimension is given within ...

    a) brackets.
    b) double quotes.
    c) parentheses.
    d) single quotes.

Q4-13) Is the following dimension a repeated feature dimension or a chamfer dimension?

2X 45°

Q4-14) Dimensioning hidden lines under some circumstances is allowed. (true, false)

Q4-15) Is a complete circle such as a hole dimensioned by its diameter or radius?

Q4-16) A _____ is located in the circular view. (Circle all that apply.)

    a) hole
    b) cylinder

Q4-17) The diameter of a _____ is given in the circular view. (Circle all that apply.)

    a) hole
    b) cylinder

Q4-18) Write the dimension text for 3 repeated holes with a diameter of 10 mm and a 2 mm chamfer dimension with equal sides.

Q4-19) Write the dimension text for a 1/2 inch blind hole that is 1 inch deep.

Q4-20) Write the dimension text for a counterbore that has a 1/4 inch drill and a 1/2 in counterbore that is 1/2 inch deep.

Q4-21) Write the dimension text for a countersink that has a 10 mm drill and a countersink that has a maximum diameter of 20 mm with a 90 degree angle.

Dimensioning/manufacturing

Q4-22) What unit of measure is most commonly used on English drawing?

Q4-23) What unit of measure is most commonly used on metric drawing?

Q4-24) How many zero's to the right of the decimal does two thousandths of an inch have?

Q4-25) Datum dimensioning is preferred over continuous dimensions because it …

   a) reduces dimensioning time.
   b) reduces error build up.
   c) increases calculation time.
   d) increases set up time.

Q4-26) A surface of the part that touches the datum plane is called a …

   a) datum.
   b) simulated datum.
   c) baseline.
   d) datum feature.

Q4-27) Non-critical inch dimensions usually have … decimal places.

   a) 0
   b) 1
   c) 2
   d) 3

Q4-28) Non-critical mm dimensions usually have … decimal places. (Circle all that apply.)

   a) 0
   b) 1
   c) 2
   d) 3

Q4-29) (Continuous, Datum) dimensioning is preferred to minimize error build up. (Circle the appropriate answer.)

DIMENSIONING PROBLEMS

Name: _____   Date: _____

P4-1) Answer questions about the following drawing.

  a) How many linear dimensions?

  b) How many diameter dimensions?

  c) How many notes-leader line dimensions?

  d) On the drawing, identify the three datums.

  e) If you were inspecting the thickness of this part and find that it measures 0.254 in, would it pass inspection?

  f) If you were inspecting the height of this part and find that it measures 1.009 in, would it pass inspection?

NOTES:

Name: _____ Date: _____

P4-2) Answer questions about the following drawing.

a) How many linear dimensions?

b) How many diameter dimensions?

c) How many angular dimensions?

d) How many notes-leader line dimensions?

e) On the drawing, identify the three datums.

f) What does "THRU" mean?

g) If you were inspecting the overall thickness of this part and find that it measures 1.002 in, would it pass inspection?

h) If you were inspecting the diameter of the two big holes and find that the right hole measures 0.6255 in, would it pass inspection?

i) Circle the explicitly stated toleranced dimensions.

NOTES:

Name: _____   Date: _____

P4-3) Answer the following questions related to the figure.

    a) Drill diameter = _____

    b) Counterbore diameter = _____

    c) Counterbore depth = _____

P4-4) Answer the following questions related to the figure.

    a) Drill diameter = _____

    b) Drill depth = _____

    c) Countersink maximum diameter = _____

    d) Countersink angle = _____

NOTES:

P4-5) The following object is dimensioned incorrectly. Identify the incorrect dimensions and list all mistakes associated with them. Then, dimension the object correctly using proper dimensioning techniques. There are five mistakes.

1)

2)

3)

4)

5)

<u>NOTES:</u>

Name: _____ Date: _____

P4-6) The following object is dimensioned incorrectly. Identify the incorrect dimensions and list all mistakes associated with them. Then, dimension the object correctly using proper dimensioning techniques. There are four mistakes.

1)

2)

3)

4)

NOTES:

Name: _____   Date: _____

P4-7) The following object is dimensioned incorrectly. Identify the incorrect dimensions and list all mistakes associated with them. Then, dimension the object correctly using proper dimensioning techniques. There are six mistakes.

1)

2)

3)

4)

5)

6)

NOTES:

Name: _____ Date: _____

P4-8) The following object is dimensioned incorrectly. Identify the incorrect dimensions and list all mistakes associated with them. Then, dimension the object correctly using proper dimensioning techniques. There are four mistakes.

1)

2)

3)

4)

NOTES:

Name: _____   Date: _____

P4-9) The following object is dimensioned incorrectly. Identify the incorrect dimensions and list all mistakes associated with them. Then, dimension the object correctly using proper dimensioning techniques. There are five mistakes.

1)

2)

3)

4)

5)

NOTES:

Name: _____ Date: _____

P4-10) Completely dimension the objects shown (by hand) using proper dimensioning techniques. Wherever a numerical dimension value is required, place an 'x'. Use dimensioning symbols where necessary.

NOTES:

Name: _____   Date: _____

P4-11) Completely dimension the objects shown (by hand) using proper dimensioning techniques. Wherever a numerical dimension value is required, place an 'x'. Use dimensioning symbols where necessary.

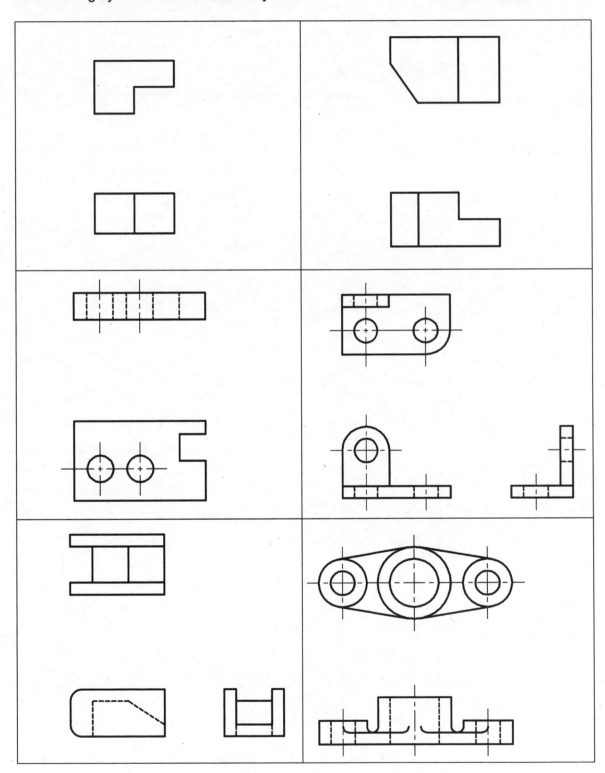

NOTES:

Name: _____ Date: _____

P4-12) Completely dimension the objects shown (by hand) using proper dimensioning techniques. Wherever a numerical dimension value is required, place an 'x'. Use dimensioning symbols where necessary.

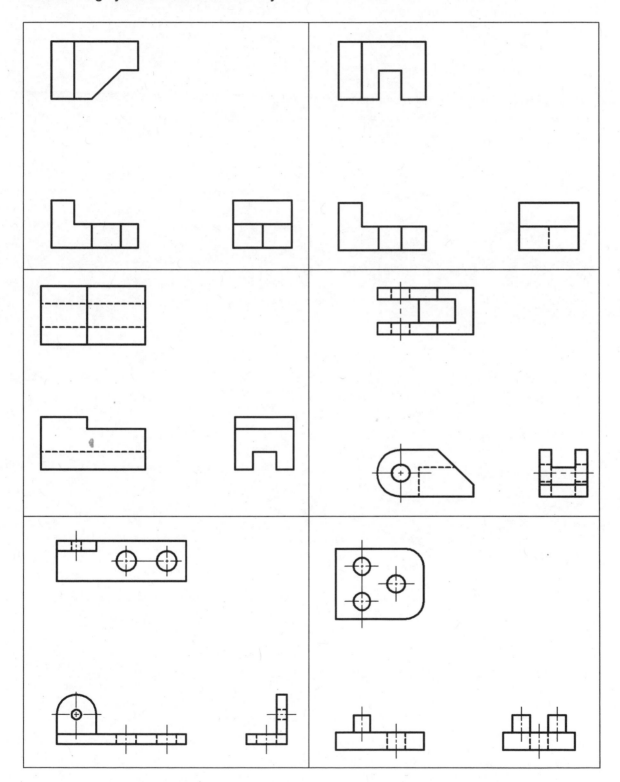

NOTES:

Name: _____ Date: _____

P4-13) Completely dimension the objects shown (by hand) using proper dimensioning techniques. Wherever a numerical dimension value is required, place an 'x'. Use dimensioning symbols where necessary.

NOTES:

P4-14) Using a CAD package, draw the necessary views and completely dimension the part shown. Do not base your 2-D dimension placement on the 3-D dimensions shown. Use proper dimensioning techniques to dimension your object.

P4-15) Using a CAD package, draw the necessary views and completely dimension the part shown. Do not base your 2-D dimension placement on the 3-D dimensions shown. Use proper dimensioning techniques to dimension your object.

P4-16) Using a CAD package, draw the necessary views and completely dimension the part shown. Do not base your 2-D dimension placement on the 3-D dimensions shown. Use proper dimensioning techniques to dimension your object.

P4-17) Using a CAD package, draw the necessary views and completely dimension the part shown. Do not base your 2-D dimension placement on the 3-D dimensions shown. Use proper dimensioning techniques to dimension your object.

P4-18) Using a CAD package, draw the necessary views and completely dimension the part shown. Do not base your 2-D dimension placement on the 3-D dimensions shown. Use proper dimensioning techniques to dimension your object.

P4-19) Using a CAD package, draw the necessary views and completely dimension the part shown. Do not base your 2-D dimension placement on the 3-D dimensions shown. Use proper dimensioning techniques to dimension your object.

NOTE: ALL FILLETS AND ROUNDS
R.12 UNLESS OTHERWISE SPECIFIED

P4-20) Using a CAD package, draw the necessary views and completely dimension the part shown. Do not base your 2-D dimension placement on the 3-D dimensions shown. Use proper dimensioning techniques to dimension your object.

P4-21) Using a CAD package, draw the necessary views and completely dimension the part shown. Do not base your 2-D dimension placement on the 3-D dimensions shown. Use proper dimensioning techniques to dimension your object.

P4-22) Using a CAD package, draw the necessary views and completely dimension the part shown. Do not base your 2-D dimension placement on the 3-D dimensions shown. Use proper dimensioning techniques to dimension your object.

P4-23) Using a CAD package, draw the necessary views and completely dimension the part shown. Do not base your 2-D dimension placement on the 3-D dimensions shown. Use proper dimensioning techniques to dimension your object.

P4-24) Using a CAD package, draw the necessary views and completely dimension the part shown. Do not base your 2-D dimension placement on the 3-D dimensions shown. Use proper dimensioning techniques to dimension your object.

P4-25) Using a CAD package, draw the necessary views and completely dimension the part shown. Do not base your 2-D dimension placement on the 3-D dimensions shown. Use proper dimensioning techniques to dimension your object.

P4-26) Using a CAD package, draw the necessary views and completely dimension the part shown. Do not base your 2-D dimension placement on the 3-D dimensions shown. Use proper dimensioning techniques to dimension your object.

P4-27) Using a CAD package, draw the necessary views and completely dimension the part shown. Do not base your 2-D dimension placement on the 3-D dimensions shown. Use proper dimensioning techniques to dimension your object.

P4-28) Using a CAD package, draw the necessary views and completely dimension the part shown. Do not base your 2-D dimension placement on the 3-D dimensions shown. Use proper dimensioning techniques to dimension your object.

P4-29) Using a CAD package, draw the necessary views and completely dimension the part shown. Do not base your 2-D dimension placement on the 3-D dimensions shown. Use proper dimensioning techniques to dimension your object.

P4-30) Using a CAD package, draw the necessary views and completely dimension the part shown. Do not base your 2-D dimension placement on the 3-D dimensions shown. Use proper dimensioning techniques to dimension your object.

P4-31) Using a CAD package, draw the necessary views and completely dimension the part shown. Do not base your 2-D dimension placement on the 3-D dimensions shown. Use proper dimensioning techniques to dimension your object.

P4-32) Using a CAD package, draw the necessary views and completely dimension the part shown. Do not base your 2-D dimension placement on the 3-D dimensions shown. Use proper dimensioning techniques to dimension your object.

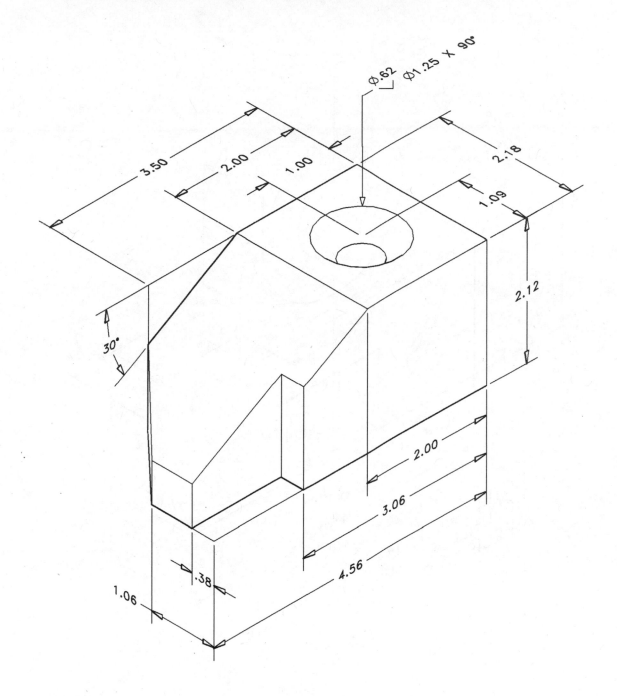

P4-33) Using a CAD package, draw the necessary views and completely dimension the part shown. Do not base your 2-D dimension placement on the 3-D dimensions shown. Use proper dimensioning techniques to dimension your object.

NOTE: ALL FILLETS AND ROUNDS R6 UNLESS OTHERWISE SPECIFIED.

SP4-1) Completely dimension the objects shown (by hand) using proper dimensioning techniques. Wherever a numerical dimension value is required, place an 'x'. Use dimensioning symbols where necessary. The answer to this problem is given in the *Independent Learning Content*.

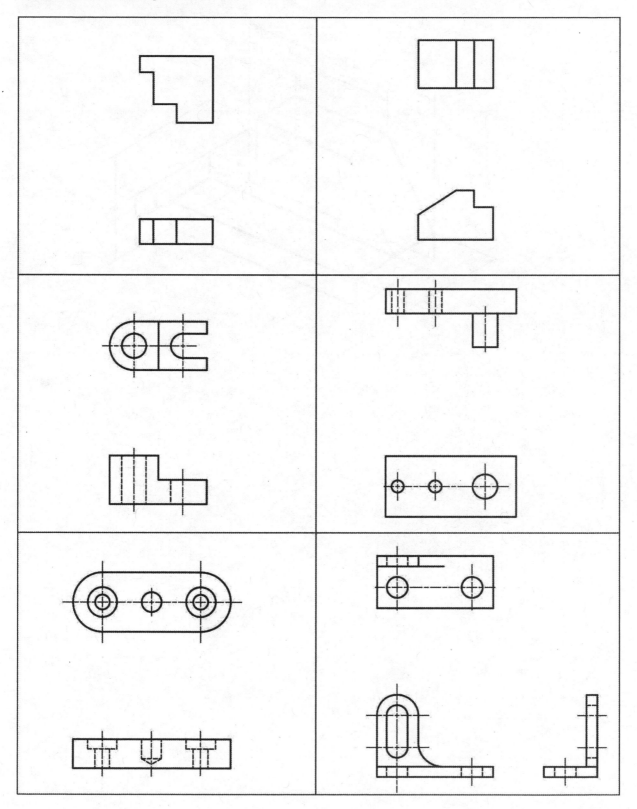

SP4-2) Using a CAD package (or sketching by hand), draw the necessary views and completely dimension the part shown. Do not base your 2-D dimension placement on the 3-D dimensions shown. Use proper dimensioning techniques to dimension your object. The answer to this problem is given in the *Independent Learning Content*.

SP4-3) Using a CAD package (or sketching by hand), draw the necessary views and completely dimension the part shown. Do not base your 2-D dimension placement on the 3-D dimensions shown. Use proper dimensioning techniques to dimension your object. The answer to this problem is given in the *Independent Learning Content*.

NOTES:

CHAPTER 5

SECTIONING

CHAPTER OUTLINE

CHAPTER SUMMARY

In this chapter you will learn how to create various types of sectional views. Sectional views allow you to see inside an object. Using a sectional view within an orthographic projection can be very useful for parts that have complex interior geometry. By the end of this chapter, you will be able to create several different types of sectional views. You will also be able to choose which type of section is the most appropriate for a given part.

5.1) SECTIONAL VIEWS

A sectional view or section looks inside an object. Sections are used to clarify the interior construction of a part that cannot be clearly described by hidden lines in exterior views. It is a cut away view of an object. Often, objects are more complex and interesting on the inside than on the outside. **By taking an imaginary cut through the object and removing a portion, the inside features may be seen more clearly.** For example, a geode is a rock that is very plain and featureless on the outside, but cut into it and you get an array of beautiful crystals.

5.1.1) Creating a section view

To produce a section view, the part is cut using an imaginary cutting plane. The portion of the part that is between the observer and the cutting plane is mentally discarded exposing the interior construction as shown in Figure 5.1-1.

A sectional view should be projected perpendicular to the cutting plane and conform to the standard arrangement of views. If there is more than one section, they should be labeled with capital letters such as A, B or C. These letters are placed near the arrows of the cutting plane line. The sectional view is then labeled with the corresponding letter (e.g. SECTION A-A) as shown in Figure 5.1-2. Letters that should not be used to label sections are I, O, Q, S, X and Z. These letters are often used for other purposes and may lead to misinterpretation.

Figure 5.1-1: Creating a section view.

Notice how the cut material is shown

SECTION A-A

Section View Label

A ▼   A ▼

Notice how the cutting plane is represented

Figure 5.1-2: Sectional view.

5.1.2) Lines used in sectional views

- Cutting Plane Line

    A cutting plane line is used to show where the object is being cut and represents the edge view of the cutting plane. Arrows are placed at the ends of the cutting plane line to indicate the direction of sight. The arrows point to the portion of the object that is kept. Cutting plane lines are thick (0.6 to 0.8 mm) and take precedence over centerlines. Figure 5.1-3 shows the two different types of cutting plane lines that are used on prints and Figure 5.1-2 illustrates its use.

Used for long distances

Used for short distances

Figure 5.1-3: Cutting plane lines.

- Section Lines

    Section lines are used to indicate where the cutting plane cuts the material (see Figure 5.1-2). Cut material is that which makes contact with the cutting plane. Section lines have the following properties:

√ Section lines are thin lines (0.3 mm).
√ Section line symbols (i.e. line type and spacing) are chosen according to the material from which the object is made. Figure 5.1-4 shows some of the more commonly used section line symbols.
√ Section lines are drawn at a 45° angle to the horizontal unless there is some advantage in using a different angle.

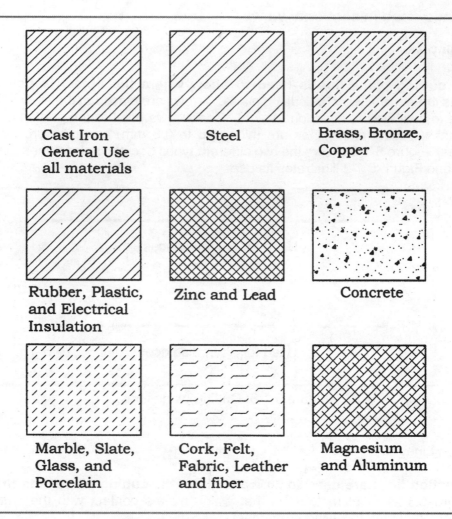

Figure 5.1-4: Section line symbols.

5.1.3) Rules of sectioning

Rule 1.   A section lined area is always completely bounded by a visible outline.

Rule 2.   The section lines in all sectioned areas should be parallel. Section lines shown in opposite directions indicate a different part.

Rule 3.   All the visible edges behind the cutting plane should be shown.

Rule 4.   Hidden features should be omitted in all areas of a section view. Exceptions include threads and broken out sections.

5.2) BASIC SECTIONS

Many types of sectioning techniques are available to use. The type chosen depends on the situation and what information needs to be conveyed.

5.2.1) Full section

To create a full section, the cutting plane passes fully through the object. The half of the object that is between the observer and the cutting plane is mentally removed. This exposes the cut surface and the interior features of the remaining portion. Full sections are used in many cases to avoid having to dimension hidden lines as shown in Figure 5.2-1.

Figure 5.2-1: Full section.

5.2.2) Half section

A half section has the advantage of exposing the interior of one half of an object while retaining the exterior of the other half. Half sections are used mainly for symmetric, nearly symmetric objects or assembly drawings. The half section is obtained by passing two cutting planes through the object, at right angles to each other, such that the intersection of the two planes coincides with the axis of symmetry. Therefore, only a quarter of the object is mentally removed. On the sectional view, a centerline is used to separate the sectioned and unsectioned halves. Hidden lines should not be shown on either half. Figure 5.2-2 shows an example of a half section.

A center line divides the halves.

This arrow may be left off.

No hidden lines on this half.

Figure 5.2-2: Half section.

5.2.3) Offset section

An offset section is produced by bending the cutting plane to show features that don't lie in the same plane. The section is drawn as if the offsets in the cutting plane were in one plane. Figure 5.2-3 shows an offset section.

Figure 5.2-3: Offset section.

Try Exercises 5.2-1 to 5.2-2 and watch Video Exercises 5.2-3 and 5.2-4

Exercise 5.2-1: Types of section views

Identify the type of section view used and the material that the part is made of.

Type of section: _____

Material: _____

Type of section: _____

Material: _____

Type of section: _____

Material: _____

Exercise 5.2-2: Full section

Given the top and right side views, sketch the front view as a full section. The material used is steel.

This way is up.

Video Exercise 5.2-3: Full Section

The following video exercise will take you through creating a full section of the objects shown.

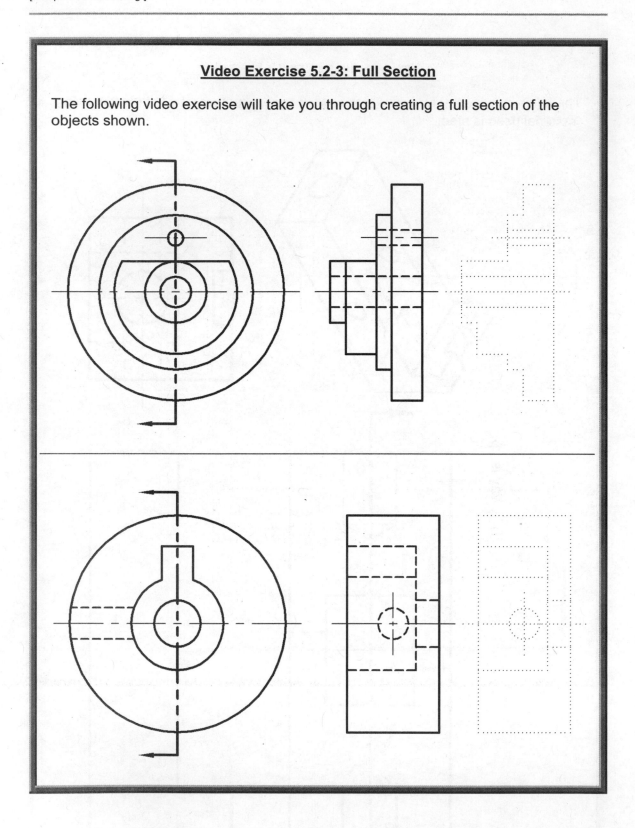

Video Exercise 5.2-4: Half Section

The following video exercise will take you through creating a half section of the objects shown.

5.3) ADVANCED SECTIONS

5.3.1) Aligned section

In order to include angled elements in a section, the cutting plane may be bent so that it passes through those features. The plane and features are then revolved, according to the convention of revolution, into the original plane.

o Convention of Revolution: Features are revolved into the projection plane, usually a vertical or horizontal plane, and then projected. The purpose of this is to show a true distance from a center or to show features that would otherwise not be seen. Figure 5.3-1 shows an aligned section employing the convention of revolution.

Figure 5.3-1: Aligned section.

5.3.2) Rib and web sections

To avoid a false impression of thickness and solidity, ribs and webs and other similar features are not sectioned even though the cutting plane passes along the center plane of the rib or web. However, if the cutting plane passes crosswise through the rib or web, the member is shown in section as indicated in Figure 5.3-2.

Figure 5.3-2: Rib and web sections.

5.3.3) Broken section

Sometimes only a portion of the object needs to be sectioned to show a single feature of the part. In this case, the sectional area is bound on one side by a break line. Hidden lines are shown in the unsectioned area of a broken section. Figure 5.3-3 shows an example of a broken section.

Figure 5.3-3: Broken section.

5.3.4) Removed section

A removed section is one that is not in direct projection of the view containing the cutting plane (Figure 5.3-4). Removed sections should be labeled (e.g. SECTION A-A) according to the letters placed at the ends of the cutting plane line. They should be arranged in alphabetical order from left to right. Frequently, removed sections are drawn to an enlarged scale, which is indicated beneath the section title.

Figure 5.3-4: Removed section.

5.3.5) Revolved section

The cross sectional shape of a bar, arm, spoke or other elongated objects may be shown in the longitudinal view by means of a revolved section. The visible lines adjacent to a revolved section may be broken out if desired. The super imposition of the revolved section requires the removal of all original lines covered by the section as shown in Figure 5.3-5. The true shape of a revolved section should be retained after the revolution regardless of the direction of the lines in the view.

Figure 5.3-5: Revolved section.

5.3.6) Non-sectioned parts

It is common practice to show standard parts like nuts, bolts, rivets, shafts and screws 'in the round' or un-sectioned. This is done because they have no internal features. Other non-sectioned parts include bearings, gear teeth, dowels, and pins.

5.3.7) Thin sections

For extremely thin parts of less than 4 mm thickness, such as sheet metal, washers, and gaskets, section lines are ineffective; therefore, the parts should be shown in solid black or without section lines.

Try Exercises 5.3-1 through 5.3-3 and watch Video Exercise 5.3-4

Exercise 5.3-1: Advanced Sections

Identify the type of section used and the material that the part is made of.

Type of section: _____

Material: _____

Type of section: _____

Material: _____

SECTION A-A   SECTION B-B   SECTION C-C

Type of section: _____

Material: _____

Type of section: _____

Material: _____

Exercise 5.3-2: Aligned section

Given the front and unrevolved right side views, sketch the right side view as an aligned section using the conventions of revolution. The material is cast iron.

Unrevolved view

Aligned section using the convention of revolution.

This way is up.

Exercise 5.3-3: Section techniques

- What features are not clearly shown in the drawing?
- What type of section would be most effective for this part?
- Draw the section view(s). The part is made of steel.

Section type(s): _____

Video Exercise 5.3-4: Aligned Section

The following video exercise will take you through creating an aligned section of the object shown.

NOTES:

5.4) APPLYING WHAT WE HAVE LEARNED

Exercise 5.4-1: Half section

Name: _____ Date: _____

Given the front and right side views, sketch the top view as a full section and create a half sectioned front view. The material is brass.

This way is up.

Exercise 5.4-2: Offset section

Name: _____ Date: _____

Given the front and top views, sketch the three missing section views in their appropriate places. The material is cast iron.

This way is up.

SECTION C-C

SECTION B-B

SECTION A-A

Exercise 5.4-3: Section techniques 3

Name: _____ Date: _____

- Draw the section view. The part is made of cast iron.

Section type(s): _____

NOTES:

SECTIONING QUESTIONS

Name: _____   Date: _____

Q5-1) The purpose of a section view is to see what is on the _____ of a part.

    a) outside
    b) inside
    c) backside
    d) otherside

Q5-2) A cutting plane line indicates where the part is being ...

    a) viewed.
    b) cut.
    c) rotated.
    d) drawn.

Q5-3) Are the arrows at the end of a cutting plane line pointing to the part of the object that is being removed or viewed?

Q5-4) Section lines are used to indicate ... (Circle all that apply.)

    a) cut material.
    b) line of sight.
    c) type of material.
    d) size of the part.

Q5-5) A full section removes one _____ of the object.

    a) half
    b) quarter
    c) third

Q5-6) A half section removes one _____ of the object.

    a) half
    b) quarter
    c) third

Q5-7) Is it permissible to show hidden lines on some portion of a half section? (yes, no)

Q5-8) Is it permissible to show hidden lines on some portion of a broken section? (yes, no)

Q5-9) The sectioned and non-sectioned halves of a half section are separated by a _____ line.

   a) visible
   b) hidden
   c) cutting plane
   d) center

Q5-10) The **convention of revolution** is used when creating a (an) ...

   a) full section
   b) half section
   c) offset section
   d) aligned section
   e) revolved section

Q5-11) The *convention of revolution* is used when creating an aligned section so that the angled features may be shown ...

   a) at an angle.
   b) aligned with the feature.
   c) true size.
   d) at a scaled size.

Q5-12) A _____ section is always labeled (for instance SECTION A-A).

Q5-13) Which type of section view is usually shown at an enlarged scale?

   a) Full
   b) Offset
   c) Aligned
   d) Removed

SECTIONING PROBLEMS

Name: _____   Date: _____

P5-1) Answer the following question regarding the section view shown.

Type of section? _____

What material is the part made of? _____

In the view that shows the cutting plane line, circle the section of the part that is being viewed.

Does this part contain counterbores or countersinks?

NOTES:

Name: _____ Date: _____

P5-2) Answer the following question regarding the section view shown.

What two sectioning techniques are used? _____ _____

What material is the part made of? _____

In the view that shows the cutting plane line, circle the section of the part that is being viewed.

NOTES:

Name: _____ Date: _____

P5-3) Circle the correct section views out of the three possibilities. One for each cutting plane.

NOTES:

Name: _____ Date: _____

P5-4) Circle the correct section view out of the three possibilities.

Would a half section been effective in this case? (Yes, no)

Why? _____

NOTES:

Name: _____   Date: _____

P5-5) Circle the correct section view out of the three possibilities.

What type of sectioning technique is being used?

NOTES:

Name: _____ Date: _____

P5-6) Circle the correct section view out of the two possibilities for both section A-A and section B-B.

SECTION A-A

SECTION A-A

SECTION B-B

SECTION B-B

NOTES:

Name: _____ Date: _____

P5-7) Sketch the sectional view as indicated. The material of the part is Steel.

P5-8) Sketch the sectional view as indicated. The material of the part is Aluminum.

NOTES:

Name: _____   Date: _____

P5-9) Sketch the sectional view as indicated. The material of the part is Rubber.

P5-10) Sketch the sectional view as indicated. The material of the part is Brass.

Name: _____   Date: _____

P5-11) Sketch the sectional view as indicated. The material of the part is Aluminum.

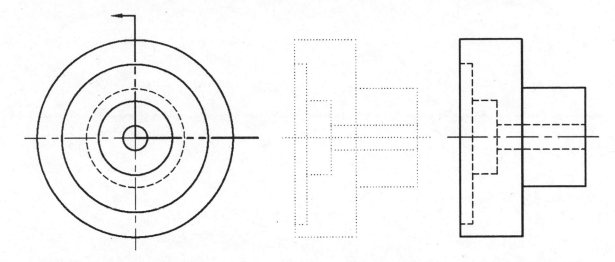

P5-12) Sketch the sectional view as indicated. The material of the part is Cast Iron.

NOTES:

Name: _____   Date: _____

P5-13) Sketch the sectional view as indicated. The material of the part is Cast Iron.

P5-14) Sketch the sectional view as indicated. The material of the part is Brass.

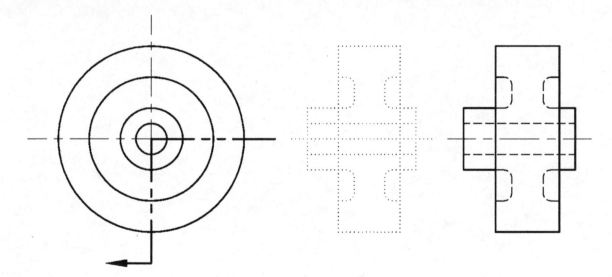

NOTES:

Name: _____ Date: _____

P5-15) Sketch the sectional view as indicated. The material of the part is Rubber.

P5-16) Sketch the sectional view as indicated. The material of the part is Steel.

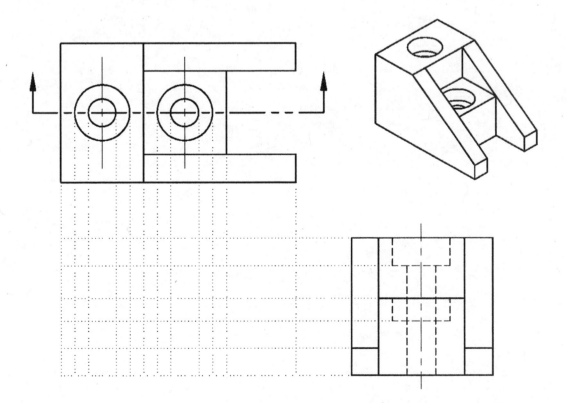

NOTES:

Name: _____ Date: _____

P5-17) Sketch the sectional view as indicated. The material of the part is Steel.

SECTION A-A

SECTION B-B

P5-18) Sketch the sectional view as indicated. The material of the part is Aluminum.

SECTION C-C

SECTION B-B

SECTION A-A

NOTES:

Name: _____ Date: _____

P5-19) Sketch the sectional view as indicated. The material of the part is Cast Iron.

SECTION B-B

SECTION A-A

NOTES:

Name: _____ Date: _____

P5-20) Sketch the sectional view as indicated. The material of the part is Steel.

SECTION B-B

SECTION A-A

SECTION C-C   SECTION D-D

P5-21) Sketch the sectional view as indicated. The material of the part is Cast Iron.

SECTION A-A   SECTION B-B

NOTES:

Name: _____   Date: _____

P5-22) Sketch the sectional view as indicated. The material of the part is Steel.

SECTION A-A   SECTION B-B   SECTION C-C

P5-23) Sketch the sectional view as indicated. The material of the part is Aluminum.

NOTES:

Name: _____ Date: _____

P5-24) Sketch an aligned section view using the conventions of revolution. The unsectioned right side view is shown true shape. The material of the part is Cast Iron.

P5-25) Sketch an aligned section view using the conventions of revolution. The unsectioned right side view is shown true shape. The material of the part is Cast Iron.

Aligned section
using the conventions
of revolution.

Unrevolved
view

NOTES:

NOTES:

P5-26) Draw the following object converting the front view into an offset section. It is not necessary to include the dimensions. The material of the part is Steel.

P5-27) Draw the following object converting the front view into an offset section. Capture as many features as possible. Draw the appropriate cutting plane line. It is not necessary to include the dimensions. The material of the part is Aluminum.

P5-28) Draw the following object converting the front view into an offset section. Capture as many features as possible. Draw the appropriate cutting plane line. It is not necessary to include the dimensions. The material of the part is Plastic.

P5-29) Draw all three views of the following object converting the front view into a full section. Draw the appropriate cutting plane line. It is not necessary to include the dimensions. The material of the part is Steel.

P5-30) Draw the following object converting the front view into a full section. Draw the appropriate cutting plane line. It is not necessary to include the dimensions. The material of the part is Cast Iron.

NOTE: ALL ROUNDS AND FILLETS .12 R

P5-31) Draw the following object converting the front view into an offset section. Capture as many features as possible. Draw the appropriate cutting plane line. It is not necessary to include the dimensions. The material of the part is Steel.

P5-32) Draw the following object converting the front view into an offset section. Capture as many features as possible. Draw the appropriate cutting plane line. It is not necessary to include the dimensions. The material of the part is Cast Iron.

NOTE: ALL FILLETS AND ROUNDS R.12
UNLESS OTHERWISE SPECIFIED

P5-33) Draw the following object converting the front view into a full section. It is not necessary to include the dimensions. The material of the part is Cast Iron.

NOTE: ALL FILLETS AND ROUNDS R.12
UNLESS OTHERWISE SPECIFIED

P5-34) Draw the following object converting the front view into a full section. It is not necessary to include the dimensions. The material of the part is Cast Iron.

NOTE: ALL FILLETS AND ROUNDS R.12
UNLESS OTHERWISE SPECIFIED.

P5-35) Draw the following object converting the front view into a full section. It is not necessary to include the dimensions. The material of the part is Plastic.

P5-36) Draw the following object converting the right side view into a half section. Draw the appropriate cutting plane line. It is not necessary to include the dimensions. The material of the part is Brass.

P5-37) Draw the following object converting the right side view into a half section. It is not necessary to include the dimensions. The material of the part is Steel.

P5-38) Draw the following object converting the right side view into a half section. It is not necessary to include the dimensions. The material of the part is Aluminum.

P5-39) Draw the following object converting the right side view into a half section. Draw the appropriate cutting plane line. It is not necessary to include the dimensions. The material of the part is Steel.

P5-40) Draw the following object converting the left side view into a half section. Draw the appropriate cutting plane line. It is not necessary to include the dimensions. The material of the part is Steel.

P5-41) Draw the following object converting the right side view into a half section. It is not necessary to include the dimensions. The material of the part is Aluminum.

P5-42) Draw the following object converting the right side view into an aligned section using the conventions of revolution. Draw the appropriate cutting plane line. It is not necessary to include the dimensions. The material of the part is Cast iron.

SP5-1) Sketch the sectional view as indicated. The material of the part is Steel. The answer to this problem is given in the *Independent Learning Content*.

SECTION B-B

SECTION A-A

SP5-2) Sketch the sectional view as indicated. The material of the part is Rubber. The answer to this problem is given in the *Independent learning Content*.

SP5-3) Draw the following object converting the right side view into an aligned section using the conventions of revolution. Draw the appropriate cutting plane line. It is not necessary to include the dimensions. The material of the part is Steel. The answer to this problem is given in the *Independent Learning Content*.

CHAPTER 6

ADVANCED DRAWING TECHNIQUES

CHAPTER OUTLINE

CHAPTER SUMMARY

In this chapter you will learn about views that are created using advanced drawing techniques. These views include removed and revolved views, detail views, partial views, and auxiliary views. You will also learn how to read orthographic projections of cast parts.

6.1) ADVANCED VIEW TECHNIQUES

Several drawing techniques will be described that enhance the standard views. These techniques are used when a feature of the part cannot be completely described using the six principal views. They may also be used to show the feature more clearly even if it is completely described in the standard views.

6.1.1) Removed and revolved orthographic views

In some instances, the size and location of an orthographic view (e.g. top, right side) interferes with other components of the drawing. In these instances the view may be removed from its normal aligned position. The view may also be rotated and scaled. When a removed or rotated view is used, view indicators with letter identifications are used to indicate from where the view was taken and its line of sight. Figure 6.1-1 shows an example of a removed orthographic view and Figure 6.1-2 shows an example of a removed view that has been rotated. Removed and rotated views are labeled with their view identification and scale. Rotated views are also labeled with their angle of rotation.

6.1.2) Detail views

If a part has intricate features that are small relative to the rest of the part, a detail view may be used to clarify these features. A detail view is usually shown at an increased scale. The detail view is identified by using a letter that matches the letter given by the circle indicating where the detail is being taken from. Figure 6.1-3 shows an example of a detail view.

6.1.3) Partial views

Partial views are used to show only pertinent features. They are used instead of drawing the complete view when the complete view does not add any new information. Many times drawing the complete view in these situations does not increase clearness. Figure 6.1-4 shows and example of a partial orthographic view and Figure 6.1-5 shows an example of a partial auxiliary view.

Figure 6.1-1: Removed orthographic view

Figure 6.1-2: Revolved orthographic view

Figure 6.1-3: Detail view

Figure 6.1-4: Partial view

6.1.4) Auxiliary views

Primary views include the six views described in the *Orthographic Projections* chapter (i.e. front, top, right side, bottom, left side, rear). These views are created by projecting the part onto the primary planes. The planes making up the glass box. **Auxiliary views** are created by projecting the part onto a plane that is at an angle to one of the primary planes as shown in Figure 6.1-5. Note that the hidden lines in this figure are omitted for clarity.

Auxiliary views are used to show the true shape of features that are not parallel to any of the principal planes of projection. In Figure 6.1-6, the counter bored hole is not shown true shape in either the top or right side views. An auxiliary view is needed to show the counter bore true size. Auxiliary views are aligned with the angled features from which they are projected. Partial auxiliary views are often used to shown only a particular feature that is not described in the principal views.

6.1.5) Related parts

If the relationship between the part being drawn and another part (i.e. related part) of the assembly is important, the related part may be shown on the detailed drawing as shown in Figure 6.1-7. The related part is drawn by outlining the part using the phantom line type. The line weight of the phantom line should be thin.

Try Exercises 6.1-1 and 6.1-2 and watch Video Exercise 6.1-3.

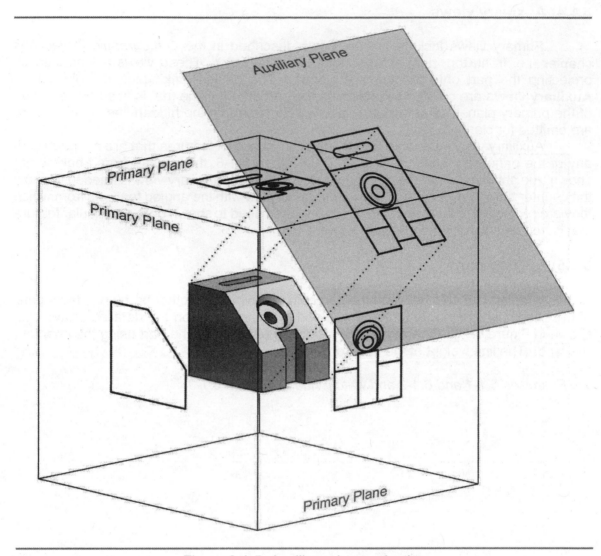

Figure 6.1-5: Auxiliary view projection

Primary view

Auxiliary view

Partial auxiliary view

Primary view

Primary view

Figure 6.1-6: Auxiliary views

Figure 6.1-7: Related part

Exercise 6.1-1: Identifying views

1. Identify the principal views.
2. Identify the auxiliary view.
3. Identify the partial views.
4. Identify the detail view.

DETAIL B
SCALE 2 : 1

Exercise 6.1-2: Auxiliary view

Draw the auxiliary view for this object.

Video Exercise 6.1-3: Auxiliary views

This video exercise takes you through creating the auxiliary views for the following object.

6.2) ADVANCED PART TECHNIQUES

There are several types of parts that required special drawing symbols. For example, cast parts use surface texture symbols and welded parts use weld symbols. We will take a look at cast and molded parts in this section.

6.2.1) Cast and molded parts

In order to fully appreciate the drawing elements of a casting or molded part, it helps to have a basic understanding of the processes used to make these parts. Cast and molded parts are similar in the sense that the parts are made by pouring or injecting a melted substance into a cavity and allowing the substance to solidify. In the case of castings, the material is usually a metal and it is poured into the mold. In the case of molded parts, the material is usually a polymer and it is injected into the mold. Cast and molded parts are most often used when the part needed is too complex to economically make using another method. Figure 6.2-1 and 6.2-2 show the different components of a casting system. Before we look at a drawing of a cast or molded part, let's go over some definitions.

- **Casting:** A process were by a part is produced by the solidification of a material in a mold. The solid part produced by this process is also called the *casting*.
- **Mold:** A form made of sand, metal, or other material. The melted material is poured or injected into the mold and allowed to solidify.
- **Parting line:** A line on the drawing that represents the mating surfaces of the mold.
- **Draft:** The taper given to a part so that it can be extracted from the mold.
- **Fillet radius:** A concaved radius on the part connecting two surfaces.
- **Corner radius:** A convex radius on the part connecting two surfaces.

In the tangible world, there are several features that allow you to immediately identify a casting. Figure 6.2-3 shows a casting of a bottle opener. Notice the following features. Cast and molded parts will often have a ridge where the parting line was located. Most sand casted metal parts have slightly rough surfaces from contact with the sand. The smooth surfaces on the casting have been machined after the completed casting process. A cast part will have both fillet and corner radii. These radii are placed in the design to avoid sharp corners which lead to stress concentrations (i.e. an increase possibility for part failure under load). Also, castings will have surfaces that are angled (i.e. drafted). Drafts allow the part to be extracted from the mold. These drafts proceed from the parting plane (i.e. the plane where the two halves of the mold meet) outward or inward depending on the drawing specifications. The most common material used for castings is cast iron. Cast iron is a relatively brittle material, therefore, you will often see supporting ribs and webs to help increase the part's strength.

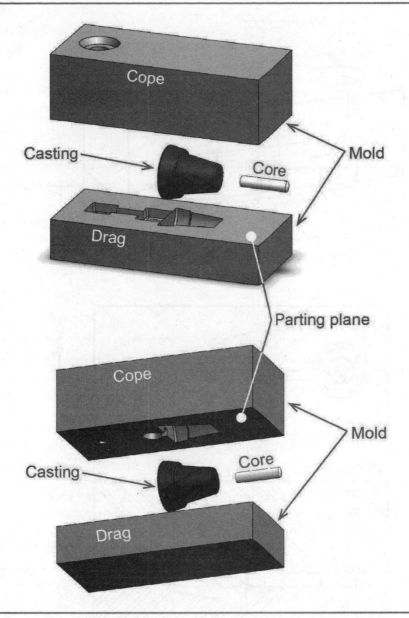

Figure 6.2-1: Casting components – exploded view

Figure 6.2-2: Casting components

Physical bottle opener

Rough surface

Machined surface

Pre-machined casting model

Fillet

Corner

Parting line

Draft
(angled surface)

Machined casting model

Machined surfaces

Machined surfaces

Figure 6.2-3: Bottle opener

In this text we will focus on the *end item drawing*. That means the drawing that shows the part after it has been cast and machined (i.e. in its final state). Here is a list of features and concepts that you should keep in mind when reading a casting drawing. See Figure 6.2-6 for illustrations of these concepts. Note that the drawing shown in Figure 6.2-6 may not be complete. It is just used for illustration purposes.

- The **radius of fillets and corners** are not dimensioned individually, but specified in a note on the drawing as shown below.
- **Dimensions are measured to the mold lines.** This means that if a dimension goes between a fillet or corner radius, the dimension is measuring from the theoretical sharp corner created by the two meeting surfaces.
- A **surface texture value** is specified for all machined surfaces.
- The **die closure tolerance** is either specified in a note or applied directly to the dimension.
- The **parting line** (i.e. where the mold halves meet) is indicated with a phantom line and the parting line symbol.

6.2.1.1) Surface texture symbol

Surface texture symbols are used to indicate surfaces of a casting that will be machined after the casting process. Figure 6.2-4 shows the three basic configurations of the surface texture symbol and Figure 6.2-6 shows their use. Figure 6.2-5 shows a surface texture symbol with roughness specifications. Getting into what each specification means is beyond the scope of this text. Further information may be obtain in the Machinery's handbook.

| The surface may be produced by any method | Material removal required | Material removal prohibited |

Figure 6.2-4: Surface texture symbols

Example

Figure 6.2-5: Surface texture symbols specifications

Figure 6.2-6: Bottle opener drawing

6.2.2) Welded parts

Welding joins pieces of metal by heating the surfaces to the point of melting using a blowtorch, electric arc, or other means. Sometimes a filler rod is used to add material to the weld joint. Welding is a permanent means of assembly. Therefore, welded parts are considered a single part and not an assembly. Weld information is given on the detailed drawing using weld symbols. Figure 6.2-7 shows examples of some common weld symbols.

There are many types of welds and weld symbols. Covering all of these symbols is beyond the scope of this book. For detailed information, refer to the Machinery's Handbook. The goal of this section is to introduce you to how welds are indicated on drawings. This will allow you to recognize these symbols as welds so that you can look up their exact meaning.

Figure 6.2-7: Weld symbol examples

ADVANCED DRAWING TECHNIQUES QUESTIONS

Name: _____ Date: _____

Q6-1) These type of views are not in the projection path. (Circle all that apply)

a) Removed
b) Revolved
c) Detail
d) Auxiliary

Q6-2) These type of views may be scaled. (Circle all that apply)

a) Removed
b) Revolved
c) Detail
d) Auxiliary

Q6-3) This type of view is created using a plane that is not parallel to one of the principal planes.

a) Removed
b) Revolved
c) Detail
d) Auxiliary

Q6-4) This type of view, for clarity, does not show everything.

a) Removed
b) Revolved
c) Partial
d) Related

Q6-5) This type of part is shown in phantom lines.

a) Adjacent
b) Revolved
c) Partial
d) Related

Q6-6) Drawings of castings use these two types of symbols. (Circle two choices)

a) Parting line
b) Weld
c) Surface texture
d) Draft

Q6-7) Weld symbols indicate the side of the weld by placing the weld symbol …

    a) above or below the line.
    b) to the right or left of the line.
    c) in bold or italics.

ADVANCED DRAWING TECHNIQUES PROBLEMS

Name: _____   Date: _____

P6-1) Sketch in a complete auxiliary view in the space indicated.

NOTES:

Name: _____ Date: _____

P6-2) Sketch in a complete auxiliary view in the space indicated.

NOTES:

Name: _____   Date: _____

P6-3) Finish the two incomplete auxiliary views.

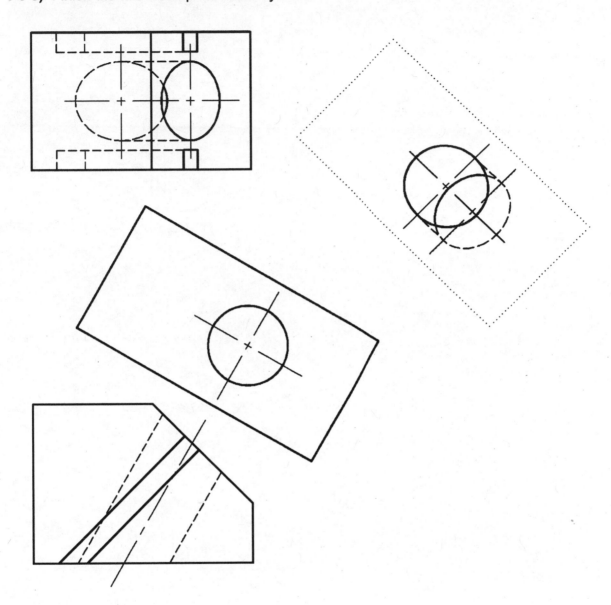

NOTES:

P6-4) Create an orthographic projection of the following object. Draw an auxiliary view that shows the angled surface true shape. Use partial views where appropriate.

P6-5) Create an orthographic projection of the following object. Draw an auxiliary view that shows the angled surface true shape. Use partial views where appropriate.

P6-6) Create an orthographic projection of the following object. Draw two auxiliary views that show the angled features true shape. Use partial views where appropriate.

P6-7) Create an orthographic projection of the following object. Draw an auxiliary view that shows the angled feature true shape. Use partial views where appropriate.

P6-8) Create an orthographic projection of the following object. Draw an auxiliary view that shows the angled surface true shape. Use partial views where appropriate.

P6-9) Create an orthographic projection of the following object. Draw an auxiliary view that shows the angled surface true shape. Use partial views where appropriate.

P6-10) Create an orthographic projection of the following object. Draw an auxiliary view that shows the angled surface true shape. Use partial views where appropriate.

P6-11) Create an orthographic projection of the following object. Draw the three standard views. Place surface roughness symbols on all finished surfaces. Note that all fillets and rounds are R3 unless otherwise specified.

P6-12) Create an orthographic projection of the following object. Draw the three standard views. Place surface roughness symbols on all finished surfaces.

P6-13) Create an orthographic projection of the following object. Draw the three standard views. Place surface roughness symbols on all finished surfaces.

NOTE: ALL FILLETS AND ROUNDS
R0.125 UNLESS OTHERWISE SPECIFIED

P6-14) Create an orthographic projection of the following object. Draw the three standard views. Place surface roughness symbols on all finished surfaces.

NOTE: ALL FILLETS AND ROUNDS R3
UNLESS OTHERWISE SPECIFIED

NOTES:

CHAPTER 7

TOLERANCING

CHAPTER OUTLINE

CHAPTER SUMMARY

In this chapter you will learn about tolerancing and how important this technique is to mass production. Tolerancing enables an engineer to design interchangeable or replacement parts. If a feature's size is toleranced, it is allowed to vary within a range of values or limits. It is no longer controlled by a single size. By the end of this chapter, you will be able to apply tolerances to a basic dimension and calculate a feature's limits.

7.1) TOLERANCING AND INTERCHANGEABILITY

Tolerancing is dimensioning for interchangeability. An interchangeable part is a part that possesses functional and physical characteristics equivalent in performance to another part for which it is intended to replace. When dimensioning an interchangeable part, the dimension is not a single value but a range of values that the part must fall within.

Interchangeability is achieved by imposing tolerances or limits on a dimension. **A tolerance is the total amount of dimensional variation permitted.** In other words, it is the difference between the maximum and minimum size of the feature. Tolerancing enables similar parts to be near enough alike so that any one of them will fit properly into the assembly. For example, you would like to replace your mountain bike's seat post with a seat post that contains a shock absorber. You expect that all seat posts designed for mountain bikes will be interchangeable.

Tolerancing and interchangeability are an essential part of mass production. **Tolerances are necessary because it is impossible to manufacture parts without some variation.** A key component of mass production is the ability to buy replacement parts that are interchangeable or can substitute for the part being replaced.

Tolerancing gives us the means of specifying dimensions with whatever degree of accuracy we may require for our design to work properly. We would like to choose a tolerance that is not unnecessarily accurate or excessively inaccurate. Choosing the correct tolerance for a particular application depends on the design intent (i.e. the end use) of the part, cost, how it is manufactured, and experience.

7.2) TOLERANCING STANDARDS

Standards are needed to establish dimensional limits for parts that are to be interchangeable. Standards make it possible for parts to be manufactured at different times and in different places with the assurance that they will meet assembly requirements. The two most common standards agencies are the American National Standards Institute (ANSI) and the International Standards Organization (ISO). The ANSI standards are now being compiled and distributed by the American Society of Mechanical Engineers (ASME). The information contained in this chapter is based on the following standards: ASME Y14.5 - 2009, USAS B4.1 – 1967 (R2004), and ANSI B4.2 – 1978 (R2004).

7.3) TOLERANCE TYPES

Tolerancing on an engineering drawing may be describing two very different forms of dimensional variation. The type of tolerancing that will be discussed in this chapter may be referred to as *standard tolerancing* or *x-y coordinate tolerancing*. This type of tolerancing is used to control position and size. The other type of tolerancing is called *geometric dimensioning and tolerancing* (i.e. GD&T). This type of tolerancing controls things such as form (i.e. feature shape), location, and position. Geometric dimensioning and tolerancing is beyond the scope of this book.

Toleranced dimensions may be presented using three general methods. The methods presented in this chapter include *limit* dimensions, *plus-minus* tolerances, and *page* or *block* tolerances.

- Limit Dimensions: Limits are the maximum and minimum size that a part can obtain and still function properly. For example, the diameter of a shaft may vary between .999 inch and 1.001 inches. On a drawing, you would see this dimension specified as the *limit tolerance* shown in Figure 7.3-1. Notice that the upper limit is placed above the lower limit in the stacked version. When both limits are placed on one line, the lower limit precedes the upper limit. Limit dimensions provide the blueprint reader with the limits of allowable variation without any calculation. It eliminates potential calculation mistakes.
- Plus-Minus Tolerances: Plus-minus tolerances give a basic size and the variation that can occur around that basic size. On a drawing, a *plus-minus tolerance* dimension would look like that shown in Figure 7.3-1. When the positive and negative variations are the same, it is referred to as an equal bilateral tolerance. When they are not the same, the specification is called an unequal bilateral and when one of the variances is zero, the tolerance is unilateral. The type of tolerance chosen depends on the direction in which variation is most detrimental. Plus-minus tolerances are convenient because a design may be initially drawn and dimensioned using basic sizes. As the design progresses, tolerances may be added.
- Page or Block Tolerances: A block tolerance is a general note that applies to all dimensions that are not covered by some other tolerancing type. The format of a block tolerance is shown in Figure 7.3-1. Block tolerances are placed in the tolerance block to the left of the title block and above the projection block. Block tolerances are used for two reasons. First, they act as a default tolerance for any dimensions that may have been overlooked when tolerances were assigned. Second, they are often used to quickly tolerance non-critical dimensions.

$\varnothing^{1.001}_{.999}$ or $\varnothing$.999 - 1.001

$10.0^{+0.1}_{-0.2}$

Limit tolerance

Plus-minus tolerance

UNLESS OTHERWISE SPECIFIED
DIM ARE IN INCHES
TOL ON ANGLE ±.XX°
2 PL ±.XX 3 PL ±.XXX
INTERPRET DIM AND TOL PER
ASME Y14.5 - XXXX

Block tolerance

Figure 7.3-1: Tolerance methods

7.4) SHAFT-HOLE ASSEMBLY

In the intervening sections, a simple shaft and hole assembly will be used to illustrate different concepts and definitions. Figure 7.4-1 shows a shaft that is designed to fit into a hole. Both the shaft and the hole are allowed to vary between a maximum and minimum diameter.

Figure 7.4-1: Shaft and hole assembly.

7.5) INCH TOLERANCES

Consider a simple shaft and hole assembly, like that shown in Figure 7.5-1, when reading the following definitions relating to tolerancing in inches. Both the diameter of the shaft and hole are allowed to vary between a maximum and minimum value.

- Limits: The limits are the maximum and minimum size that the part is allowed to be.

- Basic Size: The basic size is the size from which the limits are calculated. It is common for both the hole and the shaft and is usually the value of the closest fraction.

- Tolerance: The tolerance is the total amount a specific dimension is permitted to vary.

- Maximum Material Condition (MMC): The MMC is the size of the part when it consists of the most material.

- Least Material Condition (LMC): The LMC is the size of the part when it consists of the least material.

- Maximum Clearance: The maximum clearance is the maximum amount of space that can exist between the hole and the shaft. Don't let the word clearance fool you. The maximum clearance may be positive (a space) or negative (no space). The maximum clearance is calculated by using the following equation:

$$\text{Max. Clearance} = \text{LMC}_{hole} - \text{LMC}_{shaft}$$

- Minimum Clearance (Allowance): The minimum clearance is the minimum amount of space that can exist between the hole and the shaft. Don't let the word clearance fool you. The minimum clearance may be positive (a space) or negative (no space). The minimum clearance is calculated by using the following equation:

$$\text{Min. Clearance} = \text{MMC}_{hole} - \text{MMC}_{shaft}$$

$\varnothing\,^{.51}_{.47}$ $\varnothing\,^{.50}_{.49}$

Figure 7.5-1: Toleranced shaft and hole pair (English).

Exercise 7.5-1: Inch tolerance definitions

Referring to Figure 7.5-1, fill in the following table.

	Shaft	Hole
Limits		
Basic Size		
Tolerance		
MMC		
LMC		
Max. Clearance		
Min. Clearance (Allowance)		

7.5.1) Types of fits

Within the set of inch tolerances, there are four major types of fits. Within each fit there are several degrees or classes. The type of fit and class that you choose to implement depends on the function of your design. The major categories of fits are: *clearance*, *interference*, *transition*, and *line*. Table 7.5-1 lists and defines each of the four types of fits.

Type of Fit	Definition	When it exists
Clearance Fit	The internal member (shaft) fits into the external member (hole) and always leaves a space or clearance between the parts.	Min. Clear > 0
Interference Fit	The internal member is larger than the external member such that there is always an actual interference of metal.	Max. Clear ≤ 0
Transition Fit	The fit might result in either a clearance or interference fit condition.	Min. Clear < 0 Max. Clear > 0
Line Fit	The limits of size are specified such that a clearance or surface contact may result.	Min. Clear = 0 Max. Clear >0

Table 7.5-1: Types of fits.

Exercise 7.5-2: Types of fits

From everyday life, list some examples of clearance and interference fits.

Fit	Examples
Clearance	
Interference	

Exercise 7.5-3: Determining fit type

Determine the basic size and type of fit given the limits for the shaft and hole.

Shaft Limits	Hole Limits	Basic Size	Type of Fit
1.498 - 1.500	1.503 – 1.505		
.751 - .755	.747 - .750		
.373 - .378	.371 - .375		
.247 - .250	.250 - .255		

7.5.2) ANSI standard limits and fits (English)

The following fit types and classes are in accordance with the USAS B4.1-1967 (R2004) standard.

- Running or Sliding Clearance Fits (RC)

Running and sliding clearance fits are intended to provide running performance with suitable lubrication. Table 7.5-2 lists the different classes of running and sliding clearance fits and their design uses.

- Locational Fits (LC, LT, LN)

Locational fits are intended to determine only the location of the mating parts. They are divided into three groups: clearance fits (LC), transition fits (LT), and interference fits (LN). Table 7.5-3 lists the different classes of locational fits and their design uses.

- FN: Force Fits:

Force fits provide a constant bore pressure throughout the range of sizes. The classes are categorized from FN1 to FN5. Table 7.5-4 lists the different classes of force fits and their design uses.

Class of Fit	Description	Design use
RC9 -RC8	Loose running fit	Used with material such as cold rolled shafting and tubing made to commercial tolerances.
RC7	Free running fit	Used where accuracy is not essential, or where large temperature variations occur.
RC6 -RC5	Medium running fit	Used on accurate machinery with higher surface speeds where accurate location and minimum play is desired.
RC4	Close running fit	Used on accurate machinery with moderate surface speeds where accurate location and minimum play is desired.
RC3	Precision running fit	This is the closest fit, which can be expected to run freely. Intended for slow speeds. Not suitable for appreciable temperature changes.
RC2	Sliding fit	Used for accurate location. Parts will move and turn easily but are not intended to run freely. Parts may seize with small temperature changes.
RC1	Close Sliding fit	Used for accurate location of parts that must be assembled without perceptible play.

Table 7.5-2: Running and sliding clearance fit classes.

Class of Fit	Description	Design use
LC	Locational clearance fit	Intended for parts that are normally stationary, but which can be freely assembled or disassembled. They run from snug fits (parts requiring accuracy of location), through the medium clearance fits (parts where freedom of assembly is important). The classes are categorized from LC1 being the tightest fit to LC11 being the loosest.
LT	Locational transition fit	Used where accuracy of location is important, but a small amount of clearance or interference is permissible. The classes are categorized from LT1 to LT6.
LN	Locational interference fit	Used where accuracy of location is of prime importance, and for parts requiring rigidity and alignment with no special requirements for bore pressure. The classes are categorized from LN1 to LN3.

Table 7.5-3: Locational fit classes.

Class of Fit	Description	Design use
FN1	Light drive fit	This fit produces a light assembly pressure and a more or less permanent assembly.
FN2	Medium drive fit	Suitable for ordinary steel parts or for shrink fits on light sections. About the tightest fit that can be used with high-grade cast iron.
FN3	Heavy drive fit	Suitable for heavier steel parts or for shrink fit in medium sections.
FN4 - FN5	Force fit	Suitable for parts that can be heavily stressed, or for shrink fits where the heavy pressing forces required are impractical.

Table 7.5-4: Force fit classes.

Exercise 7.5-4: Limits and fits

Given a basic size of .50 inches and a fit of RC8, calculate the limits for both the hole and the shaft. Use the ANSI limits and fit tables given in the Appendix A.

Shaft:

Hole:

7.6) METRIC TOLERANCES

Consider a simple shaft and hole assembly, like that shown in Figure 7.6-1, when reading the following definitions relating to tolerancing in millimeters. The dimensions of both are shown in Figure 7.6-1. Both the diameter of the shaft and hole are allowed to vary between a maximum and minimum value.

Figure 7.6-1: Toleranced shaft and hole pair (metric).

- Basic Size: The basic size is the size from which the limits are calculated.

- Tolerance: The tolerance is the total amount a dimension is permitted to vary.

- Upper deviation: The upper deviation is the difference between the basic size and the permitted maximum size of the part.

  UD = | basic size – max size |

- Lower deviation: The lower deviation is the difference between the basic size and the minimum permitted size of the part.

  LD = | basic size – min size |

- Fundamental deviation: The fundamental deviation is the closest deviation to the basic size. To determine the fundamental deviation, compare the upper deviation and the lower deviation. The fundamental deviation is the smaller of the two. A letter in the fit specification represents the fundamental deviation. If the letter is capital, it is referring to the hole's fundamental deviation and a lower case letter refers to the shaft. Refer to Table 7.6-1 for metric fit designations.

- International tolerance grade number (IT#): The IT#'s are a set of tolerances that vary according to the basic size and provide the same relative level of accuracy within a given grade. The number in the fit specification represents the IT#. A smaller number provides a smaller tolerance.

- Tolerance zone: The fundamental deviation in combination with the IT# defines the tolerance zone. The IT# establishes the magnitude of the tolerance zone or the amount that the dimension can vary. The fundamental deviation establishes the position of the tolerance zone with respect to the basic size.

Exercise 7.6-1: Millimeter tolerance definitions

Referring to Figure 7.6-1, fill in the following table.

	Shaft	Hole
Limits		
Basic Size		
Tolerance		
Upper deviation		
Lower deviation		
Fundamental deviation		
Type of fit		

7.6.1) ANSI standard limits and fits (Metric)

The following fit types are in accordance with the ANSI B4.2 – 1978 (R2004) standard. Available metric fits and their descriptions are summarized in Table 7.6-1.

7.6.2) Tolerance designation

Metric fits are specified using the fundamental deviation (letter) and the IT#. When specifying the fit for the hole, an upper case letter is used. A lower case letter is used when specifying the fit for the shaft. As stated before, the IT# establishes the magnitude of the tolerance zone or the amount that the dimension can vary. The fundamental deviation establishes the position of the tolerance zone with respect to the basic size.

FIT SYMBOL			
Hole Basis	Shaft Basis	Fit	Description
H11/c11	C11/h11	Loose running fit	For wide commercial tolerances or allowances.
H9/d9	D9/h9	Free running fit	Good for large temperature variations, high running speeds, or heavy journal pressures.
H8/f7	F8/h7	Close running fit	For accurate location at moderate speeds and journal pressures.
H7/g6	G7/h6	Sliding fit	Not intended to run freely, but to move and turn freely and locate accurately.
H7/h6	H7/h6	Locational clearance fit	For locating stationary parts but can be freely assembled and disassembled.
H7/k6 and H7/n6	K7/h6 and N7/h6	Locational transition fit	For accurate location.
H7/p6	P7/h6	Locational interference fit	For parts requiring rigidity where accuracy of location is important, but without special bore pressure requirements.
H7/s6	S7/h6	Medium drive fit	For ordinary steel parts or shrink fits on light sections, the tightest fit usable with cast iron.
H7/u6	U7/h6	Force fit	Suitable for parts that can be highly stressed.

Table 7.6-1: Metric standard fits.

Exercise 7.6-2: Metric fit designation

Fill in the appropriate name for the fit component.

7.6.3) Basic hole and basic shaft systems

Notice that Table 7.6-1 gives two different tolerance designations for each type of fit. Metric limits and fits are divided into two different systems: the basic hole system and the basic shaft system. Each system has its own designation.

- Basic hole system: The basic hole system is used when you want the basic size to be attached to the hole dimension. For example, if a standard drill, reamer, broach, or another standard tool is used to produce a hole, you would want to use the hole system. In this system, the minimum hole diameter is taken as the basic size.

- Basic shaft system: The basic shaft system is used when you want the basic size to be attached to the shaft dimension. For example, you would use the shaft system if you need to tolerance a hole based on the size of a purchased standard drill rod. In this system, the maximum shaft diameter is taken as the basic size.

Exercise 7.6-3: Systems

Identify the type of fit and the system used to determine the limits of the following shaft and hole pairs.

Shaft	Hole	Type of Fit	System
9.987 – 9.972	10.000 – 10.022		
60.021 - 60.002	60.000 - 60.030		
40.000 – 39.984	39.924 – 39.949		

Exercise 7.6-4: Metric limits and fits.

Find the limits, tolerance, type of fit, and type of system for a ⌀30 H11/c11 fit. Use the tolerance tables given in Appendix A.

	Shaft	Hole
Limits		
Tolerance		
System		
Fit		

Find the limits, tolerance, type of fit, and type of system for a ⌀30 P7/h6 fit.

	Shaft	Hole
Limits		
Tolerance		
System		
Fit		

7.7) SELECTING TOLERANCES

Tolerances will govern the method of manufacturing. **When tolerances are reduced, the cost of manufacturing rises very rapidly.** Therefore, specify as generous a tolerance as possible without interfering with the function of the part.

Choosing the most appropriate tolerance depends on many factors. As stated before it depends on design intent, cost and how the part will be manufactured. Choosing a tolerance that will allow the part to function properly is the most important consideration. Things to consider are length of engagement, bearing load, speed, lubrication, temperature, humidity, and material. Experience also plays a significant role.

Table 7.7-1 may be used as a general guide for determining the machining processes that will under normal conditions, produce work within the tolerance grades indicated. As the tolerance grade number decreases the tolerance becomes smaller. Tolerance grades versus actual tolerances may be found in any Machinery's Handbook.

Machining Operation	IT Grades							
	4	5	6	7	8	9	10	11
Lapping & Honing	█							
Cylindrical Grinding		█	█					
Surface Grinding		█	█		█			
Diamond Turning		█	█	█				
Diamond Boring		█	█	█				
Broaching		█	█	█				
Reaming			█	█	█	█	█	
Turning				█	█	█	█	█
Boring					█	█	█	█
Milling							█	█
Planing & Shaping							█	█
Drilling							█	█
Punching							█	█
Die Casting								█

Table 7.7-1: Relation of machining processes to international tolerance grades.

7.8) TOLERANCE ACCUMULATION

The tolerance between two features of a part depends on the number of controlling dimensions. A distance can be controlled by a single dimension or multiple dimensions. The maximum variation between two features is equal to the sum of the tolerances placed on the controlling dimensions. As the number of controlling dimensions increases, the tolerance accumulation increases. Remember, even if the dimension does not have a stated tolerance, it has an implied tolerance.

Instructor Led Exercise 7.8-1: Tolerance accumulation

What is the tolerance accumulation for the distance between surface A and B for the three different dimensioning methods?

Tolerance accumulation between surface A and B =

Tolerance accumulation between surface A and B =

Tolerance accumulation between surface A and B =

If the accuracy of the distance between surface A and B is important, which dimensioning method should be used?

7.9) FORMATTING TOLERANCES

The conventions that are presented in this section pertain to the number of decimal places and format of tolerance dimensions and are in accordance with the ASME Y14.5M standard.

7.9.1) Metric tolerances

- If a tolerance is obtained from a standardized fit table, the limits plus the basic size and tolerance symbol should be given in one of the following three ways. It is preferred to use the forms that directly state the limits.

$$\emptyset^{20.240}_{20.110} \ (\emptyset 20 \ C11) \qquad \text{or} \qquad \emptyset 20 \ C11 \left(\emptyset^{20.240}_{20.110}\right) \qquad \text{or} \qquad \emptyset 20 \ C11$$

- Where a unilateral tolerance exists, a single zero without a plus-minus sign is shown.

$$40 \begin{array}{c} 0 \\ -0.02 \end{array} \qquad \text{or} \qquad 40 \begin{array}{c} +0.02 \\ 0 \end{array}$$

- Where a bilateral tolerance is used, both the plus and minus values have the same number of decimal places, using zeros where necessary.

$$10 \begin{array}{c} +0.25 \\ -0.10 \end{array} \qquad \text{not} \qquad 10 \begin{array}{c} +0.25 \\ -0.1 \end{array}$$

- If limit dimensions are used, both values should have the same number of decimal places, using zeros where necessary.

$$\begin{array}{c} 15.45 \\ 15.00 \end{array} \qquad \text{not} \qquad \begin{array}{c} 15.45 \\ 15 \end{array}$$

- Basic dimensions are considered absolute. When used with a tolerance, the number of decimal places in the basic dimension does not have to match the number of decimal places in the tolerance.

$$45 \pm 0.15 \qquad \text{not} \qquad 45.00 \pm 0.15$$

7.9.2) Inch tolerances

- For unilateral and bilateral tolerances, the basic dimension and the plus and minus values should be expressed with the same number of decimal places.

$$.500 \begin{array}{c} +.000 \\ -.002 \end{array} \qquad \text{not} \qquad .500 \begin{array}{c} 0 \\ -.002 \end{array}$$

$$.500 \begin{array}{c} +.001 \\ -.002 \end{array} \qquad \text{not} \qquad .50 \begin{array}{c} +.001 \\ -.002 \end{array}$$

- If limit dimensions are used, both values should have the same number of decimal places, using zeros where necessary.

$$\begin{array}{c} .252 \\ .250 \end{array} \qquad \text{not} \qquad \begin{array}{c} .252 \\ .25 \end{array}$$

- When basic dimensions are used, the number of decimal places should match the number of decimal places in the tolerance.

$$2.000 \pm 0.015 \qquad \text{not} \qquad 2.0 \pm 0.015$$

7.9.3) Angular tolerances

- Where angle dimensions are used, both the angle and the plus and minus values have the same number of decimal places.

$$30.0°±.2° \qquad \text{not} \qquad \cancel{30°±.2°}$$

<u>NOTES:</u>

7.10) APPLYING WHAT WE HAVE LEARNED

Exercise 7.10-1: Milling Jack assembly tolerances

Name: _____   Date: _____

Consider the *Milling Jack* assembly shown. Notice that there are many parts
that fit into or around other parts. Each of these parts are toleranced to ensure
proper fit and function.

Exercise 7.10-1 Cont.: Milling Jack assembly tolerances

The *V-Anvil* fits (shaft) into the *Sliding Screw* (hole) with a RC4 fit. The basic size is .375 (3/8). Determine the limits for both parts.

- V – Anvil limits: _____

- Sliding Screw limits: _____

Part#3: V - Anvil   Part#2: Sliding Screw

Exercise 7.10-1 Cont.: Milling Jack assembly tolerances

Name: _____   Date: _____

The *Sliding Screw* (shaft) fits into the *Base* (hole) with a RC5 fit. The basic size is .625 (5/8). Determine the limits for both parts.

- Sliding Screw limits: _____

- Base limits: _____

Part#1: Base

Exercise 7.10-2: Drill jig tolerances

Name: _____   Date: _____

Determine the limits for the toleranced features.

Exercise 7.10-3: Over dimensioning

Assuming that the diameter dimensions are correct, explain why this object is dimensioned incorrectly.

NOTES:

TOLERANCING QUESTIONS

Name: _____   Date: _____

Tolerancing

Q7-1) Is it possible to machine a part to an exact size? (yes, no)

Q7-2) A tolerance is the maximum amount a part is allowed to _____. Fill in the blank.

Q7-3) Circle the three different types of tolerances that you may find on a drawing.

    a) Block
    b) Plus-minus
    c) Varying
    d) Limit
    e) Design

Q7-4) A fit that always leaves space between the mating parts.

    a) clearance
    b) interference
    c) transition
    d) line

Q7-5) A fit that sometimes leaves a space between the mating parts.

    a) clearance
    b) interference
    c) transition

Q7-6) The fit that never leaves a space between the mating parts.

    a) clearance
    b) interference
    c) transition
    d) line

Q7-7) This type of dimension has the advantage of providing the print reader with the allowable variation without any calculation.

    a) limit dimension
    b) block tolerance
    c) plus minus dimension
    d) basic dimension

Q7-8) This type of tolerancing is convenient because a design may be initially drawn and dimensioned using basic sizes.

    a) limit dimension
    b) block tolerance
    c) plus minus dimension
    d) basic dimension

Q7-9) This type of tolerancing applies a tolerance to all dimensions not covered by some other tolerance type.

    a) limit dimension
    b) block tolerance
    c) plus minus dimension
    d) basic dimension

Q7-10) When specifying a limit dimension, the (lower, upper) limit go first.

Q7-11) When specifying a limit dimension, the (lower, upper) limit go on top.

Inch tolerances

Q7-12) What does the fit designation RC stand for?

Q7-13) What does the fit designation LT stand for?

Q7-14) What does the fit designation FN stand for?

Q7-15) The type of fit that provides running performance with suitable lubrication. (Choose all that apply)

    a) RC
    b) LC
    c) LT
    d) LN
    e) FN

Q7-16) The type of fit that is intended only to locate mating parts. (Choose all that apply)

    a) RC
    b) LC
    c) LT
    d) LN
    e) FN

Q7-17) The type of fit that provides constant bore pressure. (Choose all that apply)

    a) RC
    b) LC
    c) LT
    d) LN
    e) FN

Q7-18) What is the closest fit that is intended to run freely (inch)?

Q7-19) What is the tightest fit that may be used with cast iron (inch)?

Metric tolerances

Q7-20) When designating a metric fit, what does the letter represent?

    a) fundamental deviation
    b) international tolerance grade
    c) tolerance zone
    d) upper deviation

Q7-21) When designating a metric fit, what does the number represent?

    a) fundamental deviation
    b) international tolerance grade
    c) tolerance zone
    d) upper deviation

Q7-22) When specifying the tolerance zone, does a capital letter represent the fit for the hole or the shaft?

Q7-23) What are the two systems used in the metric tolerance tables?

Q7-24) What does the fit designation H11/c11 stand for?

Q7-25) What does the fit designation P7/h6 stand for?

Q7-26) Given the fit designation H11/c11, would the hypothetical fit H9/c9 be looser or tighter?

Q7-27) This type of clearance fit is good for large temperature variations. (Choose all that apply)

- a) H11/c11
- b) H9/d9
- c) H8/f7
- d) H7/g6
- e) C11/h11
- f) D9/h9
- g) F8/h7
- h) G7/h6

Q7-28) This type of locational fit is good for assemblies that need to be freely assembled and disassembled. (Choose all that apply)

- a) H7/h6
- b) H7/k6
- c) K7/h6
- d) H7/p6
- e) P7/h6

Selecting tolerances

Q7-29) What are some of the factors that influences tolerance choice? (Circle all that apply.)

- a) cost
- b) manufacturing capability
- c) design intent
- d) material

Q7-30) Will tightening a tolerance increase or decrease the cost of manufacturing?

TOLERANCING PROBLEMS

Name: _____   Date: _____

P7-1) Fill in the given table for the following shaft and hole limits.

	(a)	(b)	(c)	(d)	(e)	(f)	(g)	(h)
Shaft	.9975	4.7494	.494	5.0005	1.2513	.1256	2.5072	8.9980
Limits	.9963	4.7487	.487	4.9995	1.2507	.1254	2.5060	8.9878
Hole	1.002	4.751	.507	5.0016	1.251	.1253	2.5018	9.0018
Limits	1.000	4.750	.500	5.0000	1.250	.1250	2.5000	9.0000

	Shaft	Hole
Limits		
Basic Size		
Tolerance		
MMC		
LMC		
Max. Clearance		
Min. Clearance (Allowance)		
Type of Fit (Select one)	Clearance, Transition, Interference, Line	

	Shaft	Hole
Limits		
Basic Size		
Tolerance		
MMC		
LMC		
Max. Clearance		
Min. Clearance (Allowance)		
Type of Fit (Select one)	Clearance, Transition, Interference, Line	

	Shaft	Hole
Limits		
Basic Size		
Tolerance		
MMC		
LMC		
Max. Clearance		
Min. Clearance (Allowance)		
Type of Fit (Select one)	Clearance, Transition, Interference, Line	

NOTES:

Name: _____   Date: _____

P7-2) Find the limits of the shaft and hole for the following basic size – fit combinations.

	(a)	(b)	(c)	(d)	(e)	(f)	(g)
Basic Size	.25	.5	.75	1	1.375	2	2.125
Fit 1	RC3	RC5	RC1	RC9	RC7	RC4	RC6
Fit 2	LC2	LC7	LC11	LC6	LC1	LC9	LC4
Fit 3	LT1	LT2	LT3	LT4	LT5	LT6	LT3
Fit 4	LN2	LN1	FN1	FN5	LN3	FN4	FN2

	Shaft	Hole
Basic Size		
Limits		

	Shaft	Hole
Basic Size		
Limits		

	Shaft	Hole
Basic Size		
Limits		

	Shaft	Hole
Basic Size		
Limits		

	Shaft	Hole
Basic Size		
Limits		

	Shaft	Hole
Basic Size		
Limits		

	Shaft	Hole
Basic Size		
Limits		

	Shaft	Hole
Basic Size		
Limits		

NOTES:

Name: _____   Date: _____

P7-3) Fill in the given table for the following shaft and hole limits.

	(a)	(b)	(c)	(d)	(e)	(f)	(g)	(h)
Shaft	5.970	79.990	16.029	25.061	120.000	2.000	30.000	8.000
Limits	5.940	79.971	16.018	25.048	119.780	1.994	29.987	7.991
Hole	6.030	80.030	16.018	25.021	120.400	2.012	30.006	7.978
Limits	6.000	80.000	16.000	25.000	120.180	2.002	29.985	7.963

	Shaft	Hole
Limits		
Basic size		
Tolerance		
Upper Deviation		
Lower Deviation		
Fundamental Deviation		
System (Select one)	Shaft, Hole	
Fit (Select one)	Clearance, Transition, Interference	

	Shaft	Hole
Limits		
Basic size		
Tolerance		
Upper Deviation		
Lower Deviation		
Fundamental Deviation		
IT Grade		
System (Select one)	Shaft, Hole	
Fit (Select one)	Clearance, Transition, Interference	

	Shaft	Hole
Limits		
Basic size		
Tolerance		
Upper Deviation		
Lower Deviation		
Fundamental Deviation		
IT Grade		
System (Select one)	Shaft, Hole	
Fit (Select one)	Clearance, Transition, Interference	

NOTES:

Name: _____   Date: _____

P7-4) Find the limits of the shaft and hole for the following basic size – fit combinations.

	(a)	(b)	(c)	(d)	(e)	(f)	(g)
Basic Size	5	10	12	16	20	25	30
Fit 1	H11/c11	H7/k6	H7/p6	H7/u6	H8/f7	H7/n6	H7/s6
Fit 2	U7/h6	N7/h6	G7/h6	C11/h11	S7/h6	H7/h6	K7/h6

	Shaft	**Hole**
Basic Size		
Limits		

	Shaft	**Hole**
Basic Size		
Limits		

	Shaft	**Hole**
Basic Size		
Limits		

	Shaft	**Hole**
Basic Size		
Limits		

	Shaft	**Hole**
Basic Size		
Limits		

	Shaft	**Hole**
Basic Size		
Limits		

	Shaft	**Hole**
Basic Size		
Limits		

	Shaft	**Hole**
Basic Size		
Limits		

NOTES:

P7-5) Draw the following object including dimensions. Apply a H7/g6 Sliding clearance fit to the ∅20 hole and shaft. Apply a U7/h6 force fit to the ∅10 hole and shaft. Insert your title block and print.

P7-6) Draw and dimension the *Drive Pulley* using proper dimensioning techniques. This *Drive Pulley* is part of the *Pulley Assembly* given in the Assembly chapter problem section. Notice that the dimensioned isometric drawing does not always use the correct symbols or dimensioning techniques.
- Part name = Drive Pulley
- Part No. = 2
- Material = Steel
- Required = 1

P7-7) Draw and dimension the *Follower Pulley* using proper dimensioning techniques. This *Follower Pulley* is part of the *Pulley Assembly* given in the Assembly chapter problem section. Notice that the dimensioned isometric drawing does not always use the correct symbols or dimensioning techniques.
- Part name = Follower Pulley
- Part No. = 3
- Material = Steel
- Required = 1

P7-8) Draw and dimension the *Shaft* using proper dimensioning techniques. This *Shaft* is part of the *Pulley Assembly* given in the Assembly chapter problem section. Notice that the dimensioned isometric drawing does not always use the correct symbols or dimensioning techniques.
- Part name = Shaft
- Part No. = 4
- Material = Hardened Steel
- Required = 1

P7-9) Draw and dimension the *Bushing* using proper dimensioning techniques. This *Bushing* is part of the *Pulley Assembly* given in the Assembly chapter problem section. Notice that the dimensioned isometric drawing does not always use the correct symbols or dimensioning techniques.
- Part name = Bushing
- Part No. = 5
- Material = Brass
- Required = 1

P7-10) Draw and dimension the *V-Anvil* using proper dimensioning techniques. This *V-Anvil* is part of the *Milling Jack* given in the Assembly chapter problem section. Notice that the dimensioned isometric drawing does not always use the correct symbols or dimensioning techniques.
- Part name = V-Anvil
- Part No. = 3
- Material = SAE 1045 – Heat Treat
- Required = 1

SP7-1) Fill in the given table for the following shaft and hole limits. The answers to this problem are given in the *Independent learning content*.

	Shaft	Hole
	Shaft	**Hole**
Limits	1.2518-1.2524	1.2500-1.2510
Basic Size		
Tolerance		
MMC		
LMC		
Max. Clearance		
Min. Clearance (Allowance)		
Type of Fit		

SP7-2) Find the limits of the shaft and hole for the following basic size – fit combinations. The answers to this problem are given in the *Independent learning content*.

	Shaft	Hole
	Shaft	**Hole**
Basic Size	.625	
Fits	Limits	
RC9		
LC2		
LT3		
FN1		

SP7-3) Fill in the given table for the following shaft and hole limits. The answers to this problem are given in the *Independent learning content*.

	Shaft	Hole
	Shaft	**Hole**
Limits	1.994-2.000	1.990-2.000
Basic size		
Tolerance		
Upper Deviation		
Lower Deviation		
Fundamental Deviation		
IT Grade		
System (hole, shaft)		
Fit		

SP7-4) Find the limits of the shaft and hole for the following basic size – fit combinations. The answers to this problem are given in the *Independent learning content*.

	Shaft	Hole
	Shaft	**Hole**
Basic Size	8	
Fits	Limits	
H7/k6		
S7/h6		

NOTES:

CHAPTER 8

THREADS AND FASTENERS

CHAPTER OUTLINE

CHAPTER SUMMARY

In this chapter you will learn about fasteners. Fasteners give us the means to assemble parts and to later disassemble them if necessary. Most fasteners have threads; therefore, it is important to understand thread notation when learning about fasteners. By the end of this chapter, you will be able to draw and correctly annotate threads on an orthographic projection. You will also be able to calculate an appropriate bolt or screw clearance hole and generate a standard parts sheet. This sheet contains information about purchased items.

8.1) FASTENERS

Fasteners include items such as bolts, nuts, set screws, washers, keys, and pins, just to name a few. Fasteners are not a permanent means of assembly, such as welding or adhesives. They are used in the assembly of machines that, in the future, may need to be taken apart and serviced. The most common type of fastener is the screw. There are many types of screws and many types of screw threads or thread forms.

Fasteners and threaded features must be specified on your engineering drawing. If the fastener is purchased, specifications must be given to allow the fastener to be ordered correctly. All fasteners that are going to be purchased are specified on a standard parts sheet. Information about the type, size and quantity (among other information) is given. If the fastener is to be manufactured, a detailed drawing must be produced. The majority of this chapter will focus on how to draw and dimension threaded features.

It is important that you understand how to identify and draw threads on a print and create their respective thread notes. To save time and computer memory, threads are usually not drawn to look realistic. A thread symbol is used. The different thread symbols used and how to specify thread notes will be described in this chapter.

8.2) SCREW THREAD DEFINITIONS

Fill in *Exercise 8.2-1* as you read through these definitions.

- Screw Thread: A screw thread is a ridge of uniform section in the form of a helix (see Figure 8.2-1).

- External Thread: External threads are on the outside of a member. A chamfer on the end of the screw thread makes it easier to engage the nut. An external thread is cut using a die or lathe.

- Internal Thread: Internal threads are on the inside of a member. An internal thread is cut using a tap.

- Major DIA (D): The major diameter is the largest diameter for both internal and external threads. Sometimes referred to as the nominal or basic size.

- Minor DIA (d): The minor diameter is the smallest diameter.

- Pitch DIA (d_P): Consider a line that cuts across the threads such that the distance on the line that cuts the thread space equals the distance of the line that cuts the actual thread. The pitch diameter is the location of this line.

- Crest: The crest is the top surface of the thread.

- Root: The root is the bottom surface of the thread.

- Side: The side is the surface between the crest and root.

- <u>Depth of thread:</u> The depth of thread is the perpendicular distance between the crest and the root and is equal to (D-d)/2.

- <u>Pitch (P):</u> The pitch is the distance from a point on one thread to the corresponding point on the next thread. The pitch is given in inches per threads or millimeters per thread.

- <u>Angle of Thread (A):</u> The angle of thread is the angle between the sides of the threads.

- <u>Screw Axis:</u> The screw axis is the longitudinal centerline.

- <u>Lead:</u> The lead is the distance a screw thread advances axially in one turn.

- <u>Right Handed Thread:</u> Right handed threads advance when turned clockwise (CW). Threads are assumed RH unless specified otherwise.

- <u>Left Handed Thread:</u> Left handed threads advance when turned counter clockwise (CCW).

External Threads   Internal Threads

Figure 8.2-1: External and internal threads.

Exercise 8.2-1: Screw thread features

Identify the screw thread features using the preceding definitions as a guide.

Application Question 8.2-1

Name an example of a left handed thread.

8.3) TYPES OF THREAD

There are many different types of threads or thread forms available. The thread form is the shape of the thread. The choice of thread form used for a particular application depends on length of engagement and load among other factors. **Unified and *Metric* threads are the most widely used thread forms.** Table 8.3-1 describes just a few of the different thread forms available and their uses.

Thread Name	Figure	Uses
Unified screw thread		General use.
Metric screw thread		General use.
Square		Ideal thread for power transmission.
ACME		Stronger than square thread.
Buttress		Designed to handle heavy forces in one direction (e.g. truck jack).

Table 8.3-1: Screw thread examples

8.4) MANUFACTURING SCREW THREADS

Before proceeding with a description of how to draw screw threads, it is helpful to understand the manufacturing processes used to produce threads.

To cut internal threads, a tap drill hole is drilled first and then the threads are cut using a tap. The tap drill hole is a little bigger than the minor diameter of the mating external thread to allow engagement. The depth of the tap drill is longer than the length of the threads to allow the proper amount of threads to be cut as shown in Figure 8.4-1. There are approximately three useless threads at the end of a normal tap. A bottom tap has useful threads all the way to the end, but is more expensive than a normal tap. If a bottom tap is used, the tap drill depth is approximately the same as the thread length.

To cut external threads, you start with a shaft the same size as the major diameter. Then, the threads are cut using a die or on a lathe. For both internal and external threads, a chamfer is usually cut at the points of engagement to allow easy assembly.

Figure 8.4-1: Manufacturing screw threads.

8.5) DRAWING SCREW THREADS

There are three methods of representing screw threads on a drawing: *detailed*, *schematic*, and *simplified*. The screw thread representations and standards presented in this chapter are in accordance with the ASME Y14.6-2001 standard. The physical dimension of a particular thread may be obtained in Appendix B.

8.5.1) Detailed representation

A detailed representation is a close approximation of the appearance of an actual screw thread. The form of the thread is simplified by showing the helix structure with straight lines and the truncated crests and roots as a sharp 'V' similar to that shown in Figure 8.2-1. This method is comparatively difficult and time consuming.

8.5.2) Schematic representation

The schematic representation is nearly as effective as the detailed representation and is much easier to draw. Staggered lines are used to represent the thread roots and crests (see Figures 8.5-1 and 8.5-2). This method should not be used for hidden internal threads or sections of external threads.

Figure 8.5-1: Schematic representation of external threads.

Figure 8.5-2: Schematic representation of internal threads.

8.5.3) Simplified representation

In the simplified representation, the screw threads are drawn using visible and hidden lines to represent the major and minor diameters. Line choice depends on whether the thread is internal or external and the viewing direction (see Figures 8.5-3 through 8.5-5). Simplified threads are the simplest and fastest to draw. This method should be used whenever possible.

The major, minor, and tap drill diameters may be looked up in Appendix B. If screw thread tables are not available for reference, the minor diameter can be approximated as 75% of the major diameter.

Figure 8.5-3: Simplified representation of external threads.

Figure 8.5-4: Simplified representation of internal threads.

Figure 8.5-5: Simplified representation of internal threads cut on a blind hole.

8.6) UNIFIED THREADS

After drawing a thread using the proper representation, we need to identify the thread form and size in a thread note. Each type of thread (Unified, Metric, ACME, etc...) has its own way of being identified. Unified threads are identified in a thread note by their *major diameter*, *threads per inch*, *thread form* and *series*, *thread class*, whether the thread is *external* or *internal*, whether the thread is *right* or *left* handed, and the thread *depth* (internal only) as shown in Figures 8.6-1 and 8.6-2.

8.6.1) Unified thread note

The list on the following page enumerates all of the components that should be included in the Unified thread note. The first three components (major diameter, threads per inch, and thread form and series) should be included in all thread notes and the depth of thread should be included for all applicable internal thread notes. The other components are optional and are only used if additional refinement is needed.

Figure 8.6-1: Examples of Unified thread notes

Figure 8.6-2: Unified thread note components

1. <u>Major Diameter:</u> The major diameter is the largest diameter for both internal and external threads.
2. <u>Threads per Inch:</u> The number of threads per inch is equal to one over the pitch.
3. <u>Thread Form and Series:</u> The thread form is the shape of the thread cut (Unified) and the thread series is the number of threads per inch for a particular diameter (coarse, fine, extra fine).
   - <u>UNC:</u> UNC stands for *Unified National coarse*. Coarse threads are the most commonly used thread.
   - <u>UNF:</u> UNF stands for *Unified National fine*. Fine threads are used when high degree of tightness is required.
   - <u>UNEF:</u> UNEF stands for *Unified National extra fine*. Extra fine threads are used when the length of engagement is limited (e.g. sheet metal).
4. <u>Thread Class:</u> The thread class indicates the closeness of fit between the two mating threaded parts. There are three thread classes. A thread class of "1" indicates a generous tolerance and used when rapid assembly and disassembly is required. A thread class of "2" is a normal production fit. This fit is assumed if none is stated. A thread class of "3" is used when high accuracy is required.

5. <u>External or Internal Threads:</u> An "A" (external threads) or "B" (internal threads) is placed next to the thread class to indicate whether the threads are external or internal.
6. <u>Right handed or left handed thread:</u> Right handed threads are indicated by the symbol "RH" and left handed threads are indicated by the symbol "LH." Right handed threads are assumed if none is stated.
7. <u>Depth of thread:</u> The thread depth is given at the end of the thread note and indicates the thread depth for internal threads. The stated depth is not the tap drill depth. Remember the tap drill depth is longer than the thread depth.

<u>Exercise 8.6-1: Unified National thread note components</u>

Identify the different components of the following Unified National thread note.

$$1/4 - 20 \; UNC - 2A - RH$$

1/4	
20	
UNC	
2	
A	
RH	

8.6.2) Unified thread tables

Standard screw thread tables are available in order to look up the major diameter, threads per inch, tap drill size, and minor diameter for a particular thread. These thread tables are given in the ASME B1.1-2003 standard and are restated in Appendix B.

<u>Exercise 8.6-2: Unified National thread note</u>

Write the thread note for a #10 fine thread.

What are the major and minor diameters in inches?
- Major
- Minor

8.7) METRIC THREADS

Metric threads are identified, in a thread note, by "M" for Metric thread form, the *major diameter* followed by a lower case "x", *pitch*, *tolerance class*, whether the thread is *right* or *left* handed, and *thread depth* (internal only) as shown in Figures 8.7-1 and 8.7-2.

Figure 8.7-1: Examples of Metric thread notes

8.7.1) Metric thread note

The following is a list of components that should be included in a Metric thread note. The first three components (Metric form, major diameter, and pitch) should be included in all thread notes and the depth of thread should be included for all applicable internal thread notes. The other components are optional and are only used if additional refinement is needed.

1. <u>Metric Form:</u> Placing an "M" before the major diameter indicates the Metric thread form.
2. <u>Major Diameter:</u> This major diameter is the largest diameter for both internal and external.
3. <u>Pitch:</u> The pitch is given in millimeters per thread.

Figure 8.7-2: Metric thread note components

4. <u>Tolerance Class:</u> The tolerance class describes the looseness or tightness of fit between the internal and external threads. The tolerance class contains both a tolerance grade given by a number and tolerance position given by a letter. In a thread note, the pitch diameter tolerance is stated first followed by the crest diameter tolerance if it is different. The crest diameter tolerance is the tolerance on the major diameter for an external thread and the tolerance on the minor diameter for an internal thread. Two classes of Metric thread fits are generally recognized. For general purpose, the fit "6H/6g" should be used. This fit is assumed if none is stated. For a closer fit, use "6H/5g6g."

    -   <u>Tolerance Grade:</u> The tolerance grade is indicated by a number. The smaller the number the tighter the fit. The number "5" indicates good commercial practice. The number "6" is for general purpose threads and is equivalent to the thread class "2" used for Unified National threads.

- • Tolerance Position: The tolerance position specifies the amount of allowance and is indicated by a letter. Upper case letters are used for internal threads and lower case letters for external threads. The letter "e" is used for large allowances, "g" and "G" are used for small allowances, and "h" and "H" are used for no allowance.
5. Right handed or left handed thread: Right handed threads are indicated by the symbol "RH" and left handed threads are indicated by the symbol "LH." Right handed threads are assumed if none is stated.
6. Depth of thread: The thread depth is given at the end of the thread note and indicates the thread depth for internal threads, not the tap drill depth.

Exercise 8.7-1: Metric thread note components

Identify the different components of the following Metric thread notes.

M10 x 1.5 – 4h6h – RH

M	
10	
1.5	
4h	
6h	
Internal or External	
RH	

8.7.2) Metric thread tables

Standard screw thread tables are available in order to look up the major diameter, threads per inch, tap drill size, and minor diameter for a particular thread. These thread tables are given in the ASME B1.13M-2001 standard and are given in Appendix B.

Exercise 8.7-2: Metric thread tables

For a ∅16 internal Metric thread, what are the two available pitches and the required tap drill diameter and the corresponding minor diameter for the mating external thread?

Pitch	Tap drill size	Minor DIA

Which has the finer thread?

The finer thread is M16 x (   )

Exercise 8.7-2 Cont.: Metric thread tables

Write the thread note for a 16 mm diameter coarse thread.

8.8) DRAWING BOLTS

Figure 8.8-1 illustrates how to draw bolts. The variable D represents the major or nominal diameter of the bolt. Nuts are drawn in a similar fashion.

Figure 8.8-1: Drawing bolts.

8.9) BOLT AND SCREW CLEARANCES

Bolts and screws attach one material with a clearance hole to another material with a threaded hole. The size of the clearance hole depends on the major diameter of the fastener and the type of fit that is required for the assembly to function properly. Clearance holes can be designed to have a *normal*, *close* or *loose* fit. Table 8.9-1 gives the normal fit clearances which are illustrated in Figure 8.9-1. For detailed information on clearances for bolts and screws, refer to the ASME B18.2.8-1999 standard also given in Appendix B.

Figure 8.9-1: Bolt clearance.

Inch clearances	
Nominal screw size (D)	Clearance hole (C)
#0 - #4	D + 1/64
#5 – 7/16	D + 1/32
1/2 – 7/8	D + 1/16
1	D + 3/32
1 1/8, 1 1/4	D + 3/32
1 3/8, 1 1/2	D + 1/8

Metric clearances	
Nominal screw size (D)	Clearance hole (C)
M1.6	D + 0.2
M2, M2.5	D + 0.4
M4, M5	D + 0.5
M6	D + 0.6
M8, M10	D + 1
M12 – M16	D + 1.5
M20, M24	D + 2
M30 – M42	D + 3
M48	D + 4
M56 – M90	D + 6
M100	D + 7

Table 8.9-1: Bolt and screw normal fit clearance holes.

Sometimes bolt or screw heads need to be flush with the surface. This can be achieved by using either a counterbore or countersink depending on the fastener's head shape. Counterbores are holes that are designed to recess bolt or screw heads below the surface of a part as shown in Figure 8.9-2. Countersinks are angled holes that are designed to recess screws with angled heads as shown in Figure 8.9-3. Appendix B gives the clearance hole diameters illustrated in Figure 8.9-2 and 8.9-3. If screw clearance tables are not available, typically CH = H + 1/16 (1.5 mm) and C1 = D1 + 1/8 (3 mm).

Figure 8.9-2: Counterbore clearances.

Figure 8.9-3: Countersink clearances.

Exercise 8.9-1: Fastener tables and clearance holes

What is the normal fit clearance hole diameter for the following nominal bolt sizes?

Nominal size	Clearance hole
1/4	
3/4	

A 5/16 - 18 UNC – Socket Head Cap Screw needs to go through a piece of metal in order to screw into a plate below. The head of the screw should be flush with the surface. Fill in the following table for a normal fit clearance hole. Refer to Appendix B.

Max. Head diameter	
Max. Height of head	
Clearance hole diameter	
Counterbore diameter	
Counterbore depth	

An M8x1.25 Flat Countersunk Head Metric Cap Screw needs to go through a piece of metal in order to screw into a plate below. The clearance hole needs to be close and the head needs to go below the surface. What should the countersink diameter and clearance hole diameter be?

Major diameter	
Head diameter	
Countersink diameter	
Clearance hole diameter	

8.10) STANDARD PARTS

Standard parts include any part that can be bought off the shelf. **Standard parts do not need to be drawn.** This could include bolts, nuts, washers, keys, etc. Purchasing information is specified on a standard parts sheet attached to the back of a working drawing package. Figure 8.10-1 shows an example of a standard parts sheet which lists four different items. Keep in mind that the format of the standard parts sheet may change depending on a company's policies. The type of information given may depend on how a company identifies regularly used fasteners. If fasteners are completely identified by a part or identification number, it may not be necessary to create a standard parts sheet at all. This part information may be given in the parts list on the assembly drawing. How to create an assembly drawing and parts list will be discussed in an upcoming chapter. Some of the components of the standard parts sheet will become clearer after learning about assembly drawings.

8.10.1) General fastener specifications

The information that is usually specified on a standard parts sheet for a general fastener is listed below.

1. Thread specification (only if the fastener contains threads)
2. Head/point style or shape and name of the fastener
3. Fastener length or size
4. Fastener series
5. Material
6. Special requirements (coatings, finishes, specifications to meet)
7. QTY REQ'D (i.e. number required)

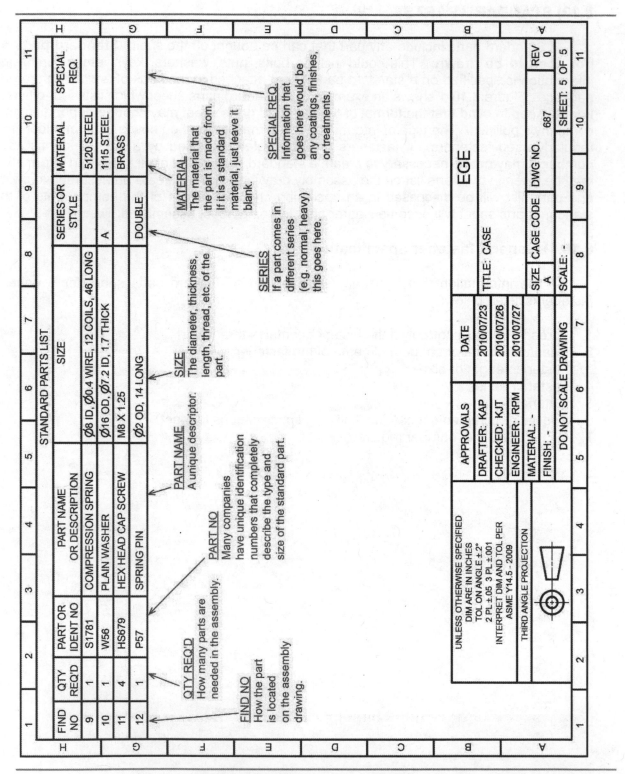

Figure 8.10-1: Standard parts sheet.

8.11) APPLYING WHAT YOU HAVE LEARNED

Exercise 8.11-1: Milling Jack assembly fasteners

Name: _____ Date: _____

Consider the *Milling Jack* assembly shown. Notice that there are many parts that fasten to other parts.

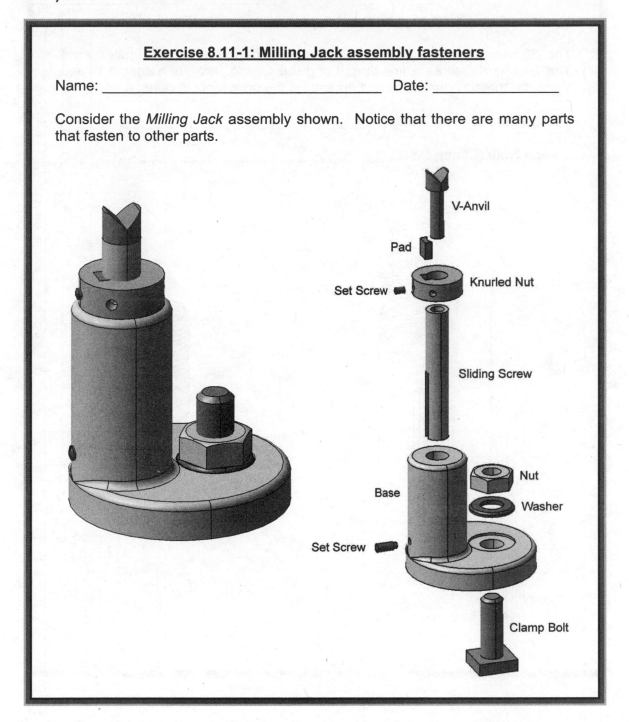

Exercise 8.11-1 Cont.: Milling Jack assembly fasteners

The *Sliding Screw* and *Clamp Bolt* have 5/8 inch thread cut into their bodies. The *Sliding Screw* as a fine thread and the *Clamp Bolt* has a coarse thread. Write the thread note that would appear on the print for both parts.

Thread Note (Sliding Screw): _____

Thread Note (Clamp Bolt): _____

Exercise 8.11-1 Cont.: Milling Jack assembly fasteners

Name: _____ Date: _____

The *Base* has a 1/4 inch course thread drilled and tapped into its body. Write the thread note that would appear on the print. What is the tap drill size?

Thread Note: _____

Tap Drill Size: _____

Ø1.62

1.56

Ø.625 RCS

Ø.56 Ø1.28
.06

NOTE: ALL FILLETS AND
ROUNDS R .12 UNLESS
OTHERWISE SPECIFIED

3.50

1.00

.62

Ø3.56

Exercise 8.11-1 Cont.: Milling Jack assembly fasteners

The *Knurled Nut* has a 0.190 inch major diameter course thread drilled and tapped into its body. Write the thread note that would appear on the print. What is the tap drill size?

Thread Note: _____

Tap Drill Size: _____

Ø1.38

.44

5/8 - 18 UNF - 2B

.20

.40

4X .24

.50

MEDIUM KNURL

3X   Ø.19
▼.25
EQUALLY SPACED
V - BOTTOM

Exercise 8.11-2: Drill jig fasteners

Determine the normal fit clearance hole and countersink dimension for the M12 x 1.75 courntersunk socket head cap screw.

Clearance hole: _____

Countersink diameter and angle: _____

Exercise 8.11-2 Cont.: Drill jig fasteners

Create a standard parts sheet for the *Drill jig*.

THREAD AND FASTENER QUESTIONS

Name: _____   Date: _____

Threads and Fasteners

Q8-1) The major diameter is the (smallest, largest) diameter of the thread.

Q8-2) The minor diameter is the (smallest, largest) diameter of the thread.

Q8-3) The units of pitch are mm or inches per _____. Fill in the blank.

Q8-4) What are the two most common thread forms (i.e. types)?

Q8-5) External threads may be cut using a (die, tap).

Q8-6) Internal threads may be cut using a (die, tap).

Q8-7) A tap drill is used when manufacturing (external, internal) threads.

Q8-8) Label the following thread representations as *Detailed*, *Schematic*, or *Simplified*.

Q8-9) The schematic thread symbol draws lines at every crest and _____. Fill in the blank.

Q8-10) The simplified thread symbol uses a _____ line to represent the minor diameter on external threads.

    a) visible
    b) hidden
    c) center
    d) phantom

Q8-11) How much longer is the tap drill depth than the thread depth when using a taper tap?

    a) 1 times the pitch
    b) 2 times the pitch
    c) 3 times the pitch
    d) 4 times the pitch

Q8-12) The tap drill diameter is closest in size to the _____ diameter.

    a) major
    b) minor
    c) pitch

Unified national threads

Q8-13) 1/4 - 20 UNC. What is 20?

    a) Major diameter
    b) Pitch
    c) One over the pitch
    d) Thread form
    e) Thread series

Q8-14) 1/2 - 13 UNC. What is UN?

    a) Major diameter
    b) Pitch
    c) One over the pitch
    d) Thread form
    e) Thread series

Q8-15) 3/8 - 24 UNF. What is F?

    a) Major diameter
    b) Pitch
    c) One over the pitch
    d) Thread form
    e) Thread series

Q8-16) 5/8 - 24 UNEF – 2A - RH. What is 2?

a) Right handed threads
b) Left handed threads
c) Thread series
d) Thread class
e) External threads
f) Internal threads

Q8-17) 1 - 8 UNC – 3B - RH. What is B?

a) Right handed threads
b) Left handed threads
c) Thread series
d) Thread class
e) External threads
f) Internal threads

Q8-18) 1/2 - 20 UNF – 2B - LH. What is LH?

a) Right handed threads
b) Left handed threads
c) Thread series
d) Thread class
e) External threads
f) Internal threads

Q8-19) #10 - 24 UNC. What is #10?

a) Major diameter
b) Pitch
c) One over the pitch
d) Thread form
e) Thread series

Metric threads

Q8-20) M5 x 0.8. M stands for _____? Fill in the blank.

Q8-21) M4 x 0.7. What is 4?

a) Major diameter
b) Pitch
c) One over the pitch
d) Thread form
e) Thread series
f) Tolerance class

Q8-22) M12 x 1.25. What is 1.25?

a) Major diameter
b) Pitch
c) One over the pitch
d) Thread form
e) Thread series
f) Tolerance class

Q8-23) M6 x 1 – 4h6h – RH. What is 4h6h?

a) Major diameter
b) Pitch
c) One over the pitch
d) Thread form
e) Thread series
f) Tolerance class

Q8-24) Of the two listed threads, circle the one that is the fine thread.

M20 x 2.5   M20 x 1.5

Bolt and screw clearances

Q8-25) A bolt or screw clearance hole diameter depends on what factors? (Circle all that apply.)

a) major diameter
b) minor diameter
c) fit
d) thread depth

Standard parts sheet

Q8-26) A standard parts sheet contains enough information about the standard parts so that they may be ...

a) manufactured
b) drawn
c) purchased
d) modeled

Q8-27) A standard parts sheet contains drawings of all purchased parts. (True, False)

THREAD AND FASTENER PROBLEMS

Name: _____   Date: _____

P8-1) Write the thread notes for the following external threads. Also, what are the minor diameter and the pitch? Thread class = 2.

	(a)	(b)	(c)	(d)	(e)	(f)	(g)
Major ⌀	1/4	7/8	3/4	1/2	1	3/8	5/16
Series	Fine	Coarse	Fine	Coarse	Fine	Extra Fine	Coarse

Thread Note	
Minor diameter	
Pitch	

Thread Note	
Minor diameter	
Pitch	

Thread Note	
Minor diameter	
Pitch	

P8-2) Write the thread notes for the following internal threads. Also, what are the tap drill size and/or diameter and the pitch? Thread class = 3.

	(a)	(b)	(c)	(d)	(e)	(f)	(g)
Major ⌀	7/16	1/4	5/8	1 ¼	3/8	1/2	1
Series	Fine	Coarse	Fine	Coarse	Fine	Extra Fine	Coarse

Thread Note	
Tap drill size and/or diameter	
Pitch	

Thread Note	
Tap drill size and/or diameter	
Pitch	

Thread Note	
Tap drill size and/or diameter	
Pitch	

P8-3) Write the thread notes for the following threads. Also, what is the major diameter in inches?

	(a)	(b)	(c)	(d)	(e)	(f)	(g)
Major ⌀	#0	#2	#4	#5	#6	#8	#10
Series	Fine	Coarse	Fine	Coarse	Fine	Fine	Coarse

Thread note	
Major diameter	

Thread note	
Major diameter	

Thread note	
Major diameter	

Name: _____ Date: _____

P8-4) Write the thread notes for the following external threads. Also, what are the minor diameter and the number of threads per mm?

	(a)	(b)	(c)	(d)	(e)	(f)	(g)
Major ⌀	M3	M4	M8	M10	M12	M20	M24
Series	Coarse	Coarse	Fine	Coarse	Fine	Fine	Coarse

Thread Note	
Minor diameter	
# of threads per mm	

Thread Note	
Minor diameter	
# of threads per mm	

Thread Note	
Minor diameter	
# of threads per mm	

P8-5) Write the thread notes for the following internal threads. Also, what are the tap drill size and/or diameter and the number of threads per mm?

	(a)	(b)	(c)	(d)	(e)	(f)	(g)
Major ⌀	M1.6	M5	M6	M12	M18	M22	M27
Series	Coarse	Coarse	Coarse	Coarse	Fine	Fine	Coarse

Thread Note	
Tap drill size and/or diameter	
# of threads per mm	

Thread Note	
Tap drill size and/or diameter	
# of threads per mm	

Thread Note	
Tap drill size and/or diameter	
# of threads per mm	

NOTES:

Name: _____   Date: _____

P8-6) Fill in the given table for a hex head bolt with the following major diameters.

	(a)	(b)	(c)	(d)	(e)	(f)	(g)	(h)
Major ⌀	1/4	5/16	1/2	7/8	1	9/16	3/8	7/16

Major diameter	
Width across flats	
Max. width across corners	
Head height	
Normal clearance hole	

Major diameter	
Width across flats	
Max. width across corners	
Head height	
Normal clearance hole	

Major diameter	
Width across flats	
Max. width across corners	
Head height	
Normal clearance hole	

P8-7) Fill in the given table for a hexagon (socket) head cap screw with the following major diameters.

	(a)	(b)	(c)	(d)	(e)	(f)	(g)	(h)
Major ⌀	1/4	5/16	1/2	#8	#5	9/16	3/8	#10

Major diameter	
Max. head diameter	
Max. head height	
Normal clearance hole	
Counterbore diameter	
Counterbore depth	

Major diameter	
Max. head diameter	
Max. head height	
Normal clearance hole	
Counterbore diameter	
Counterbore depth	

P8-8) Fill in the given table for a slotted flat countersunk head cap screw with the following major diameters.

	(a)	(b)	(c)	(d)	(e)	(f)	(g)	(h)
Major ⌀	1/4	5/16	3/8	7/16	1/2	9/16	5/8	3/4

Major diameter	
Max. head diameter	
Max. head height	
Normal clearance hole	
Countersink diameter	
Countersink angle	

Major diameter	
Max. head diameter	
Max. head height	
Normal clearance hole	
Countersink diameter	
Countersink angle	

Name: _____ Date: _____

P8-9) Fill in the given table for a hex head bolt with the following major diameters.

	(a)	(b)	(c)	(d)	(e)	(f)	(g)	(h)
Major ∅	M5	M12	M20	M30	M36	M48	M14	M24

Major diameter	
Max. width across flats	
Max. width across corners	
Max. head height	
Thread length for a screw that is shorter than 125 mm	
Normal clearance hole	

Major diameter	
Max. width across flats	
Max. width across corners	
Max. head height	
Thread length for a screw that is shorter than 125 mm	
Normal clearance hole	

P8-10) Fill in the given table for a socket head cap screw with the following major diameters.

	(a)	(b)	(c)	(d)	(e)	(f)	(g)	(h)
Major ∅	M1.6	M2.5	M4	M6	M12	M16	M24	M42

Major diameter	
Max. head diameter	
Max. head height	
Normal clearance hole	
Counterbore diameter	
Counterbore depth	

Major diameter	
Max. head diameter	
Max. head height	
Normal clearance hole	
Counterbore diameter	
Counterbore depth	

Name: _____ Date: _____

P8-11) Fill in the given table for a flat countersunk head cap screw with the following major diameters.

	(a)	(b)	(c)	(d)	(e)	(f)	(g)	(h)
Major ⌀	M16	M3	M12	M5	M6	M8	M10	M4

Major diameter	
Head diameter	
Head height	
Normal clearance hole	
Countersink diameter	
Countersink angle	

Major diameter	
Head diameter	
Head height	
Normal clearance hole	
Countersink diameter	
Countersink angle	

P8-12) Draw and dimension the *Knurled Nut* using proper dimensioning techniques. This *Knurled Nut* is part of the *Milling Jack* given in the *Assemblies* chapter problem section. Notice that the dimensioned isometric drawing does not always use the correct symbols or dimensioning techniques.
- Part name = Knurled Nut
- Part No. = 4
- Material = SAE 1045 – Heat Treat
- Required = 1

P8-13) Draw and dimension the *Pad* using proper dimensioning techniques. This *Pad* is part of the *Milling Jack* given in the *Assemblies* chapter problem section. Notice that the dimensioned isometric drawing does not always use the correct symbols or dimensioning techniques.
- Part name = Pad
- Part No. = 5
- Material = Phosphor Bronze - FAO
- Required = 1

P8-14) Draw and dimension the *Clamp Bolt* using proper dimensioning techniques. This *Clamp Bolt* is part of the *Milling Jack* given in the *Assemblies* chapter problem section. Notice that the dimensioned isometric drawing does not always use the correct symbols or dimensioning techniques.
- Part name = Clamp Bolt
- Part No. = 6
- Material = SAE 1020 – Case Hardened
- Required = 1

P8-15) Draw and dimension the *Sliding Screw* using proper dimensioning techniques. This *Sliding Screw* is part of the *Milling Jack* given in the *Assemblies* chapter problem section. Notice that the dimensioned isometric drawing does not always use the correct symbols or dimensioning techniques.
- Part name = Sliding Screw
- Part No. = 2
- Material = SAE 1045 – Heat Treat
- Required = 1

NOTES:

SP8-1) Write the thread notes for the following external threads. Also, what are the minor diameter and the pitch? Thread class = 2. The answer to this problem is given in the *Independent Learning Content*.

Major ∅	7/16
Series	Coarse
Thread Note	
Minor diameter	
Pitch	

SP8-2) Write the thread notes for the following internal threads. Also, what are the tap drill size and/or diameter and the pitch? Thread class = 3. The answer to this problem is given in the *Independent Learning Content*.

Major ∅	9/16
Series	Fine
Thread Note	
Tap drill size and/or diameter	
Pitch	

SP8-3) Write the thread notes for the following threads. Also, what is the major diameter in inches? The answer to this problem is given in the *Independent Learning Content*.

Major ∅	#3
Series	Coarse
Thread note	
Major diameter	

SP8-4) Write the thread notes for the following external threads. Also, what are the minor diameter and the number of threads per mm? The answer to this problem is given in the *Independent Learning Content*.

Major ∅	M33
Series	Fine
Thread Note	
Minor diameter	
# of threads per mm	

SP8-5) Write the thread notes for the following internal threads. Also, what are the tap drill size and/or diameter and the number of threads per mm? The answer to this problem is given in the *Independent Learning Content*.

Major ∅	M24
Series	Coarse
Thread Note	
Tap drill size and/or diameter	
# of threads per mm	

SP8-6) Fill in the given table for a hex head bolt with the following major diameters. The answer to this problem is given in the *Independent Learning Content*.

Major ∅	3/4
Width across flats	
Max. width across corners	
Head height	
Normal clearance hole	

SP8-7) Fill in the given table for a hexagon (socket) head cap screw with the following major diameters. The answer to this problem is given in the *Independent Learning Content*.

Major ∅	7/8
Max. head diameter	
Max. head height	
Normal clearance hole	
Counterbore diameter	
Counterbore depth	

SP8-8) Fill in the given table for a slotted flat countersunk head cap screw with the following major diameters. The answer to this problem is given in the *Independent Learning Content*.

Major ∅	1
Max. head diameter	
Max. head height	
Normal clearance hole	
Countersink diameter	
Countersink angle	

SP8-9) Fill in the given table for a hex head bolt with the following major diameters. The answer to this problem is given in the *Independent Learning Content*.

Major ⌀	M8
Max. width across flats	
Max. width across corners	
Max. head height	
Thread length for a screw that is shorter than 125 mm	
Normal clearance hole	

SP8-10) Fill in the given table for a socket head cap screw with the following major diameters. The answer to this problem is given in the *Independent Learning Content*.

Major ⌀	M14
Max. head diameter	
Max. head height	
Normal clearance hole	
Counterbore diameter	
Counterbore depth	

SP8-11) Fill in the given table for a flat countersunk head cap screw with the following major diameters. The answer to this problem is given in the *Independent Learning Content*.

Major ⌀	M20
Head diameter	
Head height	
Normal clearance hole	
Countersink diameter	
Countersink angle	

NOTES:

CHAPTER 9

ASSEMBLY DRAWINGS

CHAPTER OUTLINE

CHAPTER SUMMARY

In this chapter you will learn how to create an assembly drawing. An assembly drawing is a drawing of an entire machine with each part located and identified. After each part of a machine is manufactured, the assembly drawing shows us how to put these parts together. The assembly drawing together with all the detailed part drawings and the standard parts sheet is called a working drawing package. By the end of this chapter, you will be able to create a working drawing package which contains all the information necessary to manufacture a machine or system.

An assembly drawing is a drawing of an entire machine or system with all of its components located and identified.

9.1) DEFINITIONS

- Detail Drawing: A detail drawing is a drawing of an individual part, which includes an orthographic projection with dimensions. One detail/part per sheet.

- Assembly Drawing: An assembly consists of a number of parts that are joined together to perform a specific function (e.g. a bicycle). The assembly may be disassembled without destroying any part of the assembly. An assembly drawing shows the assembled machine or structure with all of the parts in their functional position.

- Subassembly Drawing: A subassembly is two or more parts that form a portion of an assembly (e.g. the drive train of a bicycle). A subassembly drawing shows only one unit of a larger machine.

- Working Drawing Package: A typical working drawing package includes an assembly drawing, detailed drawings, and a standard parts sheet. The drawing package contains the specifications that will enable the design to be manufactured.

9.1.1) Drawing order

Drawings included in a working drawing package should be presented in the following order:

1) Assembly drawing (first sheet)
2) Part Number 1
3) Part Number 2
4) ....
5) Standard parts sheet (last sheet)

9.2) COMPONENTS OF AN ASSEMBLY DRAWING

Figure 9.2-1 shows the components of an assembly drawing.

9.2.1) Assembly drawing views

Assembly drawings may contain one or more of the standard views (i.e. Front, top, right-side, left-side, bottom, rear). It may also include specialized views such as section views or auxiliary views. When deciding which view or views to include you should keep in mind the purpose of an assembly drawing. **The purpose of an assembly drawing is to show how the parts fit together** and to suggest the function of the entire unit. Its purpose is not to describe the shapes of the individual parts. Sometimes only one view is needed and sometimes it is necessary to draw all three principal views.

9.2.3) Part identification

A part is located and identified by using a circle or balloon containing a *find number* and a leader line that points to the corresponding part. A balloon containing a *find number* is placed adjacent to the part. A leader line, starting at the balloon, points to the part to which it refers. Balloons identifying different parts are placed in orderly horizontal or vertical rows. The leader lines are never allowed to cross and adjacent leader lines should be as parallel to each other as possible as shown in Figure 9.2-2.

9.2.4) Parts list / bill of material

The parts list is an itemized list of the parts that make up the assembled machine. A parts list may contain, but is not limited to, the following.

- Find number: The *find number* links the *parts list* description of the part to the balloon locating the part on the assembly drawing.
- Part number: A *part number* is an identifier of a particular part design. It is common practice, but not a requirement, to start the part number with the drawing number followed by a dash and then a unique number identifying the part. This unique number usually matches the find number. Standard parts usually do not contain the drawing number because they are used across designs not just in a particular design.
- Nomenclature or description: The part name or description.
- Number of parts required (QTY REQ'D): The number of that part used in the assembly.
- Part material: The material in which the part is made of.
- Stock size: The pre-machined size of the part.
- Cage code: A cage code is a five position code that identifies companies doing or wishing to do business with the Federal Government.
- Part weight: The weight of the finished part.

Parts lists are arranged in order of their find number. Find and part numbers are usually assigned based on the size or importance of the part. The parts list is placed either in the upper left corner of the drawing, with part number 1 at the top, or lower right corner of the drawing, with part number 1 at the bottom (see Figures 9.2-1).

Figure 9.2-1: Components of an assembly drawing.

Balloons are placed in orderly horizontal or vertical rows.

Balloons contain the find number.

SECTION A-A

Leader lines point to the part identified by the corresponding find no.

Leader lines should not cross and be as parallel as possible.

Figure 9.2-2: Part identification

9.3) SECTION VIEWS

Since assemblies often have parts fitting into or overlapping other parts, sectioning can be used to great advantage. When using sectional views in assembly drawings, it is necessary to distinguish between adjacent parts. **Section lines in adjacent parts are drawn in opposing directions.** In the largest area, the section lines are drawn at 45°. In the next largest area, the section lines are drawn at 135° (in the opposite direction of the largest area). Section line angles of 30° and 60° are used for additional parts. **The distance between the section lines may also be varied to further distinguish between parts.**

Exercise 9.3-1: Section lines in assemblies

The following assembly is sectioned. Draw in the section lines according to the rules stated above.

9.4) THINGS TO INCLUDE/NOT INCLUDE

The purpose of an assembly drawing is to show how the individual parts fit together. Therefore, each individual part must be identified. It is not, however, used as a manufacturing print. Some lines that are included and necessary in the detailed drawing may be left off the assembly drawing to enhance clearness. The assembly drawing should not look overly cluttered.

9.4.1) Hidden and center lines

Hidden and center lines are often not needed. However, they should be used wherever necessary for clearness. It is left to the judgment of the drafter whether or not to include hidden lines. A good practice is to include all hidden and center lines at first and then delete or hide the lines that impair clearness. When a section view is used, hidden lines should not be used in the sectional view.

9.4.2) Dimensions

As a rule, dimensions are not given on assembly drawings. If dimensions are given, they are limited to some function of the object as a whole.

9.5) APPLYING WHAT WE HAVE LEARNED

Exercise 9.5-1: Working drawing package

Consider the *Clamp* shown. Sheets of an incomplete working drawing package are given in the following pages. Follow the directions and complete the drawing sheets. Note that the drawing number is 31578.

Exercise 9.5-1: Working drawing package cont.

Part 1: The *Base* is made of steel.

Exercise 9.5-1: Working drawing package cont.

<u>Part 2:</u> The *Weight Plate* is made of steel.

<u>Part 3:</u> The *Pin* is made of hardened steel.

<u>Part 4:</u> The *Snap Ring* has an inner diameter of 3 mm, an outer diameter of 5 mm, and a thickness of 1 mm. The snap ring part number is SR67.

NOTES:

Exercise 9.5-1: Working drawing package cont.

Name: _____ Date: _____

Balloon the assembly and fill in the parts list and title block.

Exercise 9.5-1: Working drawing package cont.

Fill in the title block and add the 7 missing dimensions.

Exercise 9.5-1: Working drawing package cont.

Name: _____ Date: _____

Fill in the title block and add the 3 missing dimensions.

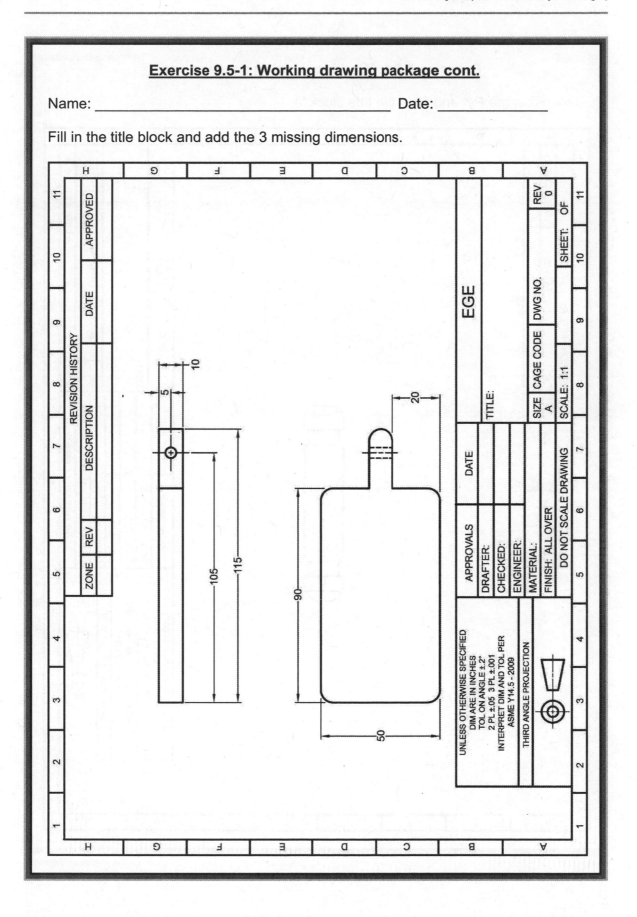

Exercise 9.5-1: Working drawing package cont.

Dimension the *Pin* and fill in the title block.

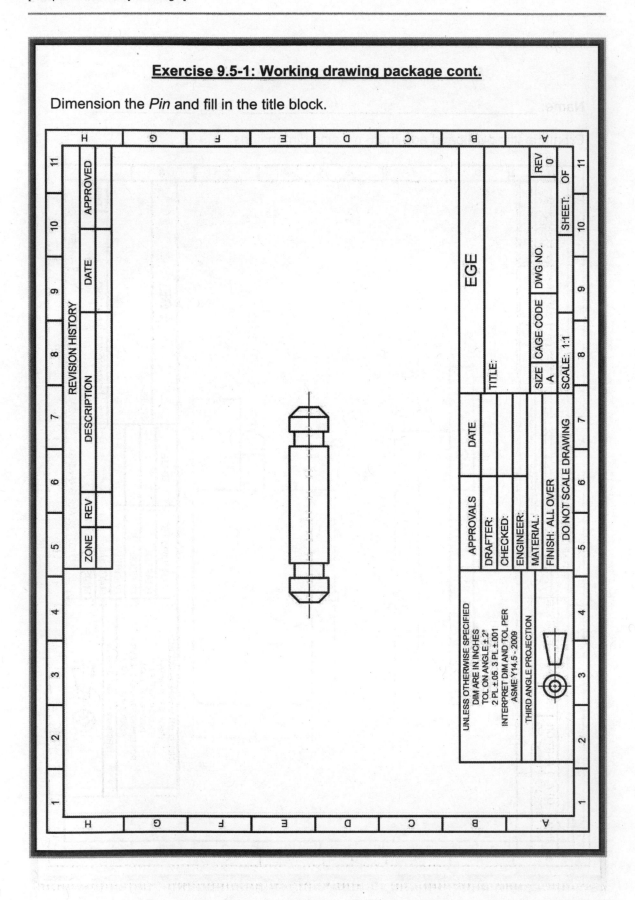

Exercise 9.5-1: Working drawing package cont.

Name: _____ Date: _____

Create a standard parts sheet.

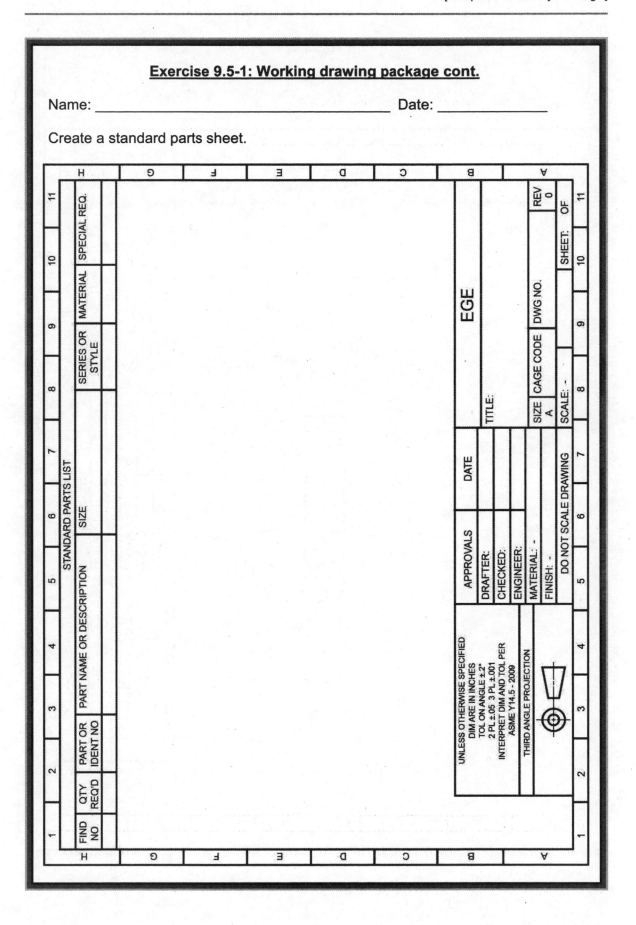

<u>NOTES:</u>

ASSEMBLY QUESTIONS

Name: _____   Date: _____

Q9-1) The purpose of an assembly drawing is to show how the individual parts _____ _____. Fill in the blank.

Q9-2) What is always included on a detailed drawing but rarely included on an assembly drawing?

    a) section lines
    b) hidden lines
    c) center lines
    d) dimensions

Q9-3) This is a place where you can get a quick overall view of all the parts that comprise an assembly and how many of each are required in the assembly. (Circle all that apply.)

    a) parts list
    b) table of contents
    c) standard parts sheet
    d) bill of materials

Q9-4) Criteria that are used to assign part numbers. (Circle all that apply.)

    a) size
    b) weight
    c) importance
    d) color

Q9-5) Section lines are drawn in opposing directions when there are ...

    a) adjacent parts
    b) small parts
    c) non-sectioned parts
    d) moving parts

Q9-6) The first sheet in a working drawing package is the ... drawing.

    a) part#1
    b) the last part
    c) assembly drawing
    d) Standard parts sheet

Q9-7) The last sheet in a working drawing package is the ... drawing.

    a) part#1
    b) the last part
    c) assembly drawing
    d) standard parts sheet

NOTES:

ASSEMBLY PROBLEMS

P9-1) Answer the following questions about the assembly drawing shown.

    a) What is the name of the assembly?

    b) How many sheets are there in the working drawing package?

    c) What is the name of part number 303200 - 4?

    d) What is the find number of the BOLT?

    e) What type of material is the WEDGE made of?

    f) How many SET SCREWS are used in the assembly?

    g) On the assembly, circle the ADJUSTING NUT.

    h) On the assembly, circle the HEX NUT.

FIND NO	QTY REQ'D	PART OR IDENT NO	NOMENCLATURE OR DESCRIPTION	MATERIAL
1	1	303200 - 1	TOOL POST BODY	CI
2	1	303200 - 2	WEDGE	1045 STEEL
3	1	303200 - 3	BOLT	1040 STEEL
4	2	303200 - 4	TOOL POST SCREW	1040 STEEL
5	1	303200 - 5	ADJUSTING SCREW	1040 STEEL
6	1	303200 - 6	ADJUSTING NUT	1020 STEEL
7	1	303200 - 7	SLOTTED WASHER	1020 STEEL
8	1	HS4590	HEX NUT	
9	2	HS3512	SET SCREW	
10	1	W654	WASHER	

PARTS LIST

EGE

APPROVALS	DATE
DRAFTER: KAP	2015/12/21
CHECKED: HYP	2015/12/23
ENGINEER: GRW	2015/12/01
MATERIAL: -	
FINISH: -	

DO NOT SCALE DRAWING

THIRD ANGLE PROJECTION

TITLE: TOOL POST

SIZE	CAGE CODE	DWG NO.	REV
A		303200	0

SCALE: 1:2   SHEET: 1 OF 11

P9-2) Consider the *Trolley* assembly shown. Sheets of an incomplete working drawing package are given in the following pages. Complete the working drawing package.

INSTRUMENT BALL BEARING
BORE = $\varnothing$.75
OD = $\varnothing$1.625
THICKNESS = .3125
2 REQ'D

SIDE PLATE
1020 STEEL
2 REQ'D

TROLLEY WHEEL
1020 STEEL
2 REQ'D

11/16 RETAINING RING
EXTERNAL
C-TYPE
2 REQ'D

AXLE
1045 COLD
DRAWN STEEL
2 REQ'D

KEEPER PLATE
1020 STEEL
2 REQ'D

10 - 24 UNC
ROUND HEAD
MACHINE SCREW
LENGTH = .62
4 REQ'D

7/8 - 9 UNC
HEX HEAD BOLT
LENGTH = 8.5
THREAD LENGTH = 2.25
2 REQ'D

7/8 - 9 UNC
HEX HEAD NUT
2 REQ'D

CROSS HEAD
1020 STEEL
1 REQ'D

7/8 PLAIN WASHER
TYPE A
NARROW
4 REQ'D

ADJUSTING SHIM
1020 STEEL
2 REQ'D

Name: _____ Date: _____

Fill in the find numbers in the appropriate balloons and complete the part list and title block information.

Name: _____ Date: _____

Draw the missing section view and complete the title block information.

Name: _____ Date: _____

Complete the title block information.

Name: _____ Date: _____

Fill in the counterbore and hole dimensions, and complete the title block information. The counterbore is .44 deep and has a diameter of 1.62. The drill diameter is .75. The holes have a diameter of .91.

Name: _____   Date: _____

Complete the title block information.

Name: _____ Date: _____

Dimension the part, and fill in the title block. When dimensioning the part, use an 'n' for the numerical value. Use the proper symbols.

Name: _____ Date: _____

Complete the title block.

Name: _____ Date: _____

Complete the information on the standard (stock) parts and fill in the title block.

FIND NO	QTY REQ'D	PART OR IDENT NO	PART NAME OR DESCRIPTION	SIZE / SERIES	MATERIAL

STANDARD PARTS LIST

UNLESS OTHERWISE SPECIFIED
DIM ARE IN INCHES
TOL ON ANGLE ±.2°
2 PL ±.05 3 PL ±.001
INTERPRET DIM AND TOL PER
ASME Y14.5 - 2009

THIRD ANGLE PROJECTION

APPROVALS	DATE
DRAFTER:	
CHECKED:	
ENGINEER:	
MATERIAL: -	
FINISH: -	

DO NOT SCALE DRAWING

EGE

TITLE:

SIZE A	CAGE CODE	DWG NO.	REV 0

SCALE: -   SHEET: OF

P9-3) Consider the *Drill Jig* assembly shown. Sheets of an incomplete working drawing package are given in the following pages. Follow the directions and complete the sheets. The *Drill Jig* dimensions are shown in the exploded assembly shown on the next page.

DRILL JIG SI

NOTE: ASSEMBLE PART 5 BEFORE PART 4

① BASE
1020 STEEL

② END BRACKET
1020 STEEL

③ CENTER PLATE
1020 STEEL

④ M20 x 2.5
HEX HEAD BOLT
60 LONG

⑤ M12 x 1.75
COUNTERSUNK SOCKET
HEAD CAP SCREW
35 LONG

⑥ M20 x 2.5
HEX HEAD NUT

Name: _____ Date: _____

Complete the section view by adding the appropriate section lines. Then, fill in the find numbers in the correct balloon, fill in the parts list, and fill in the title block.

Draw and dimension the threaded features of the BASE, fill in the title block, and answer the following questions.

- What is the tap drill size for the M12x1.75 thread? Tap drill diameter = _____
- How much further does the tap drill depth proceed past the thread depth?

Dimension the END BRACKET and fill in the title block.

Dimension the CENTER PLATE, and fill in the title block.

Create a standard parts sheet and fill in the title block.

STANDARD PARTS LIST

FIND NO	QTY REQ'D	PART OR IDENT NO	PART NAME OR DESCRIPTION	SIZE	SERIES OR STYLE	MATERIAL	SPECIAL REQ.
4		HS512					
5		HS790					
6		HS679					

UNLESS OTHERWISE SPECIFIED
DIM ARE IN INCHES
TOL ON ANGLE ± 2°
2 PL ±.05 3 PL ±.001
INTERPRET DIM AND TOL PER
ASME Y14.5 - 2009

THIRD ANGLE PROJECTION

APPROVALS | DATE

DRAFTER:
CHECKED:
ENGINEER:

MATERIAL: -
FINISH: -

DO NOT SCALE DRAWING

EGE

TITLE:

SIZE: A
CAGE CODE
DWG NO. 687
REV 0

SCALE: -
SHEET: OF

NOTES:

P9-4) Create a working drawing package for the following *Pulley Assembly*. The working drawing package should contain an assembly drawing, details of all the parts, and a standard parts sheet. Notice that some of the dimensioned isometric drawings are not dimensioned using proper dimensioning techniques. When drawing the detailed drawings use proper symbols and dimensioning techniques.

Bracket

NOTE: ALL FILLETS AND
ROUNDS R3 UNLESS
OTHERWISE SPECIFIED

130

35

35

M8 X 1.25

2X Ø25 H9/d9

20

2X Ø50

50

2X R10

2X R25

115

20

15

20

15

20

The post is
centered with
respect to the
bottom of the
bracket.

150

Ø30

Drive Pulley

Follower Pulley

Shaft

Bushing

P9-5) Create a working drawing package for the following *Milling Jack*. The working drawing package should contain an assembly drawing, details of all the parts, and a standard parts sheet. Notice that some of the dimensioned isometric drawings are not dimensioned using proper dimensioning techniques. When drawing the detailed drawings use proper symbols and dimensioning techniques.

<u>Milling Jack</u>

PAD ⑤
PHOSPHOR BRONZE
FAO
1 REQD

#10 X 1/4 ⑩
SLOTTED HEAD
SET SCREW
FLAT POINT
CASE HARDENED
1 REQD

1/4 X 5/8 ⑨
SLOTTED HEAD
SET SCREW
FULL DOG POINT
CASE HARDENED
1 REQD

③ **V-ANVIL**
SAE 1045 - HEAT TREAT
FAO
1 REQD

② **SLIDING SCREW**
SAE 1045 - HEAT TREAT
1 REQD

④ **KNURLED NUT**
SAE 1045 - HEAT TREAT
1 REQD

① **BASE**
CAST IRON
1 REQD

⑦ 5/8 - 11 UNC
HEX NUT
CASE HARDENED
1 REQD

⑧ **WASHER**
SAE 1020
CASE HARDENED
1 REQD

⑥ **CLAMP BOLT**
SAE 1020
CASE HARDENED
1 REQD

Base

NOTE: ALL FILLETS AND ROUNDS R .12 UNLESS OTHERWISE SPECIFIED

Sliding Screw

Ø .375 RC4
▽ 2.00

5/8 - 18 UNF - 2A

1.12

3.88

2.00

Ø .625 RC5

3/16 X 3/32 KEYWAY

V-Anvil

Knurled Nut

Pad

Clamp Bolt

<u>Washer</u>

SP9-1) Create a working drawing package for the following *Linear Bearing*. The working drawing package should contain an assembly drawing, details of all the parts, and a standard parts sheet. Notice that some of the dimensioned isometric drawings are not dimensioned using proper dimensioning techniques. When drawing the detailed drawings use proper symbols and dimensioning techniques. The answer to this problem is given in the *Independent Learning Content*.

<u>Part#1: Bottom Plate</u> If you are just studying the basics and have not covered threads and fasteners, replace the 12X 10 – 24 UNC dimension with a 12x ⌀.19 dimension.

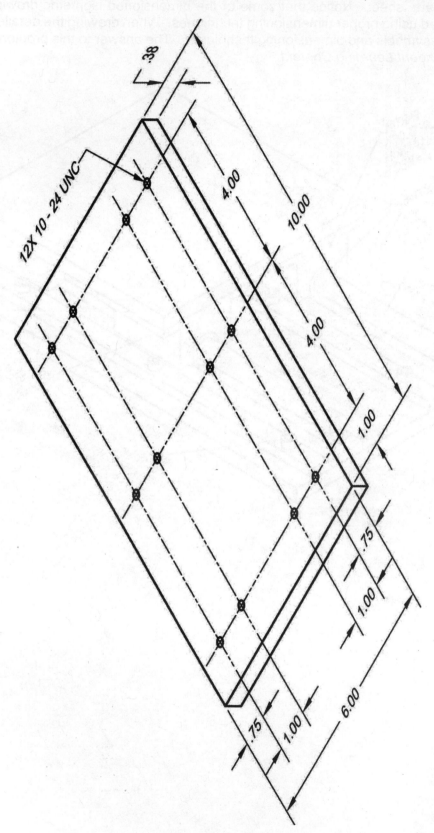

Part#2: Guide Shaft If you are just studying the basics and have not covered tolerancing, ignore the RC4 tolerance. NOTE TO DRAFTER: This part is symmetric and all fillets are R.12.

Part#3: Top Plate If you are just studying the basics and have not covered threads and fasteners, replace the 16X 10 – 24 UNC dimension with a 16x ⌀.19 dimension.

<u>Part#4: Pillow Block</u> If you are just studying the basics and have not covered tolerancing, ignore the FN1 tolerance.

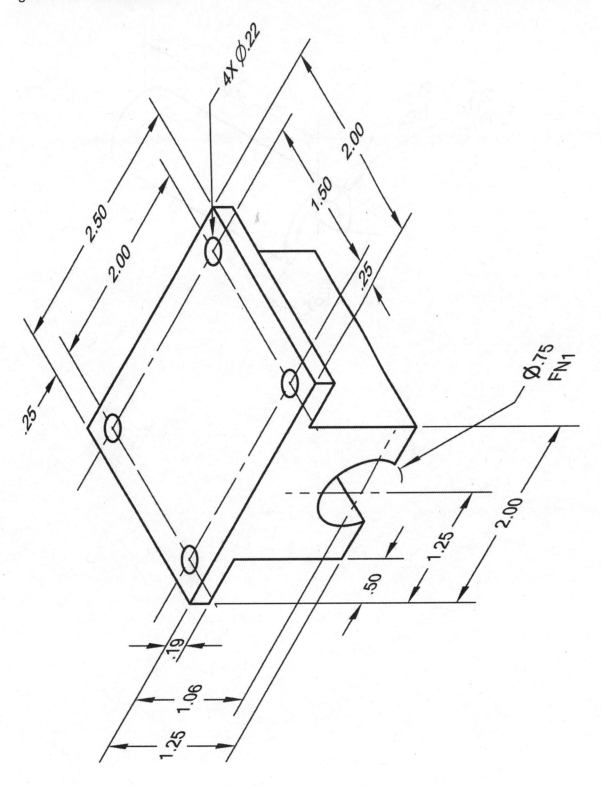

Part#5: Bearing If you are just studying the basics and have not covered tolerancing, ignore the RC4 and FN1 tolerances.

APPENDIX A

LIMITS AND FITS

APPENDIX OUTLINE

A.1) LIMITS AND FITS (INCH)

A.1.1) Running or sliding clearance fits

Basic hole system. Limits are in thousandths of an inch.
Limits for hole and shaft are applied algebraically to the basic size to obtain the limits of size for the parts.

Nominal Size Range Inches		Class RC1 Standard Limits		Class RC2 Standard Limits		Class RC3 Standard Limits		Class RC4 Standard Limits	
Over	To	Hole	Shaft	Hole	Shaft	Hole	Shaft	Hole	Shaft
0	− 0.12	+0.2 0	-0.1 -0.25	+0.25 0	-0.1 -0.3	+0.4 0	-0.3 -0.55	+0.6 0	-0.3 -0.7
0.12	− 0.24	+0.2 0	-0.15 -0.3	+0.3 0	-0.15 -0.35	+0.5 0	-0.4 -0.7	+0.7 0	-0.4 -0.9
0.24	− 0.40	+0.25 0	-0.2 -0.35	+0.4 0	-0.2 -0.45	+0.6 0	-0.5 -0.9	+0.9 0	-0.5 -1.1
0.40	− 0.71	+0.3 0	-0.25 -0.45	+0.4 0	-0.25 -0.55	+0.7 0	-0.6 -1.0	+1.0 0	-0.6 -1.3
0.71	− 1.19	+0.4 0	-0.3 -0.55	+0.5 0	-0.3 -0.7	+0.8 0	-0.8 -1.3	+1.2 0	-0.8 -1.6
1.19	− 1.97	+0.4 0	-0.4 -0.7	+0.6 0	-0.4 -0.8	+1.0 0	-1.0 -1.6	+1.6 0	-1.0 -2.0
1.97	− 3.15	+0.5 0	-0.4 -0.7	+0.7 0	-0.4 -0.9	+1.2 0	-1.2 -1.9	+1.8 0	-1.2 -2.4
3.15	− 4.73	+0.6 0	-0.5 -0.9	+0.9 0	-0.5 -1.1	+1.4 0	-1.4 -2.3	+2.2 0	-1.4 -2.8
4.73	− 7.09	+0.7 0	-0.6 -1.1	+1.0 0	-0.6 -1.3	+1.6 0	-1.6 -2.6	+2.5 0	-1.6 -3.2
7.09	− 9.85	+0.8 0	-0.6 -1.2	+1.2 0	-0.6 -1.4	+1.8 0	-2.0 -3.2	+2.8 0	-2.0 -3.8
9.85	− 12.41	+0.9 0	-0.8 -1.4	+1.2 0	-0.7 -1.6	+2.0 0	-2.5 -3.7	+3.0 0	-2.2 -4.2
12.41	− 15.75	+1.0 0	-1.0 -1.7	+1.4 0	-0.7 -1.7	+2.2 0	-3.0 -4.4	+3.5 0	-2.5 -4.7
15.75	− 19.69	+1.0 0	-1.2 -2.0	+1.6 0	-0.8 -1.8	+2.5 0	-4.0 -5.6	+4.0 0	-2.8 -5.3

Nominal Size Range Inches		Class RC5		Class RC6		Class RC7		Class RC8		Class RC9	
		Standard Limits		Standard Limits		Standard Limits		Standard Limits		Standard Limits	
Over	To	Hole	Shaft	Hole	Shaft	Hole	Shaft	Hole	Shaft	Hole	Shaft
0	− 0.12	+0.6 0	-0.6 -1.0	+1.0 0	-0.6 -1.2	+1.0 0	-1.0 -1.6	+1.6 0	-2.5 -3.5	+2.5 0	-4.0 -5.6
0.12	− 0.24	+0.7 0	-0.8 -1.3	+1.2 0	-0.8 -1.5	+1.2 0	-1.2 -1.9	+1.8 0	-2.8 -4.0	+3.0 0	-4.5 -6.0
0.24	− 0.40	+0.9 0	-1.0 -1.6	+1.4 0	-1.0 -1.9	+1.4 0	-1.6 -2.5	+2.2 0	-3.0 -4.4	+3.5 0	-5.0 -7.2
0.40	− 0.71	+1.0 0	-1.2 -1.9	+1.6 0	-1.2 -2.2	+1.6 0	-2.0 -3.0	+2.8 0	-3.5 -5.1	+4.0 0	-6.0 -8.8
0.71	− 1.19	+1.2 0	-1.6 -2.4	+2.0 0	-1.6 -2.8	+2.0 0	-2.5 -3.7	+3.5 0	-4.5 -6.5	+5.0 0	-7.0 -10.5
1.19	− 1.97	+1.6 0	-2.0 -3.0	+2.5 0	-2.0 -3.6	+2.5 0	-3.0 -4.6	+4.0 0	-5.0 -7.5	+6.0 0	-8.0 12.0
1.97	− 3.15	+1.8 0	-2.5 -3.7	+3.0 0	-2.5 -4.3	+3.0 0	-4.0 -5.8	+4.5 0	-6.0 -9.0	+7.0 0	-9.0 -13.5
3.15	− 4.73	+2.2 0	-3.0 -4.4	+3.5 0	-3.0 -5.2	+3.5 0	-5.0 -7.2	+5.0 0	-7.0 -10.5	+9.0 0	-10.0 -15.0
4.73	− 7.09	+2.5 0	-3.5 -5.1	+4.0 0	-3.5 -6.0	+4.0 0	-6.0 -8.5	+6.0 0	-8.0 -12.0	+10.0 0	-12.0 -18.0
7.09	− 9.85	+2.8 0	-4.0 -5.8	+4.5 0	-4.0 -6.8	+4.5 0	-7.0 -9.8	+7.0 0	-10.0 -14.5	+12.0 0	-15.0 -22.0
9.85	− 12.41	+3.0 0	-5.0 -7.0	+5.0 0	-5.0 -8.0	+5.0 0	-8.0 -11.0	+8.0 0	-12.0 -17.0	+12.0 0	-18.0 -26.0
12.41	− 15.75	+3.5 0	-6.0 -8.2	+6.0 0	-6.0 -9.5	+6.0 0	-10.0 -13.5	+9.0 0	-14.0 -20.0	+14.0 0	-22.0 -31.0
15.75	− 19.69	+4.0 0	-8.0 -10.5	+6.0 0	-8.0 -12.0	+6.0 0	-12.0 -16.0	+10.0 0	-16.0 -22.0	+16.0 0	-25.0 -35.0

USAS/ASME B4.1 – 1967 (R2004) Standard. For larger diameters, see the standard. ASME/ANSI B18.3.5M – 1986 (R2002) Standard. Reprinted from the standard listed by permission of the American Society of Mechanical Engineers. All rights reserved.

A.1.2) Locational clearance fits

Basic hole system. Limits are in thousandths of an inch.
Limits for hole and shaft are applied algebraically to the basic size to obtain the limits of size for the parts.

Nominal Size Range Inches		Class LC1 Standard Limits		Class LC2 Standard Limits		Class LC3 Standard Limits		Class LC4 Standard Limits	
Over	To	Hole	Shaft	Hole	Shaft	Hole	Shaft	Hole	Shaft
0	− 0.12	+0.25 0	0 -0.2	+0.4 0	0 -0.25	+0.6 0	0 -0.4	+1.6 0	0 -1.0
0.12	− 0.24	+0.3 0	0 -0.2	+0.5 0	0 -0.3	+0.7 0	0 -0.5	+1.8 0	0 -1.2
0.24	− 0.40	+0.4 0	0 -0.25	+0.6 0	0 -0.4	+0.9 0	0 -0.6	+2.2 0	0 -1.4
0.40	− 0.71	+0.4 0	0 -0.3	+0.7 0	0 -0.4	+1.0 0	0 -0.7	+2.8 0	0 -1.6
0.71	− 1.19	+0.5 0	0 -0.4	+0.8 0	0 -0.5	+1.2 0	0 -0.8	+3.5 0	0 -2.0
1.19	− 1.97	+0.6 0	0 -0.4	+1.0 0	0 -0.6	+1.6 0	0 -1.0	+4.0 0	0 -2.5
1.97	− 3.15	+0.7 0	0 -0.5	+1.2 0	0 -0.7	+1.8 0	0 -1.2	+4.5 0	0 -3.0
3.15	− 4.73	+0.9 0	0 -0.6	+1.4 0	0 -0.9	+2.2 0	0 -1.4	+5.0 0	0 -3.5
4.73	− 7.09	+1.0 0	0 -0.7	+1.6 0	0 -1.0	+2.5 0	0 -1.6	+6.0 0	0 -4.0
7.09	− 9.85	+1.2 0	0 -0.8	+1.8 0	0 -1.2	+2.8 0	0 -1.8	+7.0 0	0 -4.5
9.85	− 12.41	+1.2 0	0 -0.9	+2.0 0	0 -1.2	+3.0 0	0 -2.0	+8.0 0	0 -5.0
12.41	− 15.75	+1.4 0	0 -1.0	+2.2 0	0 -1.4	+3.5 0	0 -2.2	+9.0 0	0 -6.0
15.75	− 19.69	+1.6 0	0 -1.0	+2.5 0	0 -1.6	+4.0 0	0 -2.5	+10.0 0	0 -6.0

Nominal Size Range Inches		Class LC5 Standard Limits		Class LC6 Standard Limits		Class LC7 Standard Limits		Class LC8 Standard Limits	
Over	To	Hole	Shaft	Hole	Shaft	Hole	Shaft	Hole	Shaft
0	− 0.12	+0.4 0	-0.1 -0.35	+1.0 0	-0.3 -0.9	+1.6 0	-0.6 -1.6	+1.6 0	-1.0 -2.0
0.12	− 0.24	+0.5 0	-0.15 -0.45	+1.2 0	-0.4 -1.1	+1.8 0	-0.8 -2.0	+1.8 0	-1.2 -2.4
0.24	− 0.40	+0.6 0	-0.2 -0.6	+1.4 0	-0.5 -1.4	+2.2 0	-1.0 -2.4	+2.2 0	-1.6 -3.0
0.40	− 0.71	+0.7 0	-0.25 -0.65	+1.6 0	-0.6 -1.6	+2.8 0	-1.2 -2.8	+2.8 0	-2.0 -3.6
0.71	− 1.19	+0.8 0	-0.3 -0.8	+2.0 0	-0.8 -2.0	+3.5 0	-1.6 -3.6	+3.5 0	-2.5 -4.5
1.19	− 1.97	+1.0 0	-0.4 -1.0	+2.5 0	-1.0 -2.6	+4.0 0	-2.0 -4.5	+4.0 0	-3.0 -5.5
1.97	− 3.15	+1.2 0	-0.4 -1.1	+3.0 0	-1.2 -3.0	+4.5 0	-2.5 -5.5	+4.5 0	-4.0 -7.0
3.15	− 4.73	+1.4 0	-0.5 -1.4	+3.5 0	-1.4 -3.6	+5.0 0	-3.0 -6.5	+5.0 0	-5.0 -8.5
4.73	− 7.09	+1.6 0	-0.6 -1.6	+4.0 0	-1.6 -4.1	+6.0 0	-3.5 -7.5	+6.0 0	-6.0 -10.0
7.09	− 9.85	+1.8 0	-0.6 -1.8	+4.5 0	-2.0 -4.8	+7.0 0	-4.0 -8.5	+7.0 0	-7.0 -11.5
9.85	− 12.41	+2.0 0	-0.7 -1.9	+5.0 0	-2.2 -5.2	+8.0 0	-4.5 -9.5	+8.0 0	-7.0 -12.0
12.41	− 15.75	+2.2 0	-0.7 -2.1	+6.0 0	-2.5 -6.0	+9.0 0	-5.0 -11.0	+9.0 0	-8.0 -14.0
15.75	− 19.69	+2.5 0	-0.8 -2.4	+6.0 0	-2.8 -6.8	+10.0 0	-5.0 -11.0	+10.0 0	-9.0 -15.0

Nominal Size Range Inches		Class LC9 Standard Limits		Class LC10 Standard Limits		Class LC11 Standard Limits	
Over	To	Hole	Shaft	Hole	Shaft	Hole	Shaft
0	− 0.12	+2.5 0	-2.5 -4.1	+4.0 0	-4.0 -8.0	+6.0 0	-5.0 -11.0
0.12	− 0.24	+3.0 0	-2.8 -4.6	+5.0 0	-4.5 -9.5	+7.0 0	-6.0 -13.0
0.24	− 0.40	+3.5 0	-3.0 -5.2	+6.0 0	-5.0 -11.0	+9.0 0	-7.0 -16.0
0.40	− 0.71	+4.0 0	-3.5 -6.3	+7.0 0	-6.0 -13.0	+10.0 0	-8.0 -18.0
0.71	− 1.19	+5.0 0	-4.5 -8.0	+8.0 0	-7.0 -15.0	+12.0 0	-10.0 -22.0
1.19	− 1.97	+6.0 0	-5.0 -9.0	+10.0 0	-8.0 -18.0	+16.0 0	-12.0 -28.0
1.97	− 3.15	+7.0 0	-6.0 -10.5	+12.0 0	-10.0 -22.0	+18.0 0	-14.0 -32.0
3.15	− 4.73	+9.0 0	-7.0 -12.0	+14.0 0	-11.0 -25.0	+22.0 0	-16.0 -38.0
4.73	− 7.09	+10.0 0	-8.0 -14.0	+16.0 0	-12.0 -28.0	+25.0 0	-18.0 -43.0
7.09	− 9.85	+12.0 0	-10.0 -17.0	+18.0 0	-16.0 -34.0	+28.0 0	-22.0 -50.0
9.85	− 12.41	+12.0 0	-12.0 -20.0	+20.0 0	-20.0 -40.0	+30.0 0	-28.0 -58.0
12.41	− 15.75	+14.0 0	-14.0 -23.0	+22.0 0	-22.0 -44.0	+35.0 0	-30.0 -65.0
15.75	− 19.69	+16.0 0	-16.0 -26.0	+25.0 0	-25.0 -50.0	+40.0 0	-35.0 -75.0

USAS/ASME B4.1 − 1967 (R2004) Standard. For larger diameters, see the standard. ASME/ANSI B18.3.5M − 1986 (R2002) Standard. Reprinted from the standard listed by permission of the American Society of Mechanical Engineers. All rights reserved.

A.1.3) Locational transition fits

Basic hole system. Limits are in thousandths of an inch.
Limits for hole and shaft are applied algebraically to the basic size to obtain the limits of size for the parts.

Nominal Size Range Inches		Class LT1 Standard Limits		Class LT2 Standard Limits		Class LT3 Standard Limits	
Over	To	Hole	Shaft	Hole	Shaft	Hole	Shaft
0	− 0.12	+0.4 0	+0.10 -0.10	+0.6 0	+0.2 -0.2		
0.12	− 0.24	+0.5 0	+0.15 -0.15	+0.7 0	+0.25 -0.25		
0.24	− 0.40	+0.6 0	+0.2 -0.2	+0.9 0	+0.3 -0.3	+0.6 0	+0.5 +0.1
0.40	− 0.71	+0.7 0	+0.2 -0.2	+1.0 0	+0.35 -0.35	+0.7 0	+0.5 +0.1
0.71	− 1.19	+0.8 0	+0.25 -0.25	+1.2 0	+0.4 -0.4	+0.8 0	+0.6 +0.1
1.19	− 1.97	+1.0 0	+0.3 -0.3	+1.6 0	+0.5 -0.5	+1.0 0	+0.7 +0.1
1.97	− 3.15	+1.2 0	+0.3 -0.3	+1.8 0	+0.6 -0.6	+1.2 0	+0.8 +0.1
3.15	− 4.73	+1.4 0	+0.4 -0.4	+2.2 0	+0.7 -0.7	+1.4 0	+1.0 +0.1
4.73	− 7.09	+1.6 0	+0.5 -0.5	+2.5 0	+0.8 -0.8	+1.6 0	+1.1 +0.1
7.09	− 9.85	+1.8 0	+0.6 -0.6	+2.8 0	+0.9 -0.9	+1.8 0	+1.4 +0.2
9.85	− 12.41	+2.0 0	+0.6 -0.6	+3.0 0	+1.0 -1.0	+2.0 0	+1.4 +0.2
12.41	− 15.75	+2.2 0	+0.7 -0.7	+3.5 0	+1.0 -1.0	+2.2 0	+1.6 +0.2

Nominal Size Range Inches		Class LT4 Standard Limits		Class LT5 Standard Limits		Class LT6 Standard Limits	
Over	To	Hole	Shaft	Hole	Shaft	Hole	Shaft
0	− 0.12			+0.4 0	+0.5 +0.25	+0.4 0	-0.65 +0.25
0.12	− 0.24			+0.5 0	+0.6 +0.3	+0.5 0	+0.8 +0.3
0.24	− 0.40	+0.9 0	+0.7 +0.1	+0.6 0	+0.8 +0.4	+0.6 0	+1.0 +0.4
0.40	− 0.71	+1.0 0	+0.8 +0.1	+0.7 0	+0.9 +0.5	+0.7 0	+1.2 +0.5
0.71	− 1.19	+1.2 0	+0.9 +0.1	+0.8 0	+1.1 +0.6	+0.8 0	+1.4 +0.6
1.19	− 1.97	+1.6 0	+1.1 +0.1	+1.0 0	+1.3 +0.7	+1.0 0	+1.7 +0.7
1.97	− 3.15	+1.8 0	+1.3 +0.1	+1.2 0	+1.5 +0.8	+1.2 0	+2.0 +0.8
3.15	− 4.73	+2.2 0	+1.5 +0.1	+1.4 0	+1.9 +1.0	+1.4 0	+2.4 +1.0
4.73	− 7.09	+2.5 0	+1.7 +0.1	+1.6 0	+2.2 +1.2	+1.6 0	+2.8 +1.2
7.09	− 9.85	+2.8 0	+2.0 +0.2	+1.8 0	+2.6 +1.4	+1.8 0	+3.2 +1.4
9.85	− 12.41	+3.0 0	+2.2 +0.2	+2.0 0	+2.6 +1.4	+2.0 0	+3.4 +1.4
12.41	− 15.75	+3.5 0	+2.4 +0.2	+2.2 0	+3.0 +1.6	+2.2 0	+3.8 +1.6

A.1.4) Locational interference fits

Basic hole system. Limits are in thousandths of an inch.
Limits for hole and shaft are applied algebraically to the basic size to obtain the limits of size for the parts.

Nominal Size Range Inches		Class LN1 Standard Limits		Class LN2 Standard Limits		Class LN3 Standard Limits	
Over	To	Hole	Shaft	Hole	Shaft	Hole	Shaft
0	− 0.12	+0.25	+0.45	+0.4	+0.65	+0.4	+0.75
		0	+0.25	0	+0.4	0	+0.5
0.12	− 0.24	+0.3	+0.5	+0.5	+0.8	+0.5	+0.9
		0	+0.3	0	+0.5	0	+0.6
0.24	− 0.40	+0.4	+0.65	+0.6	+1.0	+0.6	+1.2
		0	+0.4	0	+0.6	0	+0.8
0.40	− 0.71	+0.4	+0.8	+0.7	+1.1	+0.7	+1.4
		0	+0.4	0	+0.7	0	+1.0
0.71	− 1.19	+0.5	+1.0	+0.8	+1.3	+0.8	+1.7
		0	+0.5	0	+0.8	0	+1.2
1.19	− 1.97	+0.6	+1.1	+1.0	+1.6	+1.0	+2.0
		0	+0.6	0	+1.0	0	+1.4
1.97	− 3.15	+0.7	+1.3	+1.2	+2.1	+1.2	+2.3
		0	+0.8	0	+1.4	0	+1.6
3.15	− 4.73	+0.9	+1.6	+1.4	+2.5	+1.4	+2.9
		0	+1.0	0	+1.6	0	+2.0
4.73	− 7.09	+1.0	+1.9	+1.6	+2.8	+1.6	+3.5
		0	+1.2	0	+1.8	0	+2.5
7.09	− 9.85	+1.2	+2.2	+1.8	+3.2	+1.8	+4.2
		0	+1.4	0	+2.0	0	+3.0
9.85	− 12.41	+1.2	+2.3	+2.0	+3.4	+2.0	+4.7
		0	+1.4	0	+2.2	0	+3.5
12.41	− 15.75	+1.4	+2.6	+2.2	+3.9	+2.2	+5.9
		0	+1.6	0	+2.5	0	+4.5
15.75	− 19.69	+1.6	+2.8	+2.5	+4.4	+2.5	+6.6
		0	+1.8	0	+2.8	0	+5.0

USAS/ASME B4.1 − 1967 (R2004) Standard. For larger diameters, see the standard. ASME/ANSI B18.3.5M − 1986 (R2002) Standard. Reprinted from the standard listed by permission of the American Society of Mechanical Engineers. All rights reserved.

A.1.5) Force and shrink fits

Basic hole system. Limits are in thousandths of an inch.
Limits for hole and shaft are applied algebraically to the basic size to obtain the limits of size for the parts.

Nominal Size Range Inches		Class FN1		Class FN2		Class FN3		Class FN4		Class FN5	
		Standard Limits		Standard Limits		Standard Limits		Standard Limits		Standard Limits	
Over	To	Hole	Shaft	Hole	Shaft	Hole	Shaft	Hole	Shaft	Hole	Shaft
0	− 0.12	+0.25	+0.5	+0.4	+0.85			+0.4	+0.95	+0.6	+1.3
		0	+0.3	0	+0.6			0	+0.7	0	+0.9
0.12	− 0.24	+0.3	+0.6	+0.5	+1.0			+0.5	+1.2	+0.7	+1.7
		0	+0.4	0	+0.7			0	+0.9	0	+1.2
0.24	− 0.40	+0.4	+0.75	+0.6	+1.4			+0.6	+1.6	+0.9	+2.0
		0	+0.5	0	+1.0			0	+1.2	0	+1.4
0.40	− 0.56	+0.4	+0.8	+0.7	+1.6			+0.7	+1.8	+1.0	+2.3
		0	+0.5	0	+1.2			0	+1.4	0	+1.6
0.56	− 0.71	+0.4	+0.9	+0.7	+1.6			+0.7	+1.8	+1.0	+2.5
		0	+0.6	0	+1.2			0	+1.4	0	+1.8
0.71	− 0.95	+0.5	+1.1	+0.8	+1.9			+0.8	+2.1	+1.2	+3.0
		0	+0.7	0	+1.4			0	+1.6	0	+2.2
0.95	− 1.19	+0.5	+1.2	+0.8	+1.9	+0.8	+2.1	+0.8	+2.3	+1.2	+3.3
		0	+0.8	0	+1.4	0	+1.6	0	+1.8	0	+2.5
1.19	− 1.58	+0.6	+1.3	+1.0	+2.4	+1.0	+2.6	+1.0	+3.1	+1.6	+4.0
		0	+0.9	0	+1.8	0	+2.0	0	+2.5	0	+3.0
1.58	− 1.97	+0.6	+1.4	+1.0	+2.4	+1.0	+2.8	+1.0	+3.4	+1.6	+5.0
		0	+1.0	0	+1.8	0	+2.2	0	+2.8	0	+4.0
1.97	− 2.56	+0.7	+1.8	+1.2	+2.7	+1.2	+3.2	+1.2	+4.2	+1.8	+6.2
		0	+1.3	0	+2.0	0	+2.5	0	+3.5	0	+5.0
2.56	− 3.15	+0.7	+1.9	+1.2	+2.9	+1.2	+3.7	+1.2	+4.7	+1.8	+7.2
		0	+1.4	0	+2.2	0	+3.0	0	+4.0	0	+6.0
3.15	− 3.94	+0.9	+2.4	+1.4	+3.7	+1.4	+4.4	+1.4	+5.9	+2.2	+8.4
		0	+1.8	0	+2.8	0	+3.5	0	+5.0	0	+7.0
3.94	− 4.73	+0.9	+2.6	+1.4	+3.9	+1.4	+4.9	+1.4	+6.9	+2.2	+9.4
		0	+2.0	0	+3.0	0	+4.0	0	+6.0	0	+8.0
4.73	−5.52	+1.0	+2.9	+1.6	+4.5	+1.6	+6.0	+1.6	+8.0	+2.5	+11.6
		0	+2.2	0	+3.5	0	+5.0	0	+7.0	0	+10.0
5.52	−6.30	+1.0	+3.2	+1.6	+5.0	+1.6	+6.0	+1.6	+8.0	+2.5	+13.6
		0	+2.5	0	+4.0	0	+5.0	0	+7.0	0	+12.0
6.30	−7.09	+1.0	+3.5	+1.6	+5.5	+1.6	+7.0	+1.6	+9.0	+2.5	+13.6
		0	+2.8	0	+4.5	0	+6.0	0	+8.0	0	+12.0
7.09	−7.88	+1.2	+3.8	+1.8	+6.2	+1.8	+8.2	+1.8	+10.2	+2.8	+15.8
		0	+3.0	0	+5.0	0	+7.0	0	+9.0	0	+14.0
7.88	−8.86	+1.2	+4.3	+1.8	+6.2	+1.8	+8.2	+1.8	+11.2	+2.8	+17.8
		0	+3.5	0	+5.0	0	+7.0	0	+10.0	0	+16.0
8.86	−9.86	+1.2	+4.3	+1.8	+7.2	+1.8	+9.2	+1.8	+13.2	+2.8	+17.8
		0	+3.5	0	+6.0	0	+8.0	0	+12.0	0	+16.0
9.85	−11.03	+1.2	+4.9	+2.0	+7.2	+2.0	+10.2	+2.0	+13.2	+3.0	+20.0
		0	+4.0	0	+6.0	0	+9.0	0	+12.0	0	+18.0

A.2) METRIC LIMITS AND FITS

A.2.1) Hole basis clearance fits

Preferred Hole Basis Clearance Fits. Dimensions in mm.

Basic Size	Loose Running		Free Running		Close Running		Sliding		Locational Clearance	
	Hole H11	Shaft c11	Hole H9	Shaft d9	Hole H8	Shaft f7	Hole H7	Shaft g6	Hole H7	Shaft h6
1 max	1.060	0.940	1.025	0.980	1.014	0.994	1.010	0.998	1.010	1.000
min	1.000	0.880	1.000	0.955	1.000	0.984	1.000	0.992	1.000	0.994
1.2 max	1.260	1.140	1.225	1.180	1.214	1.194	1.210	1.198	1.210	1.200
min	1.200	1.080	1.200	1.155	1.200	1.184	1.200	1.192	1.200	1.194
1.6 max	1.660	1.540	1.625	1.580	1.614	1.594	1.610	1.598	1.610	1.600
min	1.600	1.480	1.600	1.555	1.600	1.584	1.600	1.592	1.600	1.594
2 max	2.060	1.940	2.025	1.980	2.014	1.994	2.010	1.998	2.010	2.000
min	2.000	1.880	2.000	1.955	2.000	1.984	2.000	1.992	2.000	1.994
2.5 max	2.560	2.440	2.525	2.480	2.514	2.494	2.510	2.498	2.510	2.500
min	2.500	2.380	2.500	2.455	2.500	2.484	2.500	2.492	2.500	2.494
3 max	3.060	2.940	3.025	2.980	3.014	2.994	3.010	2.998	3.010	3.000
min	3.000	2.880	3.000	2.955	3.000	2.984	3.000	2.992	3.000	2.994
4 max	4.075	3.930	4.030	3.970	4.018	3.990	4.012	3.996	4.012	4.000
min	4.000	3.855	4.000	3.940	4.000	3.978	4.000	3.988	4.000	3.992
5 max	5.075	4.930	5.030	4.970	5.018	4.990	5.012	4.996	5.012	5.000
min	5.000	4.855	5.000	4.940	5.000	4.978	5.000	4.988	5.000	4.992
6 max	6.075	5.930	6.030	5.970	6.018	5.990	6.012	5.996	6.012	6.000
min	6.000	5.855	6.000	5.940	6.000	5.978	6.000	5.988	6.000	5.992
8 max	8.090	7.920	8.036	7.960	8.022	7.987	8.015	7.995	8.015	8.000
min	8.000	7.830	8.000	7.924	8.000	7.972	8.000	7.986	8.000	7.991
10 max	10.090	9.920	10.036	9.960	10.022	9.987	10.015	9.995	10.015	10.000
min	10.000	9.830	10.000	9.924	10.000	9.972	10.000	9.986	10.000	9.991
12 max	12.110	11.905	12.043	11.950	12.027	11.984	12.018	11.994	12.018	12.000
min	12.000	11.795	12.000	11.907	12.000	11.966	12.000	11.983	12.000	11.989
16 max	16.110	15.905	16.043	15.950	16.027	15.984	16.018	15.994	16.018	16.000
min	16.000	15.795	16.000	15.907	16.000	15.966	16.000	15.983	16.000	15.989
20 max	20.130	19.890	20.052	19.935	20.033	19.980	20.021	19.993	20.021	20.000
min	20.000	19.760	20.000	19.883	20.000	19.959	20.000	19.980	20.000	19.987
25 max	25.130	24.890	25.052	24.935	25.033	24.980	25.021	24.993	25.021	25.000
min	25.000	24.760	25.000	24.883	25.000	24.959	25.000	24.980	25.000	24.987
30 max	30.130	29.890	30.052	29.935	30.033	29.980	30.021	29.993	30.021	30.000
min	30.000	29.760	30.000	29.883	30.000	29.959	30.000	29.980	30.000	29.987

A.2.2) Hole basis transition and interference fits

Preferred Hole Basis Clearance Fits. Dimensions in mm.

Basic Size	Locational Transition		Locational Transition		Locational Interference		Medium Drive		Force	
	Hole H7	Shaft k6	Hole H7	Shaft n6	Hole H7	Shaft p6	Hole H7	Shaft s6	Hole H7	Shaft u6
1 max	1.010	1.006	1.010	1.010	1.010	1.012	1.010	1.020	1.010	1.024
min	1.000	1.000	1.000	1.004	1.000	1.006	1.000	1.014	1.000	1.018
1.2 max	1.210	1.206	1.210	1.210	1.210	1.212	1.210	1.220	1.210	1.224
min	1.200	1.200	1.200	1.204	1.200	1.206	1.200	1.214	1.200	1.218
1.6 max	1.610	1.606	1.610	1.610	1.610	1.612	1.610	1.620	1.610	1.624
min	1.600	1.600	1.600	1.604	1.600	1.606	1.600	1.614	1.600	1.618
2 max	2.010	2.006	2.010	2.020	2.010	2.012	2.010	2.020	2.010	2.024
min	2.000	2.000	2.000	2.004	2.000	2.006	2.000	1.014	2.000	2.018
2.5 max	2.510	2.506	2.510	2.510	2.510	2.512	2.510	2.520	2.510	2.524
min	2.500	2.500	2.500	2.504	2.500	2.506	2.500	2.514	2.500	2.518
3 max	3.010	3.006	3.010	3.010	3.010	3.012	3.010	3.020	3.010	3.024
min	3.000	3.000	3.000	3.004	3.000	3.006	3.000	3.014	3.000	3.018
4 max	4.012	4.009	4.012	4.016	4.012	4.020	4.012	4.027	4.012	4.031
min	4.000	4.001	4.000	4.008	4.000	4.012	4.000	4.019	4.000	4.023
5 max	5.012	5.009	5.012	5.016	5.012	5.020	5.012	5.027	5.012	5.031
min	5.000	5.001	5.000	5.008	5.000	5.012	5.000	5.019	5.000	5.023
6 max	6.012	6.009	6.012	6.016	6.012	6.020	6.012	6.027	6.012	6.031
min	6.000	6.001	6.000	6.008	6.000	6.012	6.000	6.019	6.000	6.023
8 max	8.015	8.010	8.015	8.019	8.015	8.024	8.015	8.032	8.015	8.037
min	8.000	8.001	8.000	8.010	8.000	8.015	8.000	8.023	8.000	8.028
10 max	10.015	10.010	10.015	10.019	10.015	10.024	10.015	10.032	10.015	10.037
min	10.000	10.001	10.000	10.010	10.000	10.015	10.000	10.023	10.000	10.028
12 max	12.018	12.012	12.018	12.023	12.018	12.029	12.018	12.039	12.018	12.044
min	12.000	12.001	12.000	12.012	12.000	12.018	12.000	12.028	12.000	12.033
16 max	16.018	16.012	16.018	16.023	16.018	16.029	16.018	16.039	16.018	16.044
min	16.000	16.001	16.000	16.012	16.000	16.018	16.000	16.028	16.000	16.033
20 max	20.021	20.015	20.021	20.028	20.021	20.035	20.021	20.048	20.021	20.054
min	20.000	20.002	20.000	20.015	20.000	20.022	20.000	20.035	20.000	20.041
25 max	25.021	25.015	25.021	25.028	25.021	25.035	25.021	25.048	25.021	25.061
min	25.000	25.002	25.000	25.015	25.000	25.022	25.000	25.035	25.000	25.048
30 max	30.021	30.015	30.021	30.028	30.021	30.035	30.021	30.048	30.021	30.061
min	30.000	30.002	30.000	30.015	30.000	30.022	30.000	30.035	30.000	30.048

ANSI B4.2 – 1978 (R2004) Standard. ASME/ANSI B18.3.5M – 1986 (R2002) Standard. Reprinted from the standard listed by permission of the American Society of Mechanical Engineers. All rights reserved.

A.2.3) Shaft basis clearance fits

Preferred Shaft Basis Clearance Fits. Dimensions in mm.

Basic Size	Loose Running		Free Running		Close Running		Sliding		Locational Clearance	
	Hole C11	Shaft h11	Hole D9	Shaft h9	Hole F8	Shaft h7	Hole G7	Shaft h6	Hole H7	Shaft h6
1 max	1.120	1.000	1.045	1.000	1.020	1.000	1.012	1.000	1.010	1.000
min	1.060	0.940	1.020	0.975	1.006	0.990	1.002	0.994	1.000	0.994
1.2 max	1.320	1.200	1.245	1.200	1.220	1.200	1.212	1.200	1.210	1.200
min	1.260	1.140	1.220	1.175	1.206	1.190	1.202	1.194	1.200	1.194
1.6 max	1.720	1.600	1.645	1.600	1.620	1.600	1.612	1.600	1.610	1.600
min	1.660	1.540	1.620	1.575	1.606	1.590	1.602	1.594	1.600	1.594
2 max	2.120	2.000	2.045	2.000	2.020	2.000	2.012	2.000	2.010	2.000
min	2.060	1.940	2.020	1.975	2.006	1.990	2.002	1.994	2.000	1.994
2.5 max	2.620	2.500	2.545	2.500	2.520	2.500	2.512	2.500	2.510	2.500
min	2.560	2.440	2.520	2.475	2.506	2.490	2.502	2.494	2.500	2.494
3 max	3.120	3.000	3.045	3.000	3.020	3.000	3.012	3.000	3.010	3.000
min	3.060	2.940	3.020	2.975	3.006	2.990	3.002	2.994	3.000	2.994
4 max	4.145	4.000	4.060	4.000	4.028	4.000	4.016	4.000	4.012	4.000
min	4.070	3.925	4.030	3.970	4.010	3.988	4.004	3.992	4.000	3.992
5 max	5.145	5.000	5.060	5.000	5.028	5.000	5.016	5.000	5.012	5.000
min	5.070	4.925	5.030	4.970	5.010	4.988	5.004	4.992	5.000	4.992
6 max	6.145	6.000	6.060	6.000	6.028	6.000	6.016	6.000	6.012	6.000
min	6.070	5.925	6.030	5.970	6.010	5.988	6.004	5.992	6.000	5.992
8 max	8.170	8.000	8.076	8.000	8.035	8.000	8.020	8.000	8.015	8.000
min	8.080	7.910	8.040	7.964	8.013	7.985	8.005	7.991	8.000	7.991
10 max	10.170	10.000	10.076	10.000	10.035	10.000	10.020	10.000	10.015	10.000
min	10.080	9.910	10.040	9.964	10.013	9.985	10.005	9.991	10.000	9.991
12 max	12.205	12.000	12.093	12.000	12.043	12.000	12.024	12.000	12.018	12.000
min	12.095	11.890	12.050	11.957	12.016	11.982	12.006	11.989	12.000	11.989
16 max	16.205	16.000	16.093	16.000	16.043	16.000	16.024	16.000	16.018	16.000
min	16.095	15.890	16.050	15.957	16.016	15.982	16.006	15.989	16.000	15.989
20 max	20.240	20.000	20.117	20.000	20.053	20.000	20.028	20.000	20.021	20.000
min	20.110	19.870	20.065	19.948	20.020	19.979	20.007	19.987	20.000	19.987
25 max	25.240	25.000	25.117	25.000	25.053	25.000	25.028	25.000	25.021	25.000
min	25.110	24.870	25.065	24.948	25.020	24.979	25.007	24.987	25.000	24.987
30 max	30.240	30.000	30.117	30.000	30.053	30.000	30.028	30.000	30.021	30.000
min	30.110	29.870	30.065	29.948	30.020	29.979	30.007	29.987	30.000	29.987

A.2.4) Shaft basis transition and interference fits

Preferred Shaft Basis Transition and Interference Fits. Dimensions in mm.

Basic Size	Locational Transition		Locational Transition		Locational Interference		Medium Drive		Force	
	Hole K7	Shaft h6	Hole N7	Shaft h6	Hole P7	Shaft h6	Hole S7	Shaft h6	Hole U7	Shaft h6
1 max	1.000	1.000	0.996	1.000	0.994	1.000	0.986	1.000	0.982	1.000
min	0.990	0.994	0.986	0.994	0.984	0.994	0.976	0.994	0.972	0.994
1.2 max	1.200	1.200	1.196	1.200	1.194	1.200	1.186	1.200	1.182	1.200
min	1.190	1.194	1.186	1.194	1.184	1.194	1.176	1.194	1.172	1.194
1.6 max	1.600	1.600	1.596	1.600	1.594	1.600	1.586	1.600	1.582	1.600
min	1.590	1.594	1.586	1.594	1.584	1.594	1.576	1.594	1.572	1.594
2 max	2.000	2.000	1.996	2.000	1.994	2.000	1.986	2.000	1.982	2.000
min	1.990	1.994	1.986	1.994	1.984	1.994	1.976	1.994	1.972	1.994
2.5 max	2.500	2.500	2.496	2.500	2.494	2.500	2.486	2.500	2.482	2.500
min	2.490	2.494	2.486	2.494	2.484	2.494	2.476	2.494	2.472	2.494
3 max	3.000	3.000	2.996	3.000	2.994	3.000	2.986	3.000	2.982	3.000
min	2.990	2.994	2.986	2.994	2.984	2.994	2.976	2.994	2.972	2.994
4 max	4.003	4.000	3.996	4.000	3.992	4.000	3.985	4.000	3.981	4.000
min	3.991	5.992	3.984	5.992	3.980	5.992	3.973	5.992	3.969	5.992
5 max	5.003	5.000	4.996	5.000	4.992	5.000	4.985	5.000	4.981	5.000
min	4.991	4.992	4.984	4.992	4.980	4.992	4.973	4.992	4.969	4.992
6 max	6.003	6.000	5.996	6.000	5.992	6.000	5.985	6.000	5.981	6.000
min	5.991	5.992	5.984	5.992	5.980	5.992	5.973	5.992	5.969	5.992
8 max	8.005	8.000	7.996	8.000	7.991	8.000	7.983	8.000	7.978	8.000
min	7.990	7.991	7.981	7.991	7.976	7.991	7.968	7.991	7.963	7.991
10 max	10.005	10.000	9.996	10.000	9.991	10.000	9.983	10.000	9.978	10.000
min	9.990	9.991	9.981	9.991	9.976	9.991	9.968	9.991	9.963	9.991
12 max	12.006	12.000	11.995	12.000	11.989	12.000	11.979	12.000	11.974	12.000
min	11.988	11.989	11.977	11.989	11.971	11.989	11.961	11.989	11.956	11.989
16 max	16.006	16.000	15.995	16.000	15.989	16.000	15.979	16.000	15.974	16.000
min	15.988	15.989	15.977	15.989	15.971	15.989	15.961	15.989	15.956	15.989
20 max	20.006	20.000	19.993	20.000	19.986	20.000	19.973	20.000	19.967	20.000
min	19.985	19.987	19.972	19.987	19.965	19.987	19.952	19.987	19.946	19.987
25 max	25.006	25.000	24.993	25.000	24.986	25.000	24.973	25.000	24.960	25.000
min	24.985	24.987	24.972	24.987	24.965	24.987	24.952	24.987	24.939	24.987
30 max	30.006	30.000	29.993	30.000	29.986	30.000	29.973	30.000	29.960	30.000
min	29.985	29.987	29.972	29.987	29.965	29.987	29.952	29.987	29.939	29.987

ANSI B4.2 – 1978 (R2004) Standard. ASME/ANSI B18.3.5M – 1986 (R2002) Standard. Reprinted from the standard listed by permission of the American Society of Mechanical Engineers. All rights reserved.

APPENDIX B

THREADS AND FASTENERS

APPENDIX OUTLINE

B.1) UNIFIED NATIONAL THREAD FORM

(External Threads) Approximate Minor diameter = $D - 1.0825P$ P = Pitch

Nominal Size, in.	Basic Major Diameter (D)	Coarse UNC		Fine UNF		Extra Fine UNEF	
		Thds. Per in.	Tap Drill Dia.	Thds. Per in.	Tap Drill Dia.	Thds. Per in.	Tap Drill Dia.
#0	0.060	...	...	80	3/64	...	...
#1	0.0730	64	0.0595	72	0.0595	...	...
#2	0.0860	56	0.0700	64	0.0700	...	...
#3	0.0990	48	0.0785	56	0.0820	...	...
#4	0.1120	40	0.0890	48	0.0935	...	...
#5	0.1250	40	0.1015	44	0.1040	...	...
#6	0.1380	32	0.1065	40	0.1130	...	...
#8	0.1640	32	0.1360	36	0.1360	...	...
#10	0.1900	24	0.1495	32	0.1590	...	...
#12	0.2160	24	0.1770	28	0.1820	32	0.1850
1/4	0.2500	20	0.2010	28	0.2130	32	7/32
5/16	0.3125	18	0.257	24	0.272	32	9/32
3/8	0.3750	16	5/16	24	0.332	32	11/32
7/16	0.4375	14	0.368	20	25/64	28	13/32
1/2	0.5000	13	27/64	20	29/64	28	15/32
9/16	0.5625	12	31/64	18	33/64	24	33/64
5/8	0.6250	11	17/32	18	37/64	24	37/64
11/16	0.675	...	...	...	...	24	41/64
3/4	0.7500	10	21/32	16	11/16	20	45/64
13/16	0.8125	...	...	...	...	20	49/64
7/8	0.8750	9	49/64	14	13/16	20	53/64
15/16	0.9375	...	...	...	...	20	57/64
1	1.0000	8	7/8	12	59/64	20	61/64
1 1/8	1.1250	7	63/64	12	1 3/64	18	1 5/64
1 1/4	1.2500	7	1 7/64	12	1 11/64	18	1 3/16
1 3/8	1.3750	6	1 7/32	12	1 19/64	18	1 5/16
1 1/2	1.5000	6	1 11/32	12	1 27/64	18	1 7/16
1 5/8	1.6250	...	...	...	...	18	1 9/16
1 3/4	1.7500	5	1 9/16	...	...	...	...
1 7/8	1.8750	...	...	...	...	...	...
2	2.0000	4 1/2	1 25/32	...	...	...	...
2 1/4	2.2500	4 1/2	2 1/32	...	...	...	...
2 1/2	2.5000	4	2 1/4	...	...	...	...
2 3/4	2.7500	4	2 1/2	...	...	...	...

B.2) METRIC THREAD FORM

(External Threads) Approximate Minor diameter = $D - 1.2075P$ P = Pitch

Preferred sizes for commercial threads and fasteners are shown in boldface type.

Coarse (general purpose)		Fine	
Nominal Size (D) & Thread Pitch	Tap Drill Diameter, mm	Nominal Size & Thread Pitch	Tap Drill Diameter, mm
M1.6 x 0.35	1.25	---	---
M1.8 x 0.35	1.45	---	---
M2 x 0.4	1.6	---	---
M2.2 x 0.45	1.75	---	---
M2.5 x 0.45	2.05	---	---
M3 x 0.5	2.5	---	---
M3.5 x 0.6	2.9	---	---
M4 x 0.7	3.3	---	---
M4.5 x 0.75	3.75	---	---
M5 x 0.8	4.2	---	---
M6 x 1	5.0	---	---
M7 x 1	6.0	---	---
M8 x 1.25	6.8	**M8 x 1**	7.0
M9 x 1.25	7.75	---	---
M10 x 1.5	8.5	**M10 x 1.25**	8.75
M11 x 1.5	9.50	---	---
M12 x 1.75	10.30	**M12 x 1.25**	10.5
M14 x 2	12.00	**M14 x 1.5**	12.5
M16 x 2	14.00	**M16 x 1.5**	14.5
M18 x 2.5	15.50	**M18 x 1.5**	16.5
M20 x 2.5	17.5	**M20 x 1.5**	18.5
M22 x 2.5[b]	19.5	**M22 x 1.5**	20.5
M24 x 3	21.0	**M24 x 2**	22.0
M27 x 3[b]	24.0	**M27 x 2**	25.0
M30 x 3.5	26.5	**M30 x 2**	28.0
M33 x 3.5	29.5	M33 x 2	31.0
M36 x 4	32.0	**M36 x 2**	33.0
M39 x 4	35.0	M39 x 2	36.0
M42 x 4.5	37.5	**M42 x 2**	39.0
M45 x 4.5	40.5	M45 x 1.5	42.0
M48 x 5	43.0	**M48 x 2**	45.0
M52 x 5	47.0	M52 x 2	49.0
M56 x 5.5	50.5	**M56 x 2**	52.0
M60 x 5.5	54.5	M60 x 1.5	56.0
M64 x 6	58.0	**M64 x 2**	60.0
M68 x 6	62.0	M68 x 2	64.0
M72 x 6	66.0	**M72 x 2**	68.0
M80 x 6	74.0	**M80 x 2**	76.0
M90 x 6	84.0	**M90 x 2**	86.0
M100 x 6	94.0	**M100 x 2**	96.0

[b]Only for high strength structural steel fasteners

B.3) FASTENERS (INCH SERIES)

CAUTION! All fastener dimensions have a tolerance. Therefore, each dimension has a maximum and minimum value. Only one size for each dimension is given in this appendix. That is all that is necessary to complete the problems given in the "Threads and Fasteners" chapter. For both values, please refer to the standards noted.

B.3.1) Dimensions of hex bolts and heavy hex bolts

Regular Hex Head Bolts

Size (D)	Head Height Basic*	Width Across Flats Basic Adjust to sixteenths	Width Across Corners Max.
1/4	H = 0.625 D + 0.016	F = 1.500 D + 0.062	
5/16 – 7/16	H = 0.625 D + 0.016		
1/2 – 7/8	H = 0.625 D + 0.031		
1 – 1 7/8	H = 0.625 D + 0.062	F = 1.500 D	Max. G = 1.1547 F
2 – 3 3/4	H = 0.625 D + 0.125		
4	H = 0.625 D + 0.188		

Heavy Hex Head Bolts

Size (D)	Head Height Basic*	Width Across Flats Basic Adjust to sixteenths	Width Across Corners Max.
1/2 - 3	Same as for regular hex head bolts.	F = 1.500 D + 0.125	Max. G = 1.1547 F

* Size to 1 in. adjusted to sixty-fourths. 1 1/8 through 2 1/2 in. sizes adjusted upward to thirty-seconds. 2 3/4 thru 4 in. sizes adjusted upward to sixteenths.

ASME B18.2.1 – 1996 Standard. Reprinted from the standard listed by permission of the American Society of Mechanical Engineers. All rights reserved.

B.3.2) Dimensions of hex nuts and hex jam nuts

Hex Nuts   Hex Jam Nuts

Hex Nuts

Nut Size (D)	Nut Thickness Basic*	Width Across Flats Basic Adjust to sixteenths	Width Across Corners Max.
1/4	$H = 0.875\,D$	$F = 1.500\,D + 0.062$	
5/16 – 5/8	$H = 0.875\,D$	$F = 1.500\,D$	Max. $G = 1.1547\,F$
3/4 – 1 1/8	$H = 0.875\,D - 0.016$		
1 1/4 – 1 1/2	$H = 0.875\,D - 0.031$		

Hex Thick Nuts

Nut Size (D)	Width Across Flats Basic Adjust to sixteenths	Width Across Corners Max.	Nut Thickness Basic
1/4	$F = 1.500\,D + 0.062$		
5/16 – 5/8	$F = 1.500\,D$	Max. $G = 1.1547\,F$	See Table
3/4 – 1 1/2	$F = 1.500\,D$		

Nut Size (D)	1/4	5/16	3/8	7/16	1/2	9/16	5/8
Nut Thickness Basic	9/32	21/64	13/32	29/64	9/16	39/64	23/32

Nut Size (D)	3/4	7/8	1	1 1/8	1 1/4	1 3/8	1 1/2
Nut Thickness Basic	13/16	29/32	1	1 5/32	1 1/4	1 3/8	1 1/2

Hex Jam Nut

Nut Size (D)	Nut Thickness Basic*	Width Across Flats Basic Adjust to sixteenths	Width Across Corners Max.
1/4	See Table	$F = 1.500 D + 0.062$	
5/16 – 5/8	See Table		Max. $G = 1.1547 F$
3/4 – 1 1/8	$H = 0.500 D – 0.047$	$F = 1.500 D$	
1 1/4 – 1 1/2	$H = 0.500 D – 0.094$		

Nut Size (D)	1/4	5/16	3/8	7/16	1/2	9/16	5/8
Nut Thickness Basic	5/32	3/16	7/32	1/4	5/16	5/16	3/8

ASME/ANSI B18.2.2 – 1987 (R1999) Standard. Reprinted from the standard listed by permission of the American Society of Mechanical Engineers. All rights reserved.

B.3.3) Dimensions of hexagon and spline socket head cap screws

Screw Size (D)	Head Diameter	Head Height
#0 - #10	See Table	Max. $H = D$
1/4 - 4	Max. $A = 1.50 D$	

Screw Size (D)	#0	#1	#2	#3	#4
Max. Head Diameter (A)	0.096	0.118	0.140	0.161	0.183

Screw Size (D)	#5	#6	#8	#10
Max. Head Diameter (A)	0.205	0.226	0.270	0.312

ASME B18.3 – 2003 Standard. Reprinted from the standard listed by permission of the American Society of Mechanical Engineers. All rights reserved.

B.3.4) Drill and counterbore sizes for socket head cap screws

Nominal Size of Screw (D)	Nominal Drill Size (A)		Counterbore Diameter (B)	Countersink (C)
	Close Fit	**Normal Fit**		
#0 (0.0600)	(#51) 0.067	(#49) 0.073	1/8	0.074
#1 (0.0730)	(#46) 0.081	(#43) 0.089	5/32	0.087
#2 (0.0860)	3/32	(#36) 0.106	3/16	0.102
#3 (0.0990)	(#36) 0.106	(#31) 0.120	7/32	0.115
#4 (0.1120)	1/8	(#29) 0.136	7/32	0.130
#5 (0.1250)	9/64	(#23) 0.154	1/4	0.145
#6 (0.1380)	(#23) 0.154	(#18) 0.170	9/32	0.158
#8 (0.1640)	(#15) 0.180	(#10) 0.194	5/16	0.188
#10 (0.1900)	(#5) 0.206	(#2) 0.221	3/8	0.218
1/4	17/64	9/32	7/16	0.278
5/16	21/64	11/32	17/32	0.346
3/8	25/64	13/32	5/8	0.415
7/16	29/64	15/32	23/32	0.483
1/2	33/64	17/32	13/16	0.552
5/8	41/64	21/32	1	0.689
3/4	49/64	25/32	1 3/16	0.828
7/8	57/64	29/32	1 3/8	0.963
1	1 1/64	1 1/32	1 5/8	1.100
1 1/4	1 9/32	1 5/16	2	1.370
1 1/2	1 17/32	1 9/16	2 3/8	1.640
1 3/4	1 25/32	1 13/16	2 3/4	1.910
2	2 1/32	2 1/16	3 1/8	2.180

Notes on next page.

Notes:

(1) *Countersink.* It is considered good practice to countersink or break the edges of holes that are smaller than F (max.) in parts having a hardness which approaches, equals, or exceeds the screw hardness. If such holes are not countersunk, the heads of screws may not seat properly or the sharp edges on holes may deform the fillets on screws thereby making them susceptible to fatigue in applications involving dynamic loading. The countersink or corner relief, however, should not be larger than is necessary to ensure that the fillet on the screw is cleared. Normally, the diameter of countersink does not heave to exceed F (max.). Countersinks or corner reliefs in excess of this diameter reduce the effective bearing area and introduce the possibility of imbedment where the parts to be fastened are softer than the screws or brinnelling or flaring of the heads of the screws where the parts to be fastened are harder than the screws.

(2) *Close Fit.* The close fit is normally limited to holes for those lengths of screws that are threaded to the head in assemblies where only one screw is to be used or where two or more screws are to be used and the mating holes are to be produced either at assembly or by matched and coordinated tooling.

(3) *Normal Fit.* The normal fit is intended for screws of relatively long length or for assemblies involving two or more screws where the mating holes are to be produced by conventional tolerancing methods. It provides for the maximum allowable eccentricity of the longest standard screws and for certain variations in the parts to be fastened, such as deviations in hole straightness, angularity between the axis of the tapped hole and that of the hole for the shank, differences in center distances of the mating holes, etc.

B.3.5) Dimensions of hexagon and spline socket flat countersunk head cap screws

Screw Size (*D*)	Head Diameter (*A*) Theor. Sharp	Max. Head Height (*H*)
#0 - #3	See Table	
#4 – 3/8	Max. $A = 2D + 0.031$	Max. $H = 0.5$ (Max. $A - D$) * cot (41°)
7/16	Max. $A = 2D - 0.031$	
1/2 – 1 1/2	Max. $A = 2D - 0.062$	

Screw Size (*D*)	Head Diameter (*A*) Theor. Sharp
#0	0.138
#2	0.168
#3	0.197
#4	0.226

B.3.6) Dimensions of slotted flat countersunk head cap screws

Screw Size (*D*)	Head Diameter (*A*) Thero. Sharp	Head Height (*H*)
1/4 through 3/8	Max. A = 2.000 D	Max. H = 0.596 D
7/16	Max. A = 2.000 D – 0.063	Max. H = 0.596 D – 0.0375
1/2 through 1	Max. A = 2.000 D – 0.125	Max. H = 0.596 D – 0.075
1 1/8 through 1 1/2	Max. A = 2.000 D – 0.188	Max. H = 0.596 D – 0.112

B.3.7) Dimensions of slotted round head cap screws

Screw Size (*D*)	Head Diameter (*A*) Thero. Sharp	Head Height (*H*)
1/4 and 5/16	Max. A = 2.000 D – 0.063	Max. H = 0.875 D – 0.028
3/8 and 7/16	Max. A = 2.000 D – 0.125	Max. H = 0.875 D – 0.055
1/2 and 9/16	Max. A = 2.000 D – 0.1875	Max. H = 0.875 D – 0.083
5/8 and 3/4	Max. A = 2.000 D – 0.250	Max. H = 0.875 D – 0.110

B.3.8) Dimensions of preferred sizes of type A plain washers

Nominal Washer Size*	Inside Diameter (A) Basic	Outside Diameter (B) Basic	Thickness (C)	Nominal Washer Size*	Inside Diameter (A) Basic	Outside Diameter (B) Basic	Thickness (C)
	0.078	0.188	0.020	1 N	1.062	2.000	0.134
	0.094	0.250	0.020	1 W	1.062	2.500	0.165
	0.125	0.312	0.032	1 1/8 N	1.250	2.250	0.134
#6 (0.138)	0.156	0.375	0.049	1 1/8 W	1.250	2.750	0.165
#8 (0.164)	0.188	0.438	0.049	1 1/4 N	1.375	2.500	0.165
#10 (0.190)	0.219	0.500	0.049	1 1/4 W	1.375	3.000	0.165
3/16	0.250	0.562	0.049	1 3/8 N	1.500	2.750	0.165
#12 (0.216)	0.250	0.562	0.065	1 3/8 W	1.500	3.250	0.180
1/4 N	0.281	0.625	0.065	1 1/2 N	1.625	3.000	0.165
1/4 W	0.312	0.734	0.065	1 1/2 W	1.625	3.500	0.180
5/16 N	0.344	0.688	0.065	1 5/8	1.750	3.750	0.180
5/16 W	0.375	0.875	0.083	1 3/4	1.875	4.000	0.180
3/8 N	0.406	0.812	0.065	1 7/8	2.000	4.250	0.180
3/8 W	0.438	1.000	0.083	2	2.125	4.500	0.180
7/16 N	0.469	0.922	0.065	2 1/4	2.375	4.750	0.220
7/16 W	0.500	1.250	0.083	2 1/2	2.625	5.000	0.238
1/2 N	0.531	1.062	0.095	2 3/4	2.875	5.250	0.259
1/2 W	0.562	1.375	0.109	3	3.125	5.500	0.284
9/16 N	0.594	1.156	0.095				
9/16 W	0.625	1.469	0.109				
5/8 N	0.656	1.312	0.095				
5/8 W	0.688	1.750	0.134				
3/4 N	0.812	1.469	0.134				
3/4 W	0.812	2.000	0.148				
7/8 N	0.938	1.750	0.134				
7/8 W	0.938	2.250	0.165				

* Nominal washer sizes are intended for use with comparable nominal screw or bolt sizes.

B.3.9) Dimensions of regular helical spring-lock washers

Enlarged Section

Nominal Washer Size	Min. Inside Diameter (A)	Max. Outside Diameter (B)	Mean Section Thickness (T)	Min. Section Width (W)	Min. Bearing Width (BW)
#2 (0.086)	0.088	0.172	0.020	0.035	0.024
#3 (0.099)	0.101	0.195	0.025	0.040	0.028
#4 (0.112)	0.114	0.209	0.025	0.040	0.028
#5 (0.125)	0.127	0.236	0.031	0.047	0.033
#6 (.0138)	0.141	0.250	0.031	0.047	0.033
#8 (0.164)	0.167	0.293	0.040	0.055	0.038
#10 (0.190)	0.193	0.334	0.047	0.062	0.043
#12 (0.216)	0.220	0.377	0.056	0.070	0.049
1/4	0.252	0.487	0.062	0.109	0.076
5/16	0.314	0.583	0.078	0.125	0.087
3/8	0.377	0.680	0.094	0.141	0.099
7/16	0.440	0.776	0.109	0.156	0.109
1/2	0.502	0.869	0.125	0.171	0.120
9/16	0.564	0.965	0.141	0.188	0.132
5/8	0.628	1.073	0.156	0.203	0.142
11/16	0.691	1.170	0.172	0.219	0.153
3/4	0.753	1.265	0.188	0.234	0.164
13/16	0.816	1.363	0.203	0.250	0.175
7/8	0.787	1.459	0.219	0.266	0.186
15/16	0.941	1.556	0.234	0.281	0.197
1	1.003	1.656	0.250	0.297	0.208
1 1/16	1.066	1.751	0.266	0.312	0.218
1 1/8	1.129	1.847	0.281	0.328	0.230
1 3/16	1.192	1.943	0.297	0.344	0.241
1 1/4	1.254	2.036	0.312	0.359	0.251
1 5/16	1.317	2.133	0.328	0.375	0.262
1 3/8	1.379	2.219	0.344	0.391	0.274
1 7/16	1.442	2.324	0.359	0.406	0.284
1 1/2	1.504	2.419	0.375	0.422	0.295
1 5/8	1.633	2.553	0.389	0.424	0.297
1 3/4	1.758	2.679	0.389	0.424	0.297
1 7/8	1.883	2.811	0.422	0.427	0.299
2	2.008	2.936	0.422	0.427	0.299
2 1/4	2.262	3.221	0.440	0.442	0.309
2 1/2	2.512	3.471	0.440	0.422	0.309
2 3/4	2.762	3.824	0.458	0.491	0.344
3	3.012	4.074	0.458	0.491	0.344

B.4) METRIC FASTENERS

B.4.1) Dimensions of hex bolts

D	D_s	S	E	K	D_a	Thread Length (B)		
Nominal Bolt Diameter and Thread Pitch	Max. Body Diameter	Max. Width Across Flats	Max. Width Across Corners	Max. Head Height	Fillet Transition Diameter	Bolt Lengths ≤ 125	Bolt Lengths > 125 and ≤ 200	Bolt Lengths > 200
M5 x 0.8	5.48	8.00	9.24	3.88	5.7	16	22	35
M6 x 1	6.19	10.00	11.55	4.38	6.8	18	24	37
M8 x 1.25	8.58	13.00	15.01	5.68	9.2	22	28	41
M10 x 1.5	10.58	16.00	18.48	6.85	11.2	26	32	45
M12 x 1.75	12.70	18.00	20.78	7.95	13.7	30	36	49
M14 x 2	14.70	21.00	24.25	9.25	15.7	34	40	53
M16 x 2	16.70	24.00	27.71	10.75	17.7	38	44	57
M20 x 2.5	20.84	30.00	34.64	13.40	22.4	46	52	65
M24 x 3	24.84	36.00	41.57	15.90	26.4	54	60	73
M30 x 3.5	30.84	46.00	53.12	19.75	33.4	66	72	85
M36 x 4	37.00	55.00	63.51	23.55	39.4	78	84	97
M42 x 4.5	43.00	65.00	75.06	27.05	45.4	90	96	109
M48 x 5	49.00	75.00	86.60	31.07	52.0	102	108	121
M56 x 5.5	57.00	85.00	98.15	36.20	62.0		124	137
M64 x 6	65.52	95.00	109.70	41.32	70.0		140	153
M72 x 6	73.84	105.00	121.24	46.45	78.0		156	169
M80 x 6	82.16	115.00	132.79	51.58	86.0		172	185
M90 x 6	92.48	130.00	150.11	57.74	96.0		192	205
M100 x 6	102.80	145.00	167.43	63.90	107.0		212	225

B.4.2) Dimensions of hex nuts, style 1

D	S	E	M	D_W	C
Nominal Bolt Diameter and Thread Pitch	Max. Width Across Flats	Max. Width Across Corners	Max. Thickness	Min. Bearing Face Diameter	Max. Washer Face Thickness
M1.6 x 0.35	3.20	3.70	1.30	2.3	
M2 x 0.4	4.00	4.62	1.60	3.1	
M2.5 x 0.45	5.00	5.77	2.00	4.1	
M3 x 0.5	5.50	6.35	2.40	4.6	
M3.5 x 0.6	6.00	6.93	2.80	5.1	
M4 x 0.7	7.00	8.08	3.20	6.0	
M5 x 0.8	8.00	9.24	4.70	7.0	
M6 x 1	10.00	11.55	5.20	8.9	
M8 x 1.25	13.00	15.01	6.80	11.6	
M10 x 1.5	15.00	17.32	9.10	13.6	
M10 x 1.5	16.00	18.45	8.40	14.6	
M12 x 1.75	18.00	20.78	10.80	16.6	
M14 x 2	21.00	24.25	12.80	19.4	
M16 x 2	24.00	27.71	14.80	22.4	
M20 x 2.5	30.00	34.64	18.00	27.9	0.8
M24 x 3	36.00	41.57	21.50	32.5	0.8
M30 x 3.5	46.00	53.12	25.60	42.5	0.8
M36 x 4	55.00	63.51	31.00	50.8	0.8

B.4.3) Dimensions of metric socket head cap screws

Dimensions in mm

Screw Size (D)	Head Diameter (A)	Head Height (H)
1.6 through 2.5	See Table	
3 through 8	Max. A = 1.5 D + 1	Max. H = D
> 10	Max. A = 1.5 D	

Screw Size (D)	1.6	2	2.5
Max. Head Diameter (A)	3.00	3.80	4.50

ASME/ANSI B18.3.1M – 1986 (R2002) Standard. Reprinted from the standard listed by permission of the American Society of Mechanical Engineers. All rights reserved.

B.4.4) Drill and counterbore sizes for socket head cap screws

Nominal Size or Basic Screw Diameter	A		X	Y
	Nominal Drill Size		Counterbore Diameter	Countersink Diameter
	Close Fit	Normal Fit		
M1.6	1.80	1.95	3.50	2.0
M2	2.20	2.40	4.40	2.6
M2.5	2.70	3.00	5.40	3.1
M3	3.40	3.70	6.50	3.6
M4	4.40	4.80	8.25	4.7
M5	5.40	5.80	9.75	5.7
M6	6.40	6.80	11.25	6.8
M8	8.40	8.80	14.25	9.2
M10	10.50	10.80	17.25	11.2
M12	12.50	12.80	19.25	14.2
M14	14.50	14.75	22.25	16.2
M16	16.50	16.75	25.50	18.2
M20	20.50	20.75	31.50	22.4
M24	24.50	24.75	37.50	26.4
M30	30.75	31.75	47.50	33.4
M36	37.00	37.50	56.50	39.4
M42	43.00	44.00	66.00	45.6
M48	49.00	50.00	75.00	52.6

B.4.5) Dimensions of metric countersunk socket head cap screws

Basic Screw Diameter and Thread Pitch	Head Diameter (A) Theor. Sharp	Head Height (H)
M3 x 0.5	6.72	1.86
M4 x 0.7	8.96	2.48
M5 x 0.8	11.20	3.10
M6 x 1	13.44	3.72
M8 x 1.25	17.92	4.96
M10 x 1.5	22.40	6.20
M12 x 1.75	26.88	7.44
M14 x 2	30.24	8.12
M16 x 2	33.60	8.80
M20 x 2.5	40.32	10.16

ASME/ANSI B18.3.5M – 1986 (R2002) Standard. Reprinted from the standard listed by permission of the American Society of Mechanical Engineers. All rights reserved.

B.4.6) Drill and countersink sizes for flat countersunk head cap screws

D	A	Y
Nominal Screw Size	**Nominal Hole Diameter**	**Min. Countersink Diameter**
M3	3.5	6.72
M4	4.6	8.96
M5	6.0	11.20
M6	7.0	13.44
M8	9.0	17.92
M10	11.5	22.40
M12	13.5	26.88
M14	16.0	30.24
M16	18.0	33.60
M20	22.4	40.32

B.5) BOLT AND SCREW CLEARANCE HOLES

B.5.1) Inch clearance holes

Nominal Screw Size	Fit Classes		
	Normal	Close	Loose
	Nominal Drill Size		
#0 (0.06)	#48 (0.0760)	#51 (0.0670)	3/32
#1 (0.073)	#43 (0.0890)	#46 (0.0810)	#37 (0.1040)
#2 (0.086)	#38 (0.1015)	3/32	#32 (0.1160)
#3 (0.099)	#32 (0.1160)	#36 (0.1065)	#30 (0.1285)
#4 (0.112)	#30 (0.1285)	#31 (0.1200)	#27 (0.1440)
#5 (0.125)	5/32	9/64	11/64
#6 (0.138)	#18 (0.1695)	#23 (0.1540)	#13 (0.1850)
#8 (0.164)	#9 (0.1960)	#15 (0.1800)	#3 (0.2130)
#10 (0.190)	#2 (0.2210)	#5 (0.2055)	B (0.238)
1/4	9/32	17/64	19/64
5/16	11/32	21/64	23/64
3/8	13/32	25/64	27/64
7/16	15/32	29/64	31/64
1/2	9/16	17/32	39/64
5/8	11/16	21/32	47/64
3/4	13/16	25/32	29/32
7/8	15/16	29/32	1 1/32
1	1 3/32	1 1/32	1 5/32
1 1/8	1 7/32	1 5/32	1 5/16
1 1/4	1 11/32	1 9/32	1 7/16
1 3/8	1 1/2	1 7/16	1 39/64
1 1/2	1 5/8	1 9/16	1 47/64

B.5.2) Metric clearance holes

Nominal Screw Size	Fit Classes		
	Normal	Close	Loose
	Nominal Drill Size		
M1.6	1.8	1.7	2
M2	2.4	2.2	2.6
M2.5	2.9	2.7	3.1
M3	3.4	3.2	3.6
M4	4.5	4.3	4.8
M5	5.5	5.3	5.8
M6	6.6	6.4	7
M8	9	8.4	10
M10	11	10.5	12
M12	13.5	13	14.5
M14	15.5	15	16.5
M16	17.5	17	18.5
M20	22	21	24
M24	26	25	28
M30	33	31	35
M36	39	37	42
M42	45	43	48
M48	52	50	56
M56	62	58	66
M64	70	66	74
M72	78	74	82
M80	86	82	91
M90	96	93	101
M100	107	104	112

NOTES:

APPENDIX C

REFERENCES

[1] "3D Master Drive Accuracy into your Business", Brochure distributed by Dassault Systemes

[2] ASME Y14.1-2012: Decimal Inch Drawing Sheet Size and Format

[3] ASME Y14.1M-2012: Metric Drawing Sheet Size and Format

[4] ASME Y14.100-2013 Engineering Drawing Practices

[5] ASMEY14.24-2012 Types and Applications of Engineering Drawings

[6] ASME Y14.2-2008: Line Conventions and Lettering

[7] ASME Y14.3-2012: Orthographic and Pictorial Views

[8] ASME Y14.5M – 2009: Dimensioning and Tolerancing

[9] ASME Y14.8-2009: Castings, Forgings, and Molded Parts

[10] Machinery's Handbook 26th Ed., Industrial Press

[11] USAS/ASME B4.1 – 1967 (R2004): Preferred Limits and Fits for Cylindrical Parts

[12] ANSI B4.2 – 1978 (R2004): Preferred Metric Limits and Fits

[13] ASME Y14.6 – 2001: Screw Thread Representation

[14] ASME B1.1 – 2003: Unified Inch Screw Threads (UN and UNR Thread Form)

[15] ASME B1.13M – 2001: Metric Screw Threads: M Profile

[16] ASME B18.2.8 – 1999: Clearance Holes for Bolts, Screws, and Studs

[17] ASME B18.2.1 – 1996: Square and Hex Bolts and Screws (Inch Series)

[18] ASME/ANSI B18.2.2 – 1987 (R1999): Square and Hex Nuts (Inch Series)

[19] ANSI B18.2.3.5M – 1979 (R2001): Metric Hex Bolts

[20] ASME B18.2.4.1M – 2002: Metric Hex Nuts, Style 1

[21] ASME B18.3 – 2003: Socket Cap, Shoulder, and Set Screws, Hex and Spline Keys (Inch Series)

[22] ASME/ANSI B18.3.1M – 1986 (R2002): Socket Head Cap Screws (Metric Series)

[23] ASME/ANSI B18.3.5M – 1986 (R2002): Hexagon Socket Flat Countersunk Head Cap Screws (Metric Series)

[24] ASME 18.6.2 – 1998: Slotted Head Cap Screws, Square Head Set Screws, and Slotted Headless Set Screws (Inch Series)

[25] ASME B18.21.1 – 1999: Lock Washers (Inch Series)

[26] ANSI B18.22.1 – 1965 (R2003): Plain Washers

NOTES:

About Us

SDC Publications specializes in creating exceptional books that are designed to seamlessly integrate into courses or help the self learner master new skills. Our commitment to meeting our customer's needs and keeping our books priced affordably are just some of the reasons our books are being used by nearly 1,200 colleges and universities across the United States and Canada.

SDC Publications is a family owned and operated company that has been creating quality books since 1985. All of our books are proudly printed in the United States.

Our technology books are updated for every new software release so you are always up to date with the newest technology. Many of our books come with video enhancements to aid students and instructor resources to aid instructors.

Take a look at all the books we have to offer you by visiting SDCpublications.com.

NEVER STOP LEARNING

Keep Going

Take the skills you learned in this book to the next level or learn something brand new. SDC Publications offers books covering a wide range of topics designed for users of all levels and experience. As you continue to improve your skills, SDC Publications will be there to provide you the tools you need to keep learning. Visit SDCpublications.com to see all our most current books.

Why SDC Publications?

- Regular and timely updates
- Priced affordably
- Designed for users of all levels
- Written by professionals and educators
- We offer a variety of learning approaches

TOPICS

3D Animation
BIM
CAD
CAM
Engineering
Engineering Graphics
FEA / CAE
Interior Design
Programming

SOFTWARE

Adams
ANSYS
AutoCAD
AutoCAD Architecture
AutoCAD Civil 3D
Autodesk 3ds Max
Autodesk Inventor
Autodesk Maya
Autodesk Revit
CATIA
Creo Parametric
Creo Simulate
Draftsight
LabVIEW
MATLAB
NX
OnShape
SketchUp
SOLIDWORKS
SOLIDWORKS Simulation